£20.

CUE.

ARISTOTLE'S THEORY OF MORAL INSIGHT

ARISTOTLE'S THEORY
OF
MORAL INSIGHT

TROELS ENGBERG-PEDERSEN

CLARENDON PRESS · OXFORD

1983

Oxford University Press, Walton Street, Oxford OX2 6DP

London Glasgow New York Toronto
Delhi Bombay Calcutta Madras Karachi
Kuala Lumpur Singapore Hong Kong Tokyo
Nairobi Dar es Salaam Cape Town
Melbourne Auckland

and associates in
Beirut Berlin Ibadan Mexico City Nicosia

Published in the United States by
Oxford University Press, New York

British Library Cataloguing in Publication Data
Engberg — Pedersen, Troels
Aristotle's theory of moral insight.
1. Aristotle — Ethics   2. Ethics
I. Title
170'.92'4   B491.E7
ISBN 0-19-824667-6

Typeset by Hope Services
Printed in Great Britain
at the University Press, Oxford
by Eric Buckley
Printer to the University

For Jonna

PREFACE

The aim of this book is to determine what, in Aristotle's ethical theory, moral goodness consists in. Aristotle's concept of moral goodness (*kyria aretē*) is complex, and one central element in it is moral insight (*phronēsis*). In trying to define Aristotelian moral goodness I shall concentrate on *phronēsis*, which is the rational, cognitive element in moral goodness, and attempt to clarify the content of that cognitive element and what the relation is of *phronēsis* to the other elements in moral goodness. Aristotle defines *phronēsis* as a state of mind that issues in (good) *praxeis* (acts proper, as opposed to *poiēsis*, 'production'), and throughout the book I shall be basically concerned to define the sense and scope of the concept of *praxis* and its connection with other central concepts in Aristotle's ethical theory such as happiness (*eudaimonia*), the noble (*to kalon*), passion (*pathos*), and desire. Nobody will deny the importance of the concept of *praxis* in Aristotelian ethics, but I believe, and this belief has been a major impulse behind writing the book, that the question of the exact sense and doctrinal implications of the concept of *praxis* has not been given its full weight in the scholarly literature, or at least that there is a need for a comprehensive account of the essentials of Aristotle's ethical theory centring on the concepts of *phronēsis* and of *praxis*. In many ways the present book is comparable, in method and subject-matter, with the recent study by J. M. Cooper, *Reason and Human Good in Aristotle* (1975), from which I have learnt a great deal. But it should also confirm Cooper's expectation that 'another person setting out to write a book on the same subject would . . . place different emphases and discover other connections of ideas' (p. xii).

The book is intended as a piece of scholarship. The best

person to write on Aristotelian ethics is no doubt the philosopher who, in connection with independent work on problems
in ethics and the philosophy of action, has become sufficiently
attracted to Aristotle's work in the area to spend the required
amount of time on the necessary painstaking analysis of his
arguments. Such a person will be able to do two things. First,
he will be able to use Aristotle's works in such a way as to
justify directly the amount of time spent on them, viz. in
order to elucidate conceptual problems with which we are
ourselves confronted. And secondly, he will be able to let
his exegetical work be guided by a grasp of conceptual
machinery that is sufficiently subtle to match that of the
philosopher himself. I am no such person, but a scholar.
The problem is, however, that since Aristotle's works are
philosophy, no firm line may be drawn between the philosophic and the scholarly approaches to them: no serious
work on Aristotle can avoid becoming philosophical. The
consequence is that since it seems true of the world as
it in fact is that there are philosophers working on Aristotle
and scholars doing so, the latter type of work will necessarily
be only second-best.

This will hold for the present work too. Thus I fear that
the concepts I shall employ in reconstructing Aristotle's
ethical position may not be sufficiently refined. Nor shall I
be able to provide any really worthwhile arguments for
taking certain results of my reading of Aristotle to be worth
the attention of modern philosophers. Still I will try, in the
final chapter of the book, to indicate the relevance of my
account for the discussion of at least some of the more
general questions in ethics.

On one point, however, I do not apologize for being
scholarly, viz. as regards the amount of heavily exegetical
work contained in the book. Recently a philosopher (D.
Wiggins) has spoken of 'the difficulty (in practice rarely
overcome) of sustaining philosophic momentum over a
prolonged examination of a large number of obscure but
relevant passages of the *Ethics* and *De Anima*'. There clearly
is a difficulty, and I fear that I may not altogether have
overcome it. Still there are a number of reasons for quoting,
paraphrasing, and discussing particular texts. First, one is

often forced to realize that no interpretation of a given passage can be counted on as being universally, or even generally, accepted. By discussing individual passages I make clear how I understand them. Secondly, well-known passages may take on a different hue when considered in a new systematic context. But then this must be brought out. And thirdly, I retain the belief that there is still some new and indisputable information to be gained from the painstaking analysis of passages which have already been extensively commented on.

On three points of scholarship special comment seems required.

(*i*) The basic texts I make use of are the *De Anima* (abbreviated as *DA*), the *Nicomachean Ethics* (*EN*), and the *Eudemian Ethics* (*EE*). I draw freely on these texts on the hypothesis that they exhibit no genuine difference of doctrine. General scholarly opinion seems to be that there are more or less substantial differences of doctrine, in particular between the *Nicomachean* and the *Eudemian Ethics*. But I do not think that we understand Aristotle's ethics, or his psychology, sufficiently well to enable us to make good such a claim. I stick, therefore, to the attempt, which is basic from the point of view of method, to make coherent and satisfactory sense of the material in its entirety.

(*ii*) I presuppose here, of course, that both the *Nicomachean* and the *Eudemian Ethics* are genuine works of Aristotle. On the authenticity of the *Magna Moralia*, by contrast, scholarly opinion is so hotly divided that I have refrained from using the book to support my reading of Aristotle. Nor have I finally made up my mind whether to accept it as genuine or not.

(*iii*) It also seems appropriate that I should indicate the relationship of the present study to other scholarly discussion of Aristotle's ethics. The book is a result of work on the *Ethics* which has been guided by what has been written during the last thirty years or so by philosophically minded commentators of, mainly, Anglo-American origin. This literature has a certain internal coherence to it, and may be said to have started with the publication in the 1950s of work by D. J. Allan (for the more scholarly approach) and

J. L. Austin and G. E. M. Anscombe (for the more directly philosophical approach). I have, of course, consulted, and benefited greatly from, scholarly comment of an older date and belonging to other traditions. But there is no point in concealing that the book springs directly from work with what is only one part of the literature on the *Ethics*. Had I been more alive, for example, to the tendencies that are reflected in the recent growing interest in Aristotle's practical philosophy among German philosophers (G. Bien, H.-G. Gadamer, M. Ganter, O. Höffe, M. Riedel, J. Ritter, to mention only a few), the book would probably have been quite different. I have endeavoured to mention, mainly in the notes, the books and articles from which I have learnt most. The bibliography cites what has seemed to me the most important work in the part of the literature that I know.

Part of the material of chapter 1 of this book has been previously published, in a paper entitled 'For Goodness' Sake: More on *Nicomachean Ethics* I.vii.5' that appeared in *Archiv für Geschichte der Philosophie*, 63, 1 (1981), 17–40. I thank the editor for permission to draw on that paper.

Finally, I wish to thank the Provost and Fellows of The Queen's College, Oxford for granting me a Florey European Studentship from 1974 to 1976. The present book is the result of efforts begun during those very stimulating two years. I have benefited greatly from discussion of Aristotelian matters, at that time and later, with a number of people at Oxford, London, and Cambridge, and with Sten Ebbesen of this university. I was much helped by Christopher Rowe at a crucial stage in the preparation of the final typescript. My thanks are also due to the staff of the Oxford University Press for their help and patience. For criticism and encouragement, however, my deepest gratitude goes to John Ackrill, Johnny Christensen, and Karsten Friis Johansen.

University of Copenhagen   T. Engberg-Pedersen
October 1981

CONTENTS

ABBREVIATIONS

AGP	*Archiv für Geschichte der Philosphie*
AJP	*American Journal of Philosophy*
APQ	*American Philosophical Quarterly*
CP	*Classical Philology*
CQ	*Classical Quarterly*
JP	*Journal of Philosophy*
M	*Mind*
PAS	*Proceedings of the Aristotelian Society*
PBA	*Proceedings of the British Academy*
Phil.	*Philosophy*
Phil. Jahr.	*Philosophisches Jahrbuch*
Phr.	*Phronesis*
PQ	*Philosophical Quarterly*
PR	*Philosophical Review*
RM	*Review of Metaphysics*
TAPA	*Transactions and Proceedings of the American Philological Association*

PART I

1
EUDAIMONIA AND *PRAXIS*

1. Aristotelian ethics is eudaimonistic. At the top of his ethical system Aristotle placed, as the supreme value, *eudaimonia* (happiness). But what does this really mean? In particular, does it follow from the fact that Aristotle relates everything else, including moral acts, to *eudaimonia* as their end that he was unable to maintain the independent, autonomous value of moral acts?

In the present chapter I shall discuss Aristotle's concepts of *eudaimonia* and of *praxis*, and the relation between the two. *Praxeis* are often understood as identical with what we should call moral acts. This is false, I believe: *praxeis* form a wider class of acts, which *includes* Aristotelian moral acts, whether good or bad. None the less, discussion of the relation between the value of *praxeis* and *eudaimonia* is a necessary preliminary to consideration of the crucial question of the relation to *eudaimonia* of the value of *moral* acts: are moral acts good because they contribute to *eudaimonia*, and if so, how can they retain their property of being intrinsically good?

The account I shall give has been prompted by recent developments in the discussion of this question. Independently of each other J. L. Ackrill[1] and J. M. Cooper[2] have suggested revisions of the traditional answer which go in the same direction. And many of the conceptual tools they have introduced play a crucial role in T. H. Irwin's recent book on *Plato*'s moral theory.[3] As will be seen, my discussion is heavily indebted to the contributions of these scholars. But

---

[1] J. L. Ackrill, 'Aristotle on *Eudaimonia*', *PBA* 60 (1974), 339–59.
[2] J. M. Cooper, *Reason and Human Good in Aristotle*, Cambridge, Mass., 1975.
[3] T. H. Irwin, *Plato's Moral Theory, The Early and Middle Dialogues*, Oxford, 1977.

it is my contention that at a fairly central point, concerning
the understanding of the concept of *eudaimonia* itself, the
three commentators do not go far enough in the direction in
which they have rightly pointed.

2.1. What may fairly be called the traditional answer to
the question of the goodness of moral action in Aristotle
detects a fundamental inconsistency in his views.[4] On the
one hand he seems to insist that moral acts are intrinsically
good, or good in themselves. On the other hand his doctrine
of certain connected concepts is such that as a consequence
moral acts must be considered good due to their being means
to *eudaimonia*.

In support of the former claim one may point to two
passages in *EN* VI where Aristotle distinguishes between
praxis and *poiēsis*: VI.v.3-4 and ii.5. The distinction may
vaguely be stated to be the one between acts that are good
in themselves and acts that are good because they produce
something other than the act itself. But moral acts are
praxeis. Hence their value cannot lie in their being means
to *eudaimonia*.

On the other hand certain passages that discuss deliberation
imply a different view. The truly good man is a man who is
able to deliberate correctly with a view to 'living well in
general', i.e. to *eudaimonia* (*EN* VI.v.1-2). But in his analysis
of deliberation (in *EN* III.iii) Aristotle takes as his model
technical sciences, and they characteristically either possess
or look for *means*, in the normal causal sense of the term,
to an end which is regarded as settled. So if, as must be the
case, what the truly good man finds as a result of deliberation
are morally good acts, they must be considered good as a
result of being means to *eudaimonia*.

2.2. This, the traditonal, diagnosis of an Aristotelian
dilemma has been challenged by J. L. Ackrill and J. M. Cooper.

---

[4] Its classic expression in post-war scholarship is Gauthier's commentary, cf.
e.g. pp. 6-7, 210, 226, 573-5 (esp. p. 575). A formulation of the problem that
was to be influential is that of D. J. Allan in 'The practical syllogism', in *Autour
d'Aristote, Recueil d'études... offert à Mgr. A. Mansion*, Louvain, 1955, 325-40,
esp. pp. 338-40.

Cooper bases his attack on a consideration of Aristotle's account of deliberation.[5] Deliberation is not just concerned with means in a strictly causal sense, but with 'things that contribute to the end' (*ta pros to telos*); and these may also be constituent parts of complex ends or particular things that a given end may be seen to consist in. Thus, to take an un-Cooperian but Aristotelian example that illustrates Cooper's point, a doctor may decide to rub a patient's limb in order to heal it, and both the rubbing, which is a means proper, and the resulting warmth of the limb, which is an element in its health, may be said to be things that 'contribute' to the end. But then if we say of the ultimate end, or *eudaimonia*, that it is something desired for its own sake, we may say the same of morally good action—if we take the way in which morally good action 'contributes' to *eudaimonia* to be that of its being a *constituent part* of it.[6] By this move the dilemma seems solved.

Ackrill takes as his starting-point a puzzling remark of Aristotle's on the very first page of the *Nicomachean Ethics*.[7] Here Aristotle is concerned to subordinate ends of acts to other ends and in the final outcome, as is clear from ii.1, to a single, truly final end. However, he has also distinguished between acts which are their own ends and acts which have ends other than themselves. And then when it comes to subordinating either type of end, he rather oddly remarks that it makes no difference as far as subordination is concerned whether a given end is of the one type or of the other. This *is* odd. In what way can an act which is its own end be subordinated to any further end? The puzzle is solved, according to Ackrill, if we introduce the relation of part to whole. Acts which are their own end may at the same time be constituents of or ingredients in or, for short, *parts* of a certain whole. The relation is illustrated by two examples: as putting is to playing golf, and as golfing is to having a good holiday. By means of this conceptual tool, Ackrill further suggests, we may solve the problem of the relation of moral acts to *eudaimonia*. For we may now sensibly say that moral acts are done for their own sake and at the same time for the sake of *eudaimonia*, viz. as parts of that whole.

⁵ Cooper, pp. 19–20.   ⁶ *Ibid.*, p. 82.   ⁷ Ackrill, pp. 342–3.

Finally, T. H. Irwin makes extensive use of the idea that moral virtue may be said to be good both in itself and because of its contribution to the final good for the reason that moral virtue should be seen as a *component* of the final good.[8] And when he introduces the distinction between 'instrumental' and 'component' means, he explicitly refers to the Aristotelian context:[9] to L. H. G. Greenwood, who introduced the distinction in connection with a certain passage in *EN* VI,[10] and to Cooper and D. Wiggins,[11] who have recently made use of it in connection with Aristotle's phrase *ta pros to telos*.

3. So should we say, and in what sense should we say, that in Aristotle a moral act, and generally a *praxis*, is considered good both in itself and also as a component, part, or constituent of *eudaimonia*?

For an answer we must turn to a crucial passage in the first book of the *Nicomachean Ethics*, vii.5. The passage itself speaks of things as chosen both 'for their own sake' and 'for the sake of *eudaimonia*'; it forms the conclusion of a piece of sustained argument (in vii.1-4) and is followed by further elucidation (in vii.6-8) of the concept of *eudaimonia* that is expressed in § 5. Perhaps renewed analysis of what comes before and after will throw light on the point of the passage itself.

4.1. First, however, we must consider the context and the point of the whole section referred to (vii.1-8).[12]

Right at the start of the *Ethics* (i-ii.1) Aristotle works out the idea of a single end of all acts which is 'the good' or 'the

---

[8] Irwin, e.g. pp. 188, 225.   [9] Ibid., p. 83 n. 53 (p. 300).

[10] L. H. G. Greenwood, *Aristotle, Nicomachean Ethics Book Six*, 1909. I believe that severe damage has been caused by Greenwood's application of his distinction, which makes perfectly good sense in connection with the passage he refers to (*EN* VI.xii.5, 1144a3-6), to the passages and problems of *EN* I that I shall discuss. In VI.xii.5 Aristotle is talking of the relationship of a certain good to a certain whole that *eudaimonia* is taken to consist in, not to *eudaimonia* itself. In the passages of *EN* I, as we shall see, he is totally reticent on what *eudaimonia* consists in and only interested in the relationship of goods to *eudaimonia* itself.

[11] D. Wiggins, 'Deliberation and Practical Reason', *PAS* 76 (1975-6), 29-51.

[12] I am relying here on J. L. Austin's '*Agathon* and *Eudaimonia* in the *Ethics* of Aristotle', in *Aristotle*, ed. J. M. E. Moravcsik, 1967, 261-96, esp. pp. 274-9.

highest good'. I shall consider the passage in more detail at
the end of this chapter (sections 10.1–2). He then asks (in
ii.3) what that single end may be and which science is concerned with it. The latter question is immediately answered
(in ii.4–8): the science is politics. The former question, of
course, is the one that guides the development of the rest
of the work. It is taken up in iv.1, following remarks (in iii)
on method and on the addressee of the work: 'what is the
thing that we claim to be what politics strives towards, and
what is the highest of all practical goods?' In terms of its
name, Aristotle continues (iv.2–3), there is general agreement:
everybody speaks of *eudaimonia* and understands living
well and doing well as synonymous with being *eudaimōn*.
But people disagree about *what eudaimonia is*, and quite
often even the same person will at different times have
different views.

Two well-known facts should be emphasized here.

First, the concept from which Aristotle takes his starting-
point in the *Nicomachean* (but not the *Eudemian*) *Ethics*
is not that of *eudaimonia*, but that of 'the good' in the form
of the highest practical good. When people talk of these
matters, they use the term *eudaimonia*, and when they disagree about what to go for, they disagree about what *eudaimonia* is; but the basic concept is that of the good as the end
of acts: *eudaimonia* is not introduced until the passage I have
paraphrased from chapter iv and then only as the more
familiar concept.

Secondly, it is quite clear from the same passage that when
Aristotle connects 'what politics strives towards' and 'the
highest of all practical goods' with *eudaimonia*, he is not
thereby assigning any determinate content to those phrases:
eudaimonia, as it is used here, signifies an 'indeterminate'
end. My discussion of vii. 1–8 is intended to bring out what
kind of indeterminacy this is.

Aristotle next (chapter v) returns to his search for 'the good
and *eudaimonia*'. He mentions the three or four things that
people normally suggest, on the basis of the well-known three
'lives',[13] to be what *eudaimonia* consists in. Corresponding

---

[13] Against tradition I translate I.v.1–2 (1095b14–19) as follows: 'For people

to the life of enjoyment there is pleasure; corresponding to
the political life there is honour, or perhaps rather the virtue
that a man is honoured for; and similarly there will presumably be, to correspond to the contemplative life, some kind
of theoretical activity — though Aristotle defers further
consideration of this till later.

These are suggestions as to what particular types of thing
or activity should be taken to 'fill in' the concept of *eudaimonia*. The following chapter (vi), on Platonic views of the
good, is clearly marked off by Aristotle, at the start of
chapter vii, as a digression. Hence when, in vii.1, he announces
a return to the question what the good that is sought may be,
one naively expects to get his own view of the determinate
content of *eudaimonia*. But this expectation, of course, is not
fulfilled until very much later in the work. What, then, is the
answer of chapter vii to the question of what the good that
is sought may be?

4.2. vii.9 is relevant. The claim, says Aristotle, that the
highest good is *eudaimonia* may seem unenlightening:[14] we
want a clearer suggestion as to what it is; but this we may
perhaps get if we consider the question whether man has a
proper activity (*ergon*). According to this paragraph chapter
vii divides into two. In vii.10 ff. Aristotle defines the highest
good, and consequently *eudaimonia*, in terms of the concept
of man's proper activity. In vii.1-8 he has defined the highest
good as — *eudaimonia*.

The latter point may seem surprising. Has not the relationship of the good and *eudaimonia* been sufficiently determined
already in chapter iv? Nevertheless there can be no doubt
that Aristotle's most overt purpose in vii.1-8 is precisely to

seem reasonably enough to understand the good and *eudaimonia* on the basis of
the (well-known) lives; the many, who are the most vulgar, (judge it to be)
pleasure — that is precisely why they love the life of enjoyment; for the prominent
lives are *three* (in number), no more no less (*malista*), viz. the one just mentioned,
the political one, and thirdly the contemplative one.' The *lives* are what people
are immediately aware of. When asked what they take *eudaimonia* to consist in,
people will answer by extrapolation from the lives. Cf. lines 22–23.

[14] In the Greek τὴν . . . εὐδαιμονίαν must be the grammatical predicate and
τὸ ἄριστον the grammatical subject. Otherwise it will be impossible to draw out
a consistent line of thought for the whole of vii.1-9. Ramsauer and Gauthier/
Jolif take it thus.

identify the good as *eudaimonia*. (*a*) Consider the line of thought in the argument of § § 1–5. The good that is sought, or the practical good, is that-for-the-sake-of-which or end; there are several types of end; so the good will be what is *most* final or final *without qualification*: it is what is always choiceworthy for its own sake and never for the sake of anything else — 'but that sort of thing *eudaimonia* seems precisely (*malista*) to be' (vii.5, 1097a34). So, as we may infer, the good is *eudaimonia*. (*b*) 'The same seems also to follow from its self-sufficiency', i.e. from the fact that it, viz. the good, is self-sufficient (b5–6).[15] § § 6–7 repeat the pattern of argument of § § 1–5. The good is self-sufficient; the self-sufficient is this and that — 'but that sort of thing we take *eudaimonia* to be' (vii.7, b15–16). So the good is *eudaimonia*.

However, it seems clear that Aristotle also has a less overt purpose in vii.1–8, which is that of defining the two properties of being final and self-sufficient, and of suggesting that they both belong to *eudaimonia*. Thus he sums up the whole section in this way (vii.8, b20–21): 'So *eudaimonia* appears to be something final and self-sufficient, being the end of acts.'

We may make sense of this seeming criss-cross of purposes, if we take Aristotle's basic aim to be that of defining the indeterminacy of the concept of *eudaimonia* by developing certain properties, viz. those of being final and self-sufficient, of his own basic concept (the good) and ascribing those properties to the concept of *eudaimonia*. Aristotle seemingly, and most overtly, argues thus: the good (his own concept) has certain properties; but look, they are precisely the properties we take *eudaimonia* to have — so the good is *eudaimonia*. But the point of the argument, in spite of its overt conclusion, lies in bringing out *that eudaimonia has* those properties. By starting from his own concept and developing that, he makes the person who only operates with the more familiar concept of *eudaimonia* realize what the properties are of that concept, and consequently what kind of indeterminacy it expresses.

---

[15] In the quotation 'its' is a translation of τῆς. That it is the good (not *eudaimonia*) whose self-sufficiency is the starting-point of the argument is once more clear from the structure of the section as a whole.

5.1. What, then, are the two properties that are ascribed to the good and *eudaimonia* in vii.1-8? The good and *eudaimonia* is something final (*teleion*) and self-sufficient (*autarkes*). Before looking at the paragraphs in detail it is worth considering Aristotle's general use of those two concepts. Although they are evidently closely related, it seems possible to maintain a certain difference between them.

The final, according to Aristotle, is 'that beyond which one cannot lay hand on anything'.[16] It seems clear that Aristotle intends this definition in the sense of that beyond which one can *no longer* lay hand on anything. In other words, the final is to be understood as the terminus of a chain that consists in constantly going beyond what was first taken as final. Thus the final is essentially relative to what lies 'before' the thing that is called final.

The case is different, I believe, for the concept of the self-sufficient. What is self-sufficient is 'what lacks nothing in addition'.[17] Here too there will be something relative to which the self-sufficient will be so called. But the former thing will not be something that lies 'before' the self-sufficient. Rather, it is some demand that is raised by the context in which the concept of self-sufficiency is introduced. Thus when Aristotle describes certain types of practical science as exact and self-sufficient (*EN* III.iii.8, 1112a34-b1), he means that they know the answers to all the questions that may be asked about how to produce something that is covered by those sciences. In this context there is a demand for a type of knowledge that will enable a person to answer all practical questions in a certain area: when the self-sufficient is present, there is knowledge that satisfies that demand.

The important point about the general use of the two concepts is, then, that the final is, but the self-sufficient is not, relative to something that lies 'before' itself.[18]

5.2. Let us now turn to vii.1-8. It will be convenient to start from § § 6-7.

---

[16] See, e.g., *Metaph.* 1021b12-13 and 1021b32-1022a1 in the chapter in the *Metaphysics* on the concept (Delta 16). And cf. *Metaph.* Iota 4, 1055a11-16.

[17] See, e.g., *EN* IX.ix.1, 1169b5-6 and X.vi.2, 1176b5-6.

[18] I do not wish to be dogmatic here. It is sufficient for my purpose that 'final' and 'self-sufficient' are sometimes used in these slightly different ways.

We know the direction of Aristotle's argument. That 'the good' is *eudaimonia* may be seen to follow from its self-sufficiency; for the final good is in fact self-sufficient; now the self-sufficient is 'that which when taken alone makes one's life choiceworthy and lacking in nothing' — 'and that is the sort of thing we take *eudaimonia* to be'; so the good is *eudaimonia*.

Let us consider the definition of the self-sufficient. The self-sufficient makes one's life choiceworthy. Aristotle is talking of a whole life, not just of living; but what does he mean by his claim that in being self-sufficient a whole life will be choiceworthy? We may make use of the fact that in his definition Aristotle glosses 'choiceworthy' as 'lacking in nothing'. If one's life is lacking in nothing, there will be no desires which are not satisfied. Perhaps, then, Aristotle's idea is that the value of living lies in the satisfaction of desires: the feeling of need, in so far as this is the only thing that fills a person's consciousness, will necessarily make non-living preferable to living. But if for the self-sufficient to be present the whole life must be choiceworthy in the sense of leaving no desires unsatisfied, then, since a life is a stretch of time that is made up of smaller stretches, and since it seems likely that Aristotle means what holds of the whole life to hold of the smaller stretches too, the consquence will be that at any particular moment during the life that is self-sufficient living will be in all respects preferable to non-living; there will be no desire which is not satisfied.

This may seem a strange conception. How, if at any particular moment all the desires of a given person are satisfied, may he 'move' from one situation to another, since there will be no desires to guide such a move? Nor will it be at all possible for human beings to come to lead such a life; for they do in fact get desires for things which are not immediately present. However, I insist that this precisely *is* Aristotle's conception of a state which is properly called self-sufficient. What the two oddities point to is just that human beings will never attain to the self-sufficient state; they do not show that the concept of that state is incoherent.

The self-sufficient, then, is the state that satisfies all the desires of a given person, and hence makes him want to live,

during the whole of his life. It is, furthermore, a state of a
person during the whole of his life which is such that at any
particular moment during that life all his desires are satisfied
and he prefers living to non-living. This state cannot in fact
be obtained by human beings, but that does not render the
concept of the state incoherent. It hardly could be incoherent
without severe consequences, since it is the concept of the
point of all the desires of a given person.

Aristotle also claims that the self-sufficient is what 'when
taken alone' makes a life choiceworthy and lacking in nothing.
His point is simply that the self-sufficient is, logically speaking, sufficient to make a whole life choiceworthy and lacking
in nothing in the manner I have explained.

So the self-sufficient is a state with the formal property of
being the point of all the desires of a given person. Therefore,
since it is relative to what desires the person in fact has, it is
indeterminate with respect to its substantial content.

'. . . and that is the sort of thing we take *eudaimonia* to
be': on the account I have given of the self-sufficient, what
Aristotle has done in vii.6–7 is to define in more precise
terms the understanding of the concept of *eudaimonia* that
seemed implied in his remarks in chapter iv concerning the
role of the concept in everyday usage.

It is worth pointing out already at this stage that Aristotle's
definition of *eudaimonia* as the self-sufficient leaves absolutely
open the question whether just one thing or more things than
one fall under the state that it is. Nor is there any implication
in his definition that if more things than one fall under the
state, they either will or will not form some ordered compound. The self-sufficient is a state that satisfies all the desires
of a given person, and there is absolutely no restriction on
how many, or how few, desires a person may have, nor on
what type of object they may be for.

In what follows I shall speak of the 'eudaimonic' state and
mean thereby a state of a person during the whole of his life
which is such that if a person is in it, all his desires will be
satisfied and he will at any time, and in all respects, prefer
living to non-living.

5.3. Let us now turn to Aristotle's account in vii.1–5 of

the good that is sought.

vii.1 starts from the question of what the good that is sought may be and suggests, in a careful progression of thought, first, that it is that-for-the-sake-of-which other things are done and then, that it is the end — for the end *is* that-for-the-sake-of-which other things are done (1097a21–22). 'So if there is a single end of all acts, that will be the practical good; if there are more than one, they will be that good' (a22–24).

vii.3 distinguishes between types of end. Some ends are subordinate: though ends of other things, they are themselves chosen for some further end. Other ends are truly end-like or final. 'So if there is only one final thing, that will be the good that is sought; if there are more than one, the most final among them will be that good' (a28–30). Two questions should concern us here. If the good is the most final among final things, what has happened to those other things which are truly final, though not the most final thing? And what sense should be given to the claim that among things which are themselves truly final something may be 'most' final?

vii.4 is clearly intended by Aristotle to help clear up these questions. The important distinction that is introduced here is the one between on the one hand things that are choice-worthy both in themselves and for the sake of something else and on the other hand what is always choiceworthy in itself and never for the sake of anything else: the latter is implied to be that most final thing and stated to be final 'without qualification'.

vii.5: 'and that is precisely the sort of thing *eudaimonia* seems to be; for . . . ' (a34–b1).

5.4. What is the good, and *eudaimonia*, if it is the most final thing or the thing which is final without qualification, i.e. what is always choiceworthy in itself and never for the sake of anything else?

I take it that Aristotle wishes to give expression, in vii.1–5, to the conception of the good and *eudaimonia* that he is also expressing in vii.6–7 when he introduces the concept of self-sufficiency. In vii.1–5 he wishes to bring out that same conception by the use of other concepts.

He glosses 'the good that is sought' as 'the practical good' and suggests that it is an end of acts. So we are in the realm of acting, which immediately brings in the concept of an end: any act is for an end, according to Aristotle. Now a concept that is closely connected with those of acting and of an end is that of choosing (*haireisthai*). Choosing is a bad translation for Aristotle's concept, which is that of 'deciding on some act with a view to getting something'.[19] There is something one wants to have; one decides on some act that will make one get it: one 'chooses'. Thus when there is choice (*hairesis*), there is some end, and some act that is supposed to bring about the end. And when one 'chooses', one *wants* to do the act with a view to bringing about the end. I wish to suggest that when Aristotle glosses 'the good that is sought' as 'the practical good', when he introduces the concept of an end, and when he draws the crucial distinction between ends that have, and ends that do not have, other things as their end, he is wishing to define the good in relation to the concept of 'choosing'. And I suggest that when he defines the good as the most final thing or the thing which is final without qualification, and hence as what is always choiceworthy in itself and never for the sake of something else, he is claiming the good to be the point of all choice. Any choice has as its 'ideal' object the state where its end has been reached. When this state is present, the choice has, as it were, made itself superfluous. But then, once more, we may introduce the idea of a state of a person during the whole of his life in which all the choices that he makes have made themselves superfluous. This, the 'eudaimonic', state is the point of all his choice.

5.5. I am evidently relying here on my interpretation of the self-sufficient. But note also that the suggested interpretation

---

[19] I suspect that this is also the precise point of *pro-* in *prohairesis* and *prohaireisthai*. Others take it, on the basis of *EN* III.ii.17 (1112a15–17), that *pro-* has a temporal significance, e.g. Joachim in his commentary (pp. 100–1) and Gauthier (ad loc.). The latter expresses agreement with Joachim and believes that the view to be combated is that *pro-* signifies *preference*. However, the point of the passage referred to is not so much that *prohairesis presupposes* deliberation, i.e. presupposes it *in time*, as that it presupposes *deliberation*, i.e. presupposes it *logically*; and deliberation is precisely a process that seeks for what to do with a view to having something else, viz. for the *means* (in some sense). Cf. also Hardie's remarks about the literal meaning of *prohairesis*, in W. F. R. Hardie, *Aristotle's Ethical Theory*, Oxford, 1968, pp. 165–8.

throws light on the crucial stages of the argument of vii.1–5.

First, of course, it explains why Aristotle connects the good that is sought with acts and with ends of acts: he is construing the good that is sought as something that may be brought about by choice, i.e. by purposeful activity.

Secondly, one can see why Aristotle introduces the distinction between ends that are and ends that are not subordinate to other ends. The distinction may seem natural enough once the concept of an end has been introduced. But note that Aristotle's aim in drawing it is not so much to discard ends that are subordinate to other ends from qualifying as the good that is sought. Rather, it is to discard even ends which, in the dichotomy as it is first drawn, are *not* subordinate to other ends, in favour of some even higher end. Thus by his use of the distinction Aristotle may now be seen to turn the reader's attention in the direction of his peculiar conception of the good as not just an end among others, but *the* end, the point of *all* the choices of a given person.

Thirdly, one can see why Aristotle restricts the good to being the most final among final ends, and what he means by the phrase 'most final among final ends'. The 'eudaimonic' state is different from ends that are final since, while the latter are the point of each their particular chain of choices, the former is the point of all the choices that a person will make during the whole of his life. This means that all particular final ends will *fall under* the 'eudaimonic' state. There is therefore no problem about Aristotle's restricting the good to being the most final among final ends: the final ends have not been accidentally left out.

Nor is it difficult to see what he means when he talks of the most final among final ends. The 'eudaimonic' state is an end that belongs at a different level from that of particular final ends, inasmuch as they fall under it; and the point of Aristotle's use of the superlative form is to bring out that difference of level. Similarly the point of 'without qualification' and, in the definition of the end that is final without qualification, 'always' and 'never' is to bring out that the good is *the* choiceworthy thing, the thing or state which puts an end to the activity of choosing, since all the things that are the objects of the choices of a given person have been acquired when he is in that state. And the choiceworthy thing, thus understood, belongs at a different level from particular choiceworthy things, inasmuch as the latter fall under the former.

5.6. It is noteworthy that it is precisely this force of the superlative form that Aristotle strives to bring out in vii.8. *Eudaimonia* is there stated to be the most choiceworthy of all things — without being counted among them; for were it so counted, it would clearly become more choiceworthy by having added to it even the slightest of those other goods — and, as we may conclude the argument, if *eudaimonia* is such a thing that it will become more choiceworthy by having goods added to it, it will not be the most choiceworthy of all things in the sense intended. *Eudaimonia*, then, is most choiceworthy in the sense of absolutely or perfectly so; it belongs at a different level from that of particular choiceworthy things.

5.7. In vii.1–5, then, Aristotle defines the good and *eudaimonia* as the point of all the choices of a given person; in vii.6–7 he defines it as the state where all the person's desires are satisfied. Thus interpreted the two definitions look similar. But note that they differ in a way that is consonant with the general difference between the concepts of being final and being self-sufficient that I brought out in section 5.1. *Eudaimonia* as final without qualification is precisely the terminus of a chain or chains of things, viz. choices and their (particular) ends (whether themselves subordinate or not), that lie 'below' the absolutely final end. *Eudaimonia* as final without qualification is at the top of a hierarchy (whether one-stringed or not is irrelevant) of things that are subordinate to it.

Not so for *eudaimonia* when it is defined as the self-sufficient. Here *eudaimonia* is simply relative to the desires that the person has at any particular moment, and there is no implication that these desires are connected with other desires in a chain or hierarchy. *Eudaimonia* as something self-sufficient is the state that satisfies the person's desires at any particular moment during the whole of his life, just as a practical science which is self-sufficient is one that contains the answer to any question one may be forced to raise as one goes through life.

The difference between the two accounts lies in the fact that while they both make use of the concept of desire, the definition of the self-sufficient does just that, whereas the definition of the final uses desire in connection with the realm of action; and this area is in fact such that one must introduce first, a distinction between what is done and what it is done for (the end) and next, a distinction between ends that are and ends that are not, subordinate to other things as their end. *Eudaimonia* as what is final without qualification is the point of all choice and action, but the area of choosing and acting is itself articulated in terms of these distinctions. *Eudaimonia* as something self-sufficient, on the other hand, is just the state where all desires are satisfied, and in itself the area of desire is not articulated in any specific way.

6.1. I have been concerned, till now, to bring out the sense of the definition of the good and *eudaimonia* as absolutely final and as self-sufficient. Two questions in connection with vii.5 have not been discussed. First, what is the sense of choosing something 'for the sake of *eudaimonia*'? And secondly, what is meant when we are said to choose something, e.g. honour, *both* for its own sake *and* for the sake of *eudaimonia*?

For the moment I shall concentrate on the former question. On the suggested reading of *eudaimonia* as the point of all choice and the state where all desires are satisfied, *eudaimonia* is an indeterminate state with a certain 'formal' property. It is indeterminate because it is dependent for its 'substantial' content on what choices a given person will in fact make and what desires he will in fact have. What, then, can be meant when something is stated to be chosen 'for the sake of' that indeterminate end?

If we are to keep *eudaimonia* as an indeterminate end, the point of the phrase 'for the sake of *eudaimonia*' cannot be to introduce something that will explain why the thing that is referred to *eudaimonia* is considered choiceworthy. The reference to *eudaimonia* cannot in any way add to the value that the thing is taken to have anyway. When e.g. honour is chosen for the sake of *eudaimonia*, the reference to *eudaimonia* does not confer additional value on honour. Honour is considered choiceworthy, and it is *also* stated to stand in a certain relationship to *eudaimonia*.

But then it is not difficult to see what that relationship must be. It is that of 'falling under' the 'eudaimonic' state, of being one thing that makes determinate (to that extent) that indeterminate state. Thus understood the reference to *eudaimonia* does have explanatory value. It introduces the concept of a very wide state, viz. the state of a person during the whole of his life, and a state which though indeterminate as regards its substantial content, nevertheless exhibits a certain precise formal property. When honour is related to this concept, we do become wiser concerning the description under which the given person considers honour choiceworthy, but our enlightenment is not due to the fact that we can now see more clearly why the person values honour as he does: what has happened is that the person's estimation of honour has now been inserted into a wider conceptual framework. He is now seen as a person who operates with the notion of *eudaimonia* and who is apparently prepared to mention honour as one thing that goes into *eudaimonia*. When we know that, we know more about the person's attitude to honour. But again we do not know any more about why he considers honour choiceworthy in the first place.

Note here that when honour is referred to *eudaimonia* as that for the sake of which it is chosen, there is absolutely no implication that there either are or are not other things that fall under *eudaimonia* in addition to honour. The reference to *eudaimonia* is a reference to a purely indeterminate state, which is the point of all choice and the state where all desires are satisfied. It is not a reference to any considered view of what things make up that state. One may of course attempt to relate honour to other such things: this, however, is not what is done when honour is referred to *eudaimonia* as what it is chosen for.

6.2. This is the point where my account of the relation 'for the sake of *eudaimonia*' differs from those I mentioned earlier. For in these accounts it does seem to be presupposed that the reference to *eudaimonia* will add to the value of the thing that is referred to *eudaimonia*. Thus when in connection with Plato's *Republic* T. H. Irwin discusses the idea that justice is good both in itself and for the sake of the final good, or *eudaimonia*, he insists that the final good is 'an ordered compound'.[20] Here the underlying idea seems to be that only thus will the reference to *eudaimonia* have any point. But this, of course, is only so if one expects that point to be the one of 'conferring value' on the thing that is referred to *eudaimonia*, of adding to the value which it is taken to have anyway.

A similar expectation seems to be entertained by J. L. Ackrill when he remarks that if *eudaimonia* is viewed as an aggregate instead of an organized system, the move, i.e. the reference, to *eudaimonia* will be trivial.[21] The reference to an aggregate *eudaimonia* will only be trivial if one expects it to provide a reason *why* the thing that is referred to *eudaimonia* is considered choiceworthy — and this is more than the reference is intended to do.

Why do Ackrill and Irwin take the reference to *eudaimonia* to have 'substantial' explanatory value in this way? The reason seems to be that although they have introduced and stressed the importance of certain points I have made use of in the above account of *eudaimonia*, e.g. that it is an indeterminate end[22] and that it may be glossed as 'the perfectly satisfying life',[23] they do not always keep in view the difference between *eudaimonia* as an indeterminate state and the inclusive determinate conception of that state that we are likely to come out with as our final view of what the state *consists in*. But these two types of end must be kept apart; for the explanatory value of referring something to the two things is different.

It will not do, therefore, to explicate the relationship between a thing and *eudaimonia*, where the former is referred

---

[20] Irwin, *Plato's Moral Theory*, p. 225.
[21] Ackrill, 'Aristotle on *Eudaimonia*', p. 347. Cf. also Irwin in his 'First Principles In Aristotle's Ethics', *Midwest Studies in Philosophy, vol. III: Studies in Ethical Theory*, University of Minnesota, Morris, 1978, 252–72, p. 259.
[22] Irwin, *Plato's Moral Theory, passim.*   [23] Ackrill, p. 351.

to the latter, by means of the following two examples: as putting is to playing golf, or as golfing is to having a good holiday. For the relationship in either example is a different one, and only the latter example is apposite. In the former case the thing is referred to a whole which is equivalent to what I called an inclusive determinate conception of *eudaimonia*. In the latter case, however, the thing is referred to something which is equivalent to the indeterminate 'eudaimonic' state: in fact having a good holiday *is* being *eudaimōn* — during one's holiday.

J. M. Cooper too wants to *infer* the intrinsic value of the components of the ultimate end from the intrinsic value of that end itself. *Because* the ultimate end is something, in fact the only thing, which is desired for its own sake, *therefore* the components of that end are themselves desired for their own sake (and, of course, for the sake of the ultimate end too).[24] It would presumably be unjust to charge Cooper with the claim that the reference to the ultimate end adds to the value of the component. But it is still clear that in the passage I have just referred to, and elsewhere, when Cooper talks of the ultimate end, he is talking of some conception of that end, not of the entirely formal state that it is. Thus in an important section he states that the ultimate end is 'an inclusive second-order end'.[25] This looks promising. But what he is really thinking of is a certain '*conception* of human flourishing' (my emphasis), which though it is claimed, validly enough, to allow for the independent value of a number of different activities and interests is also described as 'an orderly scheme' and 'an overall plan of life'.

As against this I claim that when something is referred to *eudaimonia*, it is referred, not to some (inclusive or dominant)[26] conception of what *eudaimonia* consists in, but to the state itself which has the one property of being

---

[24] Cooper, *Reason and Human Good in Aristotle*, p. 82 with footnote.

[25] Ibid., pp. 96–9.

[26] This is the terminology that was introduced by W. F. R. Hardie in an influential article, 'The Final Good in Aristotle's *Ethics*', *Phil.* 40 (1965), 277–95. As will be clear from this chapter and chapter 4, I do not consider the ascription to Aristotle of a 'dominant' conception of the supreme end very helpful. Hardie has developed his views in 'Aristotle on the Best Life for a Man', *Phil.* 54 (1979), 35–50.

the point of all the choices and desires of a given person, and none in addition.

7.1. I have discussed, in connection with vii.1-8, the sense of the concept of *eudaimonia* and the sense of referring a thing to *eudaimonia* by means of the phrase 'for the sake of *eudaimonia*'. However, Aristotle also says that one may choose something, e.g. honour, *both* for its own sake and (at the same time, I take it) *also* for the sake of *eudaimonia*. What is meant here? What is the relationship between 'for its own sake' and 'for the sake of *eudaimonia*'?

If one accepts the interpretation I have suggested of the concept of *eudaimonia* and the sense of referring something to *eudaimonia*, one might contend that the latter reference adds nothing significant to the claim that the thing is choice-worthy for its own sake. The 'eudaimonic' state will consist of all the things that are considered choiceworthy in themselves, but then could we not altogether dispense with the concept of that state?

This is not to say that Aristotle is wrong to spend time on elucidating the concept. For, as we have seen, people do talk of *eudaimonia*; hence it is well worth bringing out what they mean. However, I shall contend that the concept of *eudaimonia* has a much more important role to play. The concept is put to use at a theoretically central point.

7.2. There are good grounds for ascribing to Aristotle a view of the concept of rational want (in effect his notion of *prohairesis*)²⁷ according to which it is a necessary condition

---

²⁷ I am claiming here that we should understand Aristotle's notion of *prohairesis* along the general lines introduced by G. E. M. Anscombe to define the concept of intentional action (*Intention*, Oxford, 1963², esp. pp. 25-33). It is true that the most important form of *prohairesis* in the ethical context is the one that results in genuine *praxeis* and is therefore, as we shall see, directly related to *eudaimonia*; but there is no reason to believe, as Anscombe herself does throughout her 'Thought and Action in Aristotle', that this is the only form of *prohairesis* allowed for by Aristotle. Aristotle develops his concept of *prohairesis* (in *EN* III.iii) by drawing on the notion of *technical* deliberation. Technical justification will therefore be sufficient to qualify a want as a *prohairesis* — even technical justification as had by the incontinent man when he has deliberated about how to reach a goal that he wants only incontinently. (G. E. M. Anscombe, 'Thought and Action in Aristotle, What is 'Practical Truth'?' in *New Essays in Plato and Aristotle*, ed. R. Bambrough, London, 1965, 143-58.)

for a want to be rational that the person who has it is able to mention something that he considers the wanted object good *for*. He must, in Aristotelian terms, be able to mention some *telos* (end) or other. A paradigm case is the want which is had by a technician for an act which is considered a means proper to some end. His want is rationalized by being referred to the end, and the expression that is used to bring about this reference is the phrase 'for the sake of', where what is for the sake of is a different thing from what it is for the sake of. It also seems clear that Aristotle is prepared to use the phrase 'for the sake of' not only where what is related are two different things, but also where the phrase brings in some further description of the original thing, e.g. when something is stated to be choiceworthy or good 'for the sake of the noble'.

When, however, the two things that are brought into relation with each other by means of 'for the sake of' are one and the same thing under the same description, it is much less easy to see how the want is rationalized by means of that phrase. 'x is good for its own sake or because of itself', 'x has as its end itself': one might think that these sentences are unproblematic in the way in which talk of a mathematical set as being empty is. However, when the point of talking of an 'end' of something and of using the phrase 'for the sake of' is to rationalize or make intelligible some want, it can hardly be sufficient just to use the concepts of an end and 'for the sake of': the wanted object must be connected *by means of* those concepts with *other* things, whether it be truly different things or just different descriptions of the same thing. So the sentence 'x is choiceworthy or good for its own sake' is problematic as an expression that is intended to rationalize the want for x.

However, we cannot dispense with the phrase 'good for its own sake'. People do, or bring about, certain things for the sake of other things, but the chain of explanation cannot go on for ever. Any chain must stop somewhere, otherwise the initial desire will be pointless. And in fact people do stop chains by stating of something that they choose that thing for its own sake. Moreover, since the function of that statement is to put a stop to chains of explanation that *rationalize* wants, by the use of the phrase 'for the sake of something else', the statement must itself rationalize or make intelligible the want for the thing that is claimed to stop the given chain. But we saw that precisely as a rationalizing concept it is problematic.[28]

7.3. This is where the concept of *eudaimonia* comes in. The problem about the phrase 'for its own sake' is that we want it to put a stop to chains of explanation, but that it is not fully intelligible as a concept that rationalizes a want. The concept of *eudaimonia* is both sufficient to rationalize a want and eminently suited to put a stop to chains of explanation. It is sufficient to rationalize a want since, being the concept of the state whose existence is implied in the very notion of choosing (it is the concept of a state which is the point of all choice), it is itself so eminently rational. And it is well suited to put a stop to chains of explanation since it is the very concept of a state where all chains of explanation come to a stop. It seems, therefore, that we may make use of the concept of *eudaimonia* to put a stop to any particular chain of explanation at the point at which we do wish to stop, and that the way in which we may use the concept is by saying that we choose this thing not for the sake of anything else but 'for the sake of *eudaimonia*', i.e. as one thing that has the role of filling in that indeterminate concept or of falling under the by itself indeterminate 'eudaimonic' state.

However, what we in fact normally say is not immediately that we choose the thing for the sake of *eudaimonia*, but that we choose it for its own sake. I suggest that we take the phrase 'for the sake of *eudaimonia*' as an *explication* of the phrase 'for its own sake' or, in other words, that we take the reference to the state where there is no room at all for any more choices to rationalize the suggestion of some particular thing as something that puts a stop to *one* set of choices. We may say, then, that properly understood the phrase 'for its own sake' *introduces* the concept of *eudaimonia*. The latter concept is the one that renders the phrase sufficiently informative for it to rationalize the want for the given thing.

---

[28] The formulation of the problem, but not the solution I suggest in the following section, is indebted to Jaakko Hintikka's paper 'Remarks on praxis, poiesis and ergon in Plato and in Aristotle', in *Studia philosophica in honorem Sven Krohn*, Annales universitatis turkuensis, series B, tom. 126, 1972, 53–62.

So the concept of *eudaimonia* has a most important role to play at a crucial point for our understanding of the system of concepts that are implied by the concept of choice. The latter concept implies the notion of an end of something, and the notion of an end implies the distinction between ends that are themselves related to other things as their end, and ends which are not themselves so related. But in order to make sufficiently rational sense of the latter type of end we must introduce the concept that is basic to the concept of choice, viz. that of the 'ideal object' or point of all choice: the state where all choice has made itself superfluous since the ends of all choices have been reached. When the phrase 'for its own sake' is seen to introduce *this* concept, we shall be rationally satisfied by a claim that makes use of the phrase and states that something is chosen as an end which is not related to other things as its end, but is its own end.[29]

7.4. But is this view of the theoretical role of the reference to *eudaimonia* in its relation to the phrase 'for its own sake' Aristotle's? What he says in vii.1-8 is just that we may choose, e.g., honour, *both* for its own sake *and* for the sake of *eudaimonia*. I shall come back to the question in a moment (below, sections 9.1-9.2).

At present we should note that there is no danger of circularity in that view. It is true that in vii.1-8 Aristotle brings out his conception of *eudaimonia* by means of the distinction between ends that are chosen for the sake of other things and ends that are chosen for their own sake. But the conception of *eudaimonia*, as the point of all choice, that he brings out in this way does not rely for its intelligibility on the notion of a thing's being choiceworthy for its own sake. The definition of *eudaimonia* as the point of all choice makes use of the following two conceptual connections: that choosing implies the existence of some end, and that choosing *qua* a type of desire, viz. a desire for acts, implies the existence

[29] Basically the same account of the role of the concept of *eudaimonia* is given in an article that appeared after I had formulated my own view: K. Jacobi, 'Aristoteles' Einführung des Begriffs "eudaimonia" im I. Buch der "Nikomachischen Ethik", Eine Antwort auf einige neuere Inkonsistenzkritiken', *Phil. Jahr.* 86 (1979), 300-25, esp. pp. 318-20.

of a state where all desire is satisfied and made superfluous. Aristotle makes use of the distinction between subordinate and non-subordinate ends as a *way* of bringing out his conception of *eudaimonia*, but the distinction plays no role in that conception itself.

8.1. For the sake of completeness I will comment briefly on the lines that conclude the section we have been discussing: 'So *eudaimonia* seems to be something final and self-sufficient, being the end of acts' (vii.8, 1097b20-21). What is the exact force of the participle? Commentators suggest that the sense is: '*and* it is the end of acts'.[30] This is, of course, a possible interpretation of the Greek form, and it may well be right. By itself, however, it does not settle the question of the precise point of those last few words. What message are they intended to convey?

It is not very likely that the participle has a causal sense: 'because it is the end of acts'. Aristotle is entitled to conclude from the preceding section that *eudaimonia* is something final and self-sufficient, but hardly that it is so *because* it is the end of acts. Rather, that it is the end of acts is something that might seem, if anything, to *follow* from the definition of it as final as that definition was reached through the argument of vii.1-5. However, I am not quite happy about this suggestion either. vii.1-5 are the crucial paragraphs in as much as they talk, as vii.6-7 do not, of acts and ends of acts. They do so, as we know, because they attempt to define the good and *eudaimonia* relative to the concept of choice, and that concept involves those other concepts. Hence when, in vii.5, *eudaimonia* is identified with the absolutely final *as defined in* § *4, eudaimonia* is identified as the absolutely final *end of acts*. But in that case it is unlikely that Aristotle should have wanted, in the closing words of the passage, to sever the connection between *eudaimonia*'s being something final and its being an end of acts, and to intimate that its being the latter *follows* from its being the former.

If this view of the connection, in vii.4, between the definition of the absolutely final and its being an end of acts is correct, a third interpretation of the concluding four words

---

[30] So, e.g., Burnet.

suggests itself. We have seen that being final, and for that matter being self-sufficient, are general concepts that may be used in very different areas. We have also just seen that in vii.1–5 being final is used in connection with the realm of acts. Therefore, when Aristotle adds the words under consideration, his aim is probably to spell out that in summing up *eudaimonia* as something final (and self-sufficient) he is using 'final' in connection with the end of *acts*: 'Final, then, in some way, and self-sufficient is what *eudaimonia* seems to be, and (when I say it is final I mean that) it is the end of *acts*.' This reading gives satisfactory sense to the emphatic positions in the Greek of 'final' and of 'acts', and it suits perfectly the use of the participial form: *eudaimonia* is final (and self-sufficient) *in the way that* it is the end of *acts*.

8.2. One more word on Aristotle's summary of the whole passage. We know that Aristotle concludes that *eudaimonia* is both something final and something self-sufficient, and it is of course wholly appropriate that he should do so. However, if the above remarks on the summary are correct, it will still be the case that the main emphasis lies on the point that *eudaimonia* is something final (and final in the realm of acts). This is worth a few comments.

I have suggested that though closely connected the two concepts of being final and being self-sufficient differ in an important respect. Being final involves a reference to something that lies 'before' the final thing; being self-sufficient does not. I have also suggested that the concept of being self-sufficient has an important role to play in the passage as a whole. First, it helps us to make sense of Aristotle's definition of the most final or final without qualification. And secondly, the concept is of vital importance for my suggestion that while the idea of being choiceworthy for its own sake is problematic, the problem that it raises will disappear with the introduction of the concept of *eudaimonia*. For if it were not possible to define *eudaimonia* in other ways than by making use of the idea I take to be problematic, my whole suggestion would evidently be wrecked; due to the way it influences our understanding of the definition of *eudaimonia* as final, viz. as the point of all choice, the concept of self-sufficiency saves my suggestion from that wreck.

But now though the definition of *eudaimonia* as self-sufficient is important in these ways, it remains the case that the basic consideration by which Aristotle reaches his definition of *eudaimonia* is the one that connects the concept with that of choice and consequently talks of acts, of their goodness in terms of their ends, and of ends of acts in terms of their being choiceworthy for the sake of something else or for their own sake. Sections 10.1–10.2 below will confirm that this is in fact the basic consideration.

9.1. What argument, then, can I bring for my suggestion that the relationship between the phrases 'for its own sake' and 'for the sake of *eudaimonia*' is more complex than the simple one of both one thing and the other?

A passage I have already alluded to will provide material for an argument, *EN* VI.v.4, 1140b6–7. Here Aristotle defines the difference between *praxis* and *poiēsis* in the following way: '. . . while in the case of *poiēsis* the end is different (from the act which is the *poiēsis*),[31] in the case of *praxis* it is not; for the very "acting well" (*eupraxia*) that it itself is, is the end.'[32]

I shall assume that the concept of *eupraxia* is basically equivalent to that of *eudaimonia*, but suggest that there is the following point to operating with both concepts. As a state of a person during the whole of his life in which all of his desires are satisfied, *eudaimonia* will consist ('substantially') in those particular things or activities that satisfy any given person's desires. In fact, however, it is an Aristotelian point that the state which has the proper claim to being the 'eudaimonic' one, viz. the state in which all the desires are satisfied that are had by man *as he truly is* − that this state is one of *activity* (see *EN* I.vii.10 ff.). I believe that when in passages in which he is really working with the concept of the 'eudaimonic' state Aristotle uses *eupraxia* instead of *eudaimonia*,

[31] This is the traditional interpretation. It has recently been questioned by Theodor Ebert in 'Praxis und Poiesis, Zu einer handlungstheoretischen Unterscheidung bei Aristoteles', *Zeitschrift für philosophische Forschung*, 30 (1976), 12–30.

[32] Note αὐτή and ἡ in the last sentence: 'for it is precisely (αὐτή) the *eupraxia* that it itself is (ἡ) that is the end.' See a little further on in the text, section 9.3.

he is smuggling into the concept of that state the idea that
the state will be one of activity. And if it is questioned
whether in *eupraxia*-passages Aristotle really is working with
the concept of the 'eudaimonic' state, I believe that the
connection between *EN* VI.v.4, 1140b6-7 and VI.ii.5,
1139b1-4, on the one hand, and between the latter passage
and I.vii.1-5 and i-ii.1 on the other is sufficient to settle any
doubts. *Eupraxia* is *eudaimonia*, in the realm of acts. So
when something is done with *eupraxia* as its end or for the
sake of *eupraxia*, it is done as one thing that falls under the
'eudaimonic' state of activity.

9.2. But if this is accepted, then I may use the account of
praxis at 1140b6-7 in support of my suggestion concerning
the phrase 'for its own sake'. For what Aristotle will then be
saying of a *praxis* is this: the end of a *praxis* is the *praxis*
itself (it is its own end or done for its own sake); *for* its end
is *eupraxia* (it is done for the sake of *eupraxia* or as one thing
that falls under the 'eudaimonic' state of activity). Here the
crucial point for present purposes lies in Aristotle's use of
'for'. While in I.vii.5 he stated that honour and a number of
other things, including moral virtue, are chosen both for their
own sake and for the sake of *eudaimonia*, in the present
passage he is claiming *praxeis* to be chosen for their own sake
because they are chosen for the sake of *eupraxia*. With the
sense that we should give to the phrase 'for the sake of
eupraxia', i.e. when it is remembered that *eupraxia* is the
purely indeterminate 'eudaimonic' state of activity, this can
only mean that the very sense of the claim that a *praxis* is its
own end or is done for its own sake lies in the fact that by
these locutions the act is seen as falling under the state of
eupraxia. *Eupraxia* is the concept under which the phrase
'its own end' makes rationally satisfactory sense.

So if I am right in my assumption concerning the relationship of *eudaimonia* and *eupraxia*, the passage we have considered provides some support for my earlier suggestion
concerning the mutual relationship of the phrases 'for its
own sake' and 'for the sake of *eudaimonia*'. It is not just that
things may be said to be chosen or done both for their own
sake and also, more or less gratuitously, for the sake of

eudaimonia or, in connection with acts, because they are acting well. Rather, the very reason why they may be satisfactorily said to be chosen or done for their own sake is that they are referred to *eudaimonia* and *eupraxia*, and are seen to fall under those states.

9.3. One more point should be noted about the definition of *praxis*. Aristotle is saying, in my contorted translation, that in the case of a *praxis* 'the very "acting well" that it itself is, is the end'. The point of 'very' and 'itself' may be seen if we consider the other passage that helps to define the difference between *praxis* and *poiēsis*, *EN* VI.ii.5, 1139b1-4. Practical thought, says Aristotle, rules productive knowledge too;

for everybody who produces produces for the sake of some end, and the result that is produced (*to poiēton*) is not an end without qualification — that thing [sc. the *poiēton*] is (good) relative to some other thing and (the result) of some particular (process); rather, it is the result of *praxis* (*to prakton*) that is an end without qualification — for the *eupraxia* that it [sc. the *praxis*] is, is the end — and the desire [viz. the one that guides even the *poiēsis*] is for this [viz. the *prakton*].

I will not argue for the details of this translation. Aristotle's main point is clear, viz. that the final end, even of an act which is a *poiēsis*, is 'the result of *praxis*', or *eupraxia*.

But then the point of 'very' and 'itself' in the former passage will be that in the case of a *praxis*, as opposed to *poiēsis*, there are no intermediaries between the act and *eupraxia*. *Eupraxia* is *directly* the end of an act which is a *praxis*.

We may sum up these remarks on 1140b6-7 in the following definition of an Aristotelian *praxis*. A *praxis* is an act which is done for its own sake, i.e. which is *itself* considered as one thing that falls under the 'eudaimonic' state of *eupraxia*. This is my answer to the question I formulated at the beginning of section 3.

10.1. I now wish to go back to the very first page of the *Ethics*. I shall try to show that the conception of *eudaimonia* I have argued to be Aristotle's helps to solve a problem that has puzzled commentators, and that the passage provides support for the truth of my claim that this conception is Aristotle's.

The passage is i–ii.1. The division into chapters is unfortunate here. Chapter ii ought, if anywhere, to start between what is now ii.1 and ii.2. For ii.1 forms the conclusion of the argument of i.

Aristotle is introducing the basic concept of his ethical system: 'the good'. The good is what is aimed at (i.1). But there are different types of end; some are (the) activities (themselves), others are certain results of activities (i.2). And there are many ends (i.3). But then some are subordinate to others (i.4). And here, with respect to subordination, 'it makes no difference whether the ends are the activities themselves that the acts are, or the ends are something else beyond the acts' (i.5, 1094a16–17). We have already been puzzled by this remark (section 2.2). But Aristotle crowns his argument in this way (ii.1, 1094a18–22):

> If, then, there is a (single) end of acts which we want for its own sake while we want the rest for it, and (if) we do not choose everything for some further thing (for in that case the chain will continue *ad infinitum* with the consequence that the desire becomes empty and pointless), it is clear that that will be the good or (rather) the highest good.

10.2. This paragraph has puzzled commentators.[33] Is it not the case that Aristotle argues, invalidly, from the point (in the second part of the *protasis*) that any chain of choice must stop *some*where to the claim (in the first part of the *protasis*) that there must be a single place where *all* chains of choice come to a stop?

I agree that it is most natural to take Aristotle to be arguing from the latter to the former part of the *protasis*. But with the conception of *eudaimonia* and the good that I have argued for, we can see that it is in fact quite legitimate for him to do so. I have suggested that *eudaimonia* is the state which is the point of all choice, and that in vii.1–5 Aristotle reaches this concept via the concept of an end, the idea of subordination of some ends to others, and finally via the concept of an end which is not subordinate to

---

[33] See, e.g., Anscombe, *Intention*, p. 34; B. A. O. Williams, 'Aristotle on the Good: a Formal Sketch', *PQ* 12 (1962), 289–96, p. 292; A. J. P. Kenny, 'Happiness', *PAS* 66 (1965-6), 93–102, pp. 94–5; C. A. Kirwan, 'Logic and the Good in Aristotle', *PQ* 17 (1967), 97–114, pp. 107–11; Ackrill, 'Aristotle on *Eudaimonia*', pp. 349–51; Irwin, *Plato's Moral Theory*, p. 52.

any other end. The same line of thought runs through the whole of chapter i and the first part of the *protasis* of ii.1.[34] It seems, then, that this line of thought is in fact, as I have suggested, the basic one for the development of Aristotle's peculiar conception of the good and *eudaimonia*. But I have also suggested that Aristotle needs the concept of the good and *eudaimonia* as the state that is the point of all choice, in order to make sufficiently rational sense of the idea of stopping *particular* chains of choice each at its own particular place. And this is precisely the logical relationship that must hold between the latter and the former part of the *protasis* of ii.1. *Because* we cannot choose everything for the sake of some further thing, i.e. because any particular chain of choice must come to an end *some*where (and this must be so since otherwise the desire will become empty and vain), *therefore* there must be a single end of all choice, *viz. the 'eudaimonic' state*. Without the concept of this end we could not make sufficient sense of stopping any particular chain at any particular place.

I conclude that the conception of *eudaimonia* I have argued to be Aristotle's does help to solve the puzzle of ii.1. Furthermore, ii.1 itself supports my point concerning the logical role of the concept of *eudaimonia vis-à-vis* the phrase 'for its own sake'.[35]

It is perhaps worth pointing out that in the argument of i–ii.1 for the existence of the single ultimate end it is left absolutely open whether just one thing or activity or more things or activities than one should in the end be said to fill in *eudaimonia*. The answer may of course be, and presumably

[34] I suggest that when, in I.vii.2, Aristotle states that 'the argument has come round to its starting-point', he is drawing attention to the fact that by introducing, in vii.1, the concepts of that-for-the-sake-of-which and an end of acts he once more finds himself in the position from which he began right at the start of chapter i. From this position he argued, via the notion of subordination of some ends to others, to the formulation, in ii.1, of the concept of the single end of all acts; and in an exactly similar way he starts, *in vii.3*, by considering the notion of subordination and eventually reaches, in vii.4 and 5, his concept of the single end of all acts. Thus vii.2 does not, as it is normally taken, refer directly back to ii.1, but to the very beginning of the work.

[35] It would have been reassuring if K. Jacobi, who sees the general point about Aristotle's use of the concept of *eudaimonia*, had used that point for the interpretation of ii.1, which he does discuss. Jacobi, pp. 300–2.

will be, 'more than one'; but it might equally well be, 'just one thing or activity'. Just as this question was not raised in vii.1–8, so it is totally irrelevant to the logical point concerning the concept of *eudaimonia* that Aristotle wants to make in i–ii.1. For even if it were the case that only one thing should be taken to fill in *eudaimonia*, that thing, which would then be *the* thing that everything else is done for, would still be different from the 'eudaimonic' state. It would be the only thing that falls under, but would not be identical with, the state which is the point of all a man's choices and desires: the satisfactory life.

11.1. So far I have discussed Aristotle's concept of *eudaimonia*, and attempted to define his concept of *praxis* by drawing on the sense he attaches to the former concept. A *praxis* is an act which is chosen for its own sake, i.e. which is considered to be one thing that goes directly into the satisfactory life (of activity). However, this is hardly sufficient to define the concept of *praxis*. A central further question is whether there will be any restrictions on the description under which an act may be chosen for its own sake. In particular, may that description be allowed to contain a reference to a *result* of the act? The danger that seems to threaten here is in fact that of a total breakdown of the distinction between *praxis* and *poiēsis*. If the act-description contains a reference to a *result* of the act, the point of that reference will presumably be to indicate what it is that gives the act *value*, but in that case it seems impossible to distinguish an act under such a description from an act which is a case of *poiēsis*: in neither case, so it seems, is the act referred *directly* to *eudaimonia*. On the other hand, it does seem necessary that one should be able to perform a *praxis* under a description which contains a reference to an act-result. For moral acts are *praxeis*, according to Aristotle, and the description of most moral acts, like 'trying to save a child from drowning', will in fact contain a reference to an intended result of the act.

11.2. The distinction I am relying on here when talking of acts and their (immediate) results is Aristotle's own distinction

between two general types of movement, *energeia* and *kinēsis*.
The *locus classicus* for the distinction is *Metaph.* Theta 6,
1048b18–35. For present purposes it is sufficient to define
the distinction as follows. A movement is a *kinēsis* if an
explicit or implicit reference is contained in its description to
a possible state of the world in which the movement has
stopped, other than the bare, negative state of the movement's having stopped. Otherwise a movement is an *energeia*.
Thus 'dancing' is an *energeia*, since it contains no explicit or
implicit reference to any state of the world other than the
simple, negative one of 'not-dancing'. Similarly 'living' is an
energeia since, though it may perhaps be said to contain a
reference to the state of 'being dead', the latter state is just
the bare, negative state of 'not-living'. 'Building a house' or
'trying to save a child from drowning', on the other hand, are
kinēseis. For these descriptions refer directly to a different
state of the world with its own, 'positive' description, viz.
the state of there being a house or of the child's being safe.

In this account of the difference between *energeia* and
kinēsis it is already implied (in the examples) that I take the
distinction between *praxis* and *poiēsis* to cut across the one
between *energeia* and *kinēsis*.[36] I shall now try to justify
this assumption.

The problem that I raised in section 11.1 is basically, we
may now say, whether an act that according to its description
is a *kinēsis* may also be a *praxis* or not. The implication of
taking this as a problem is that since an act of the *kinēsis*-
type contains a reference to an intended act-result, the act
will necessarily get its value from the act-result and cannot
therefore be referred directly to the concept of *eudaimonia*:
it will necessarily be a case of *poiēsis*. This implication is
false, however. It is of course true that in the case of acts
like 'building a house' and 'trying to save a child from drown-

---

[36] In so doing I differ from the view that is normally taken by commentators
(when elucidating the *praxis/poiēsis* pair) and from some of the recent literature
on the distinction between *energeia* and *kinēsis*. See, e.g., A. J. P. Kenny, *Action,
Emotion and Will*, London, 1963, ch. VI, p. 173. J. L. Ackrill is more cautious
when he claims that the distinction between *energeia* and *kinēsis* is 'closely
related to the distinction between action (*praxis*) and production (*poiesis*)':
Ackrill, 'Aristotle's Distinction between *Energeia* and *Kinesis*', in *New Essays
in Plato and Aristotle*, ed. R. Bambrough, London, 1965, 121–41, p. 121.

ing', the act will in a sense get its value from the fact that it is
directed towards a certain act-result. But it does not follow
that 'the end of the act is different from the act itself' in the
sense that this phrase is intended to have in Aristotle's
definition of *poiēsis*. In *kineseis* such as 'building a house'
and 'trying to save a child from drowning' we cannot sever,
logically, 'the act' from the intended act-result, since no act
will be left once that logical operation has been performed.
The definition of *poiēsis*, on the other hand, relies on the
possibility of such severance. It follows that the fact that an
act is a *kinēsis* has no implications whatever for the question
whether it is a *praxis* or *poiēsis*; to answer the latter question
for a given *kinēsis* we must consider whether it is possible in
some *further* respect to 'sever' the act (*with* its intended act-
result, since it is a *kinēsis*) from an 'end' of the act that is
different from the act itself (with its intended act-result).

11.3. I shall suggest the following answer. For an act to be
a *praxis* it must be the direct expression of a settled state of
desires on the part of the agent, or of his character. That is,
an act is a *praxis* if the agent wants to perform it (with its
intended act-result, if it is a *kinēsis*) *irrespective of any reasons*
for the goodness of the act (with its intended act-result, in
the case of a *kinēsis*) which he may also be able to give. By
contrast an act is a *poiēsis* if it is a *kinēsis* and if the agent
would not have performed it had it not been for certain
reasons he has for (*i*) the goodness of the act *as* directed
towards the given act-result, and consequently for (*ii*) the
goodness of the result. Thus take the act of trying to save a
child from drowning. For this act to be a *praxis* the agent
must want just that act independently of any reasons for its
goodness that he may be able to give. This act, of course, is
a *kinēsis*, since it contains a reference to the act-result of the
child's being safe, and it clearly gets its value from being
directed towards bringing that result into existence. But the
act may still be a *praxis*, since the agent may want to do it
under the description according to which it is connected with
a certain result of the act, but independently of any reasons
he may be able to give for the goodness of the act (as directed
towards that result — and consequently for the goodness

of the result). If the agent in fact wants it in that way, it is a
direct expression of the state of his desires. And if in addition,
and as a consequence of the fact that this want is an expression of a *settled* state of his desires, he has 'conceptualized'
that want of his by referring it to the rational concept of
eudaimonia, his act will be a *praxis*.

I believe that this interpretation of the concepts of *praxis*
and *poiēsis* in relation to that of *kinēsis* allows us to perform,
in a precise and satisfactory way, the 'severance' of the act
and the end of the act that is implied in Aristotle's definition
of *poiēsis*. If an act is a *poiēsis*, it is performed because the
agent has independent reasons for the goodness of the act-
result, and the existence and motivational force of these
reasons do make the act–result more than just the intended
result of the act: they turn that result into an independent
end that is in fact 'different' from the act itself (with its
intended act-result).

By contrast my account of *praxis* explains why in a *praxis*
the end of the act cannot be severed from the act itself, even
where the act, according to its description, is a *kinēsis*. It is
of course true that if an act is a *kinēsis*, it will get its value
from the fact that the intended act-result is considered
valuable. Still an act of that type may be a *praxis* if it is
wanted under that description, but independently of whatever reasons the agent may be able to give for the goodness
of the act *as* directed towards the given act-result and consequently for the goodness of the result — and if it is at the
same time wanted as an expression of a settled state of desires
on his part which is 'conceptualized' by him in such a way
that acts that issue from that state of desire are considered
by him to be things that go into the satisfactory life.

The important point is that in one way the concept of
praxis is so very closely connected with the idea of a settled
state of the agent's *desires*: he wants to perform just that act,
e.g. trying to save the child from drowning; he clearly wants
it (in this *kinēsis*-case) because he wants the intended result
to obtain, but still even if the act is unsuccessful, it is not
thereby rendered otiose or pointless — *for the agent has been
doing what he wanted to do*. In another way, however, the
concept of *praxis* is a *rational* one and connected with the idea

of the agent's view of what *eudaimonia* consists in: only if an act that is wanted in the above way is 'conceptualized' by being referred to the concept of *eudaimonia* will it be a *praxis*.

11.4. But is this interpretation of the concept of *praxis* valid? I made two moves in the above account. The first one (section 11.2) was to insist that the fact that an act according to its description is a *kinēsis* has no implications whatever for the question whether it is a *praxis* or a *poiēsis*. For the severance of the act and its end that is implied in Aristotle's definition of *poiēsis* (and will therefore also be relevant to his definition of *praxis*) cannot be performed on a *kinēsis* as just that. This point, I believe, is justified in itself.

The second move (section 11.3) was to connect the concept of *praxis* with that of the agent's character. The person who performs a *praxis* may well have reasons to give for the goodness of the act (with its result, if it is a *kinēsis*), but independently of any such reasons he will want to do the act as one thing that goes into *eudaimonia simply because*, as Aristotle would say, he is that sort of man: it is in his character to do so. This is a suggestion that I cannot argue for here. Its theoretical backing is a certain view of the relationship between the cognitive and the desiderative elements in moral goodness which will be developed in detail in the second part of this book. I hope, however, that it will seem intuitively plausible. It is in fact a direct consequence of the interpretation of *eudaimonia* as an entirely formal concept that I have propounded in this chapter.

12. But now I have allowed that in addition to wanting an act as a *praxis*, or as one thing that goes directly into *eudaimonia*, an agent may well have reasons for the goodness of the act (or of its intended result, in the case of a *kinēsis*). Thus the good man too may have reasons for the goodness of his acts, though reasons which only add to the desire for the acts that he has anyway. In the next chapter I shall discuss the most important reason that he will have.

The clue lies in the fact that Aristotle's morally good man not only performs *praxeis*: he also acts 'for the sake of the noble'.

2

MORALITY

1. The virtuous man does more than perform *praxeis*: he also acts 'for the sake of the noble' (*tou kalou heneka*). But exactly what is meant by that phrase? In the present chapter I shall suggest an answer to this question. I first (sections 2.1–3.4) sketch my answer on the basis of two passages: *EN* IX.viii (on self-love) and *EE* VIII.iii.1–10 (on *kalokagathia*: nobility of mind or 'noble-and-goodness'); next (sections 4.1–4.8) I compare my account of the noble with certain remarks of Aristotle's on the virtue of justice (in *EN* V). In the following chapter I shall confront my interpretation of the noble with Aristotle's remarks on the topic in his discussion of the remaining moral virtues (primarily in *EN* III.vi–IV).

2.1. I begin, then, with *EN* IX.viii, on the question whether one should primarily love oneself or rather one's neighbour.[1]

The structure of the chapter is this. Aristotle first presents an argument for the view that one should primarily love others (§ 1) and then an argument for the opposite view (§ 2). So we are in a dilemma of the usual Aristotelian type; both arguments seem to contain some part of the truth. Aristotle will resolve the dilemma by considering how far each of the two arguments is valid, and he will do this by analysing in what way the two arguments use the term 'self-centred' (*philautos*) (§ 3). His solution consists, then, in

---

[1] The chapter has hardly received the attention it deserves. W. F. R. Hardie has some good remarks about it in his *Aristotle's Ethical Theory*, Oxford, 1968, pp. 323–35. See also O. Gigon, 'Die Selbstliebe in der Nikomachischen Ethik des Aristoteles', in Δώρημα, *Hans Diller zum 70. Geburtstag, Dauer und Überleben des antiken Geistes*, Griechische humanistische Gesellschaft, Internationales Zentrum für klassisch-humanistische Forschung, Zweite Reihe: Studien und Untersuchungen 27, Athens, 1975, 77–113.

showing that there are two different types of person who
may in two different senses be called self-centred, and of
these two types the one ought, and the other ought not,
primarily to love himself (§ § 4–7).

Let us consider the argument to the effect that one ought
primarily to love others (§ 1). Normally, says Aristotle,
people are blamed for loving first of all themselves: they are
said to be 'self-centred' (*philautoi*, 1168a30), and that is
something base (*aischron*, ibid.). The morally bad man, it is
said, does everything for his own sake (and the more so, the
worse he is): he is criticized for doing nothing 'without paying attention to himself' (*aph' heautou*, a33).[2] The morally
good man, by contrast, is said to act for the sake of the noble
(and the more so, the better he is) and for the sake of his
friend; and he pays no attention to his own interests (*to . . .
hautou pariēsin*, a35).

The argument is basically this. (*a*) Moral badness consists
in doing everything for one's own sake, moral goodness in
acting for the sake of the noble, i.e. for the sake of others
and without paying attention to one's own interests; (*b*) one
ought to be morally good; (*c*) hence one ought primarily
to love others. In the argument itself premiss (*a*) is stated to
be true on the basis of the way words are normally used,
while premiss (*b*) is just taken for granted. In the rest of
the chapter Aristotle accepts the connections made by
premiss (*a*) between being morally good, acting for the sake
of the noble, and acting for the sake of others, and I shall
argue that he also hints at an argument *why* one ought to
act for the sake of the noble and hence, by (*a*), why one

---

[2] For the proper understanding of this suggestive phrase one must go back to the
pre-Burnet commentaries of the nineteenth century. It is inexplicable to me how
it could come to be doubted that the sense is, as these commentaries have it, that
the bad man does nothing 'away from himself'. (People criticize him on the count
that *nihil ita agit ut sui cogitationem deponat* (Ramsauer) or that he never acts
'without thinking of self' (Stewart).) But since Burnet ('he does nothing of himself' or 'unless he has to') it has been doubted by almost all translators and
commentators: Rackham, Ross (he does nothing 'of his own accord'), Dirlmeier,
Gauthier (whose note, as always, sums up well). The latest translation into English,
by H. G. Apostle, is an honourable exception (people criticize the bad man 'for
never going out of his way to do something for others') and so is the German
translation by Rolfes ('man klagt ihn an, dass er nichts tut, als was ihm Vorteil
bringt').

ought to be morally good (*b*). But since he also accepts part
of the argument of § 2 to the effect that one ought primarily
to love oneself, he accepts the conclusion (*c*) of the above
argument only partly. In the immediate context of § 1,
however, it is worth emphasizing that the argument of that
paragraph only implies, but does not argue for, (*b*), that one
ought to be morally good and hence, by (*a*), which *is* backed
by argument, that one ought to act for the sake of the
noble. For the plausibility of Aristotle's doctrine on self-love
in the chapter clearly depends on whether he in fact has an
argument for these two claims. I have promised to argue that
he does in fact hint at such an argument, but we shall see
that it is no more than a hint (sections 2.3–2.4, below).

In § 4 Aristotle starts his analysis of the term 'self-centred'.
I must paraphrase.

People are reproached for being self-centred if they assign
to themselves the greater share of material goods, or honours,
or bodily pleasures — for these are the things 'the many' desire
and are eager to get in the belief that they are the best things
— that is why such things are fought about (*perimachēta*,
1168b19). But people who are grasping (*pleonektai*, ibid.)
with regard to such things gratify their appetites and generally
their passions and the irrational part of soul (and such are the
many). So people who are self-centred in that way are
rightly reproached for being so (§ 4).

But, as Aristotle continues, there is another type of person
who might also be called self-centred. If a man were always
eager first of all to act justly himself, or moderately, or in accordance with the rest of the virtues, if, that is, he always tried
to secure for himself the noble, then nobody would call him
self-centred (nor would anybody blame him); but such a person
would in fact seem to be self-centred in the truest sense. For
he assigns to himself what is most noble and what is in the
truest sense good (*agathon*), and he gratifies the most authori-
tative part of himself; hence the person who loves and gratifies
that is self-centred in the truest sense — though of course of a
different type from the one who is reproached: they differ as
much as living in accordance with reason differs from living in
accordance with passion, and as desiring what is noble differs
from desiring what only seems advantageous (§§ 5–6).

What Aristotle has been doing in § § 4-6 is to contrast a type of person who is self-centred in what is implied to be the more usual sense of the term, with a type of person who is self-centred in a different and more exalted way. Aristotle argues that the latter person is in fact self-centred, but admits that this is not normal usage. Normally, being self-centred is coupled with being grasping or (we may say) egotistical in the sense of keeping for oneself more than one's share of the goods that are fought about. The person who is self-centred in the more exalted way is not egotistical in that sense. For the effect, so it seems, of the fact that he acts in accordance with the virtues is precisely that he does not share out to himself more than his own of the goods that are fought about. This (implied) point already goes some way towards showing what being virtuous and 'trying to secure the noble for oneself' consists in. But Aristotle's explicit point is just that the term self-centred may be used, and with some degree of justification, of what are in fact two radically different types of person: of people as they mostly are and of the morally good man. And he mentions a corresponding difference: whereas the one type of self-centred person is normally, and rightly, reproached for being so, the other type of person is not, nor (it is implied) ought he to be.

The latter point is taken up in the paragraph which immediately follows (§ 7). Everybody, says Aristotle, praises people who show outstanding eagerness to perform actions that are noble; and if everybody strove to act nobly, everything would be as it should for the community (*koinēi*), and each single person would get the greatest of goods, since virtue is such a thing.

I take it that the latter part of this sentence is intended to justify the correctness of the normal attitude to people who want to act nobly, as described in the former part of the sentence. People are right to praise lovers of the noble; for noble action benefits the community and oneself. So Aristotle has provided us with what looks like a criterion for the appropriateness of acting nobly: one ought to act nobly because by so doing one will benefit the community and oneself. In fact, in the lines that follow immediately, in which he at last comes to answer the question he raised at the start of the chapter, Aristotle makes use of precisely that criterion. He concludes: so that the morally good man ought to be self-centred (for by acting nobly he will himself profit, and he will benefit others), whereas the morally bad person ought not to be so (for when he follows his bad passions he will do harm to himself as well as to his neighbour) (§ 7, 1169a11-15).

2.2. I have been paraphrasing, but here interpretation must start. Why is the criterion for the rightness of acting nobly that by so doing one will benefit the community and oneself? And why is the criterion for the appropriateness of self-centredness whether by being so one will benefit the community and oneself or not? Aristotle says that this is so, but why? And what is meant by benefiting oneself and the others?

Let us ask: In what sense does one benefit oneself, and in what sense does one benefit others, when one acts nobly? And why ought one to benefit oneself, and why others?

Let us take the second part of these questions: In what sense does one benefit others by acting nobly and why ought one to benefit others?

Consideration of the way in which Aristotle contrasts, in §§ 1 and 4-6, the morally bad man and the morally good man makes it likely that he considers noble action beneficial to others in the sense that in acting nobly one will share out to others what is their due of the goods that are fought about. Other people benefit from my noble act since when I act nobly I do not grasp more than my due of the goods that are fought about, but give to others their due.

But why ought I to benefit others? Aristotle himself does not raise this question. We saw, in connection with § 1, that he takes it for granted that one ought to be virtuous and act nobly so as to benefit others. But the question certainly remains of why one ought to do so: why ought one to act nobly and why, consequently, ought one to benefit others?

However, let us first consider the other part of the questions we raised: in what sense does one benefit oneself by acting nobly, and why ought one to benefit oneself?

§ 8 points the way. It follows, says Aristotle, from the answer that was just given to the basic question of the chapter, that there is a clash, in the case of the morally bad man, between what he ought to do and what he actually does, whereas the morally good man does exactly what he ought to do; 'for reason everywhere chooses what is best for itself, and the morally good man follows his reason'.

We may infer that the good man himself, who follows his reason (1169a17–18, cf. 1168b31) and (as § § 5–6 have it) in a sense *is* his reason, chooses 'what is best for himself'. What this means is, I suggest, that by acting nobly the good man 'benefits' himself in the sense that he does *what his eudaimonia consists in* as the rational being that he is. The idea is certainly not that he shares out to himself some fairly large amount of the goods that are fought about — in that case we may suppose that he ought rather to act as most people do. Nor is the idea, as 1169a22 a little further down in the text might tempt one to believe, that the good man benefits from acting nobly in the sense that he gets some special type of (adventitious) *pleasure* from his consciousness that he does what he ought to do. The idea is simply that he benefits in the sense that he does what reason tells him that his happiness, the good for him, consists in.

But in that case the latter part of our present question is easily answered. A man ought to benefit himself by acting nobly, for when he acts nobly, he benefits himself in the sense of doing what his happiness consists in, and it is analytic that one ought to do what one's happiness consists in.

It seems, then, that we have answered one part of our original questions: we understand in what sense a man benefits himself by acting nobly, and we understand why he ought to benefit himself by acting in that way. But once more it is clear that the crucial question remains unanswered: why does reason say that acting nobly is (at least part of) what one's happiness consists in? Why ought one to act nobly? And that, of course, is exactly the question we ended up with when we tried to answer the other part of those questions. The question, then, is basic: why ought one, why is it one's good, to act nobly?

2.3. Aristotle does not attempt to answer this basic question in the chapter. He does indicate that *reason sees* that acting nobly is part of one's happiness, and he thereby implies that there is some sort of argument to show that that is the case. What, then, is it that reason sees, which explains why acting nobly and consequently benefiting *others* is in fact one thing that goes into one's *own* happiness?

I shall now attempt to sketch a line of thought that will entail a certain answer to this question. Although I start from the chapter we have been considering and return to it at the end, I do not claim that the view of the noble and related matters that I am going to advance can be unequivocally ascribed to Aristotle on the basis of that text, or indeed of any other. I shall claim, however, that it makes good sense of an important point that is made in that chapter. And when I come to consider *EE* VIII.iii.1–10, I shall claim that that passage should be seen to contain some of the central elements in that view.

In § § 1 and 4 of the chapter on self-love it is implied that the act of assigning to oneself more than one's share of the goods that are fought about is normally, and rightly, said to be morally bad, something *aischron*. Suppose now that the acts that are introduced in § 5, and are said to be noble, also consist in 'sharing out' (*aponemein*, cf. viii.4, 1168b16) those same goods — but precisely not assigning to oneself more than one's share.

Aristotle's examples of the goods in question were: material goods, honour, and bodily pleasures; and this makes it clear that he is thinking of a special type of thing, which is introduced in a number of places in his ethical treatises. In *EE* VIII.iii, which I shall discuss in a moment, he provides the following list: honour, wealth, bodily excellences (including health and bodily strength, cf. iii.4, 1248b23–24), goods of fortune, and 'capacities' of whatever sort (1248b28–29). In that passage the goods are described (iii.3–5) as (*i*) choiceworthy *in themselves*, or as ends, but without being praiseworthy (for the things that are choiceworthy in themselves *and* praiseworthy are just the moral virtues and the acts that spring from them); as (*ii*) fought about (*perimachēta*); as (*iii*) goods that are normally taken to be the greatest goods, but falsely; and finally as (*iv*) natural goods (*physei agatha*). It is difficult to provide an exact definition of the type of thing in question – a point that Aristotle himself makes (in *EN* V.ii.6, 1130b2-3). Still it is reasonably clear what Aristotle is thinking of: things for which human beings have more or less basic needs (the things are *natural* goods, and the many do not go entirely astray when they consider them the greatest of goods), and things of such a kind that human beings are not in absolute control of their attainment (the things are to be contrasted with the 'psychic' good, moral virtue, and the acts that are its actualizations).

Suppose, then, that noble acts consist in sharing out such natural goods. According to the chapter on self-love, it is reason that states how they should be shared out. What is it that reason states?

2.4. Reason is universal and impersonal. If reason ordains acts that fail to gratify the person's irrational part of soul, i.e. his appetites and generally his passions (cf. *EN* IX.viii.4), and if, furthermore, these passions concern the natural goods, it seems likely that what reason sees and states is that where there are natural goods to be shared no preference can justifiably be given, initially, to one's own desires for those goods. What is relevant to the question of deciding how the goods should be shared is (*i*) that they are good for human beings as such and (*ii*) that there are more such beings than oneself. What reason sees, then, is that one cannot ground any claim for a certain share of natural goods just on the fact that one has oneself certain desires for them; initially the claims of all human beings are equally strong, at least of all those who will, in some definable sense, be affected by the goods being shared out in one way or another.

According to this line of thought, when a person 'pays no attention to himself', as opposed to doing everything for his own sake (cf. viii.1), what he does is to leave out of account 'his own' desires. But the point is not that he pays no attention whatever to himself or neglects all his desires. What he does is just to take account of himself *as one among others*. Thus he may well share out to himself a certain portion of the natural goods, viz. precisely his share, as opposed to sharing out to himself *to pleion* (viii.4, 1168b16), or more than his share. The contrast is not so much the one between oneself and the others. Rather, it is that between oneself by oneself and oneself as one among others.

Our question was what reason sees and what may justify its verdict that one should act in the way that is noble. And the answer is that since the basic problem is that of how natural goods should be shared, reason can find no foothold for a criterion anywhere else than in properties that are impersonal; reason sees that initially all human beings have an equal claim.

This is the first point I want to make, and it is the point that expresses the conception of nobility that I wish to ascribe to Aristotle. An act is noble if it is done 'for the sake of the noble', i.e. in order to comply with the rational insight that in the sharing of natural goods one's own claim is initially no stronger than that of any other human being.

2.5. But there is a second point, which answers the following question. If reason does not prescribe that natural goods should be divided equally among all concerned (and according to Aristotle it does not), what will the criterion be for the rational sharing out of the goods?

In *EE* VIII.iii we shall see Aristotle at work with two ideas that are also mentioned elsewhere (cf., e.g., *EN* I.iii.3, 1094b16–19). (1) By nature natural goods are, indeed, good for human beings; in actual fact, however, they are not good for all humans; morally bad people may be harmed by them; it is the morally good man who is able to use them to his benefit — in fact this is even what defines a man as morally good (*EE* VIII.iii.5, 1248b26–34). (2) Similarly it is the morally good man who has a right to natural goods (iii.8, 1249a8–9: he is *axios*, or worthy, of them). The two ideas may be connected: the morally good man has a right to natural goods *because* he is able to put them to the proper use, i.e. to use them to his benefit.

There can be little doubt about what is meant here by 'his benefit' (the term is *oninasthai*, iii.5, 1248b31). The morally good man will use whatever natural goods he obtains in such a way that he will not thereby lose any other natural good that he already possesses. By contrast, when the morally bad man is enabled to satisfy his vicious desires, he will often be harmed in the sense of losing natural goods that he already has. This is the reason why 'natural goods seem to have nothing fixed about them: people are often harmed by them — e.g. when people perish because of wealth' (*EN* I.iii.3, 1094b17-19). The profligate who becomes able to satisfy his desires may as a result impair his health, even die.

If this is the point Aristotle is making when he talks of the benefit the good man will get from natural goods, we may generalize the point and conclude that the criterion in accordance with which reason will share out natural goods is that of the greatest possible satisfaction of natural needs for such goods as will result from the act. The morally good man has a right to natural goods in precedence over the morally bad man because the *over-all* good, in terms of the satisfaction of natural needs, will be greater if the former obtains the goods than if the latter does. Underlying this there must be a view that there is a state of a human being, viz. the natural one, in which all basic needs are satisfied and which is harmonious in the sense that the satisfaction of any particular need does not necessitate the non-satisfaction of any other.

But now we know that reason does not ordain acts with a view to the good of any particular person. It follows that although reason will assign a large share of natural goods to the morally good man, it will not do so for his sake. Rather, it will do it because in that way the greatest possible satisfaction of natural needs will result for the community of humans involved as a whole. Reason will consider where natural goods will have, as it were, the greatest effect, and will assign a certain amount of the goods to a given person because his getting that amount will entail that the goods do have the greatest effect. But this will *imply* that the entity whose good, in terms of the satisfaction of natural needs, reason is bent on furthering is the community of humans involved as a whole. Thus we may conclude that the criterion adopted by reason for sharing out natural goods is that of the greatest possible satisfaction of needs for such goods *in the community*.

2.6. Now the question I suggested would be answered when we came to know what reason sees was why acting nobly, so as to benefit others, is part of one's own happiness. We now know that reason makes two observations. The first is that where the question is the one of how natural goods should be shared there is no legitimate ground for ascribing to oneself a claim to the goods that is any stronger than that of any other human being who will be affected by the goods being shared out in one way or another. The second observation is that the final aim of the sharing out of the goods is the greatest possible satisfaction of needs in the community of humans involved as a whole. The first principle is a principle of *nobility*; it represents the basic insight that Aristotle wishes to express by his concept of *to kalon*. The second principle is one of *utility*, in the sense of the satisfaction of needs for natural goods. How, then, does insight into these two principles explain how noble, other-regarding behaviour forms part of one's own happiness?

In order to answer this question we must consider the difference between the two claims of reason that I have been operating with. We started, in connection with the chapter on self-love, from the claim that acting nobly, so as to benefit others, is part of one's own happiness. But we have now reached the conclusion that it is part of one's own happiness to perform acts that aim at the greatest possible satisfaction of needs for natural goods on the part of all humans in the community. What lies between the two formulations is the realization that reason sees that with respect to possession of natural goods one is oneself just one among others — the principle of nobility. When this is realized there is no longer any problem about taking one's own happiness to consist (in part) in the performance of acts that benefit others. For in performing such acts what one is really doing is acting so as to benefit oneself and the others, viz. *the community as a whole*. And the effect of reason's grasp of the principle of nobility is that the best state one may oneself be in (but only with respect to possession of natural goods) is identical with the best state (in that respect) of the community: with respect to possession of natural goods one's own interests and those of the community become identical because one is oneself (but only in that respect) in a certain sense identical with the community — one is just one among others.

So I am suggesting the following move. According to the chapter on self-love, one should act nobly so as to benefit others because acting in that way is part of one's own happiness; but the latter is so because in the relevant respect (i.e. with respect to possession of natural goods, which is what noble behaviour is all about) the best state for oneself is identical with the best state for the community. Thus the criterion of the goodness of noble behaviour is 'the common weal', in terms of the satisfaction of needs for natural goods.

This is in fact precisely what Aristotle seems to be saying in the chapter on self-love itself when, in a passage I have already paraphrased, he claims that if everybody were to strive to act nobly the consequence would be both that 'everything would be as it should in the community' (*koinēi t'an pant' eiē ta deonta*) and that each individual would have the greatest of goods — since virtue is such a thing (viii.7, 1169a8-11). For the sense of the quoted words is presumably that 'all common needs would be supplied' (this, in fact, is how they are rendered in the most recent translation, that of H. G. Apostle). The criterion of the goodness of noble behaviour is that common needs for natural goods are satisfied in the best possible way. And reason sees that this is the criterion because, since the behaviour it is trying to define is concerned with natural goods, it will see that with regard to possession of natural goods no individual has, basically, any stronger claim to the goods than any other: with respect to possession of such goods each individual is just one among others.

2.7. If we now go back to the chapter on self-love, we can make sense of an important point that is made in that chapter, but has not yet been touched on. The point is Aristotle's suggestion, in viii.9-11, 1169a18-b1, that the good man, while claiming for himself the noble (a21-22), will be prepared to give up 'material goods and honours and generally the goods that are fought about' (including even his life) for the sake of his friends or his country (a18-22). Even if there is a risk that the good man will lose his life in battle for his country, he will remain at his post. And the justification we may provide is this: he views himself as one among others, and hence does not place any special value on the natural good which is his life due to the mere fact that it is his own life. What he does is to weigh the value of his keeping that good against the value of the good he may provide for the community of humans involved as a whole, viz. for his country. He may therefore decide to risk his own life, but will at the same time choose for himself the greater good (a28-29), viz. the good that it is to act in accordance with his insight into the principle of nobility.

3.1. I have not argued properly for the proposed interpretation of acting nobly. I shall now discuss a passage I have already made use of, *EE* VIII.iii.1-10, and try to show that it implies two points that are central to that interpretation, viz. the idea that noble acts consist in sharing out natural goods, and the idea that one has oneself no special claim to those goods just because one is the individual one is, viz. oneself.

The topic of the passage is the virtue of *kalokagathia*, nobility of mind or 'noble-and-goodness'. Aristotle starts (§§ 3-4) by dividing goods that are choiceworthy as ends, i.e. in themselves, into two groups. We already know the two groups: they are the ('final') goods that are praiseworthy and those that are not. He then (§§ 5-6) uses this division to define two different types of person, one who is 'merely' good (he is *agathos*) and one who is noble-and-good (*kalokagathos*). The former is a man who, in contrast to the man who is morally bad, will profit from coming to possess natural goods. The latter is a man who values for their own sake things that are noble, viz. the other type of 'final' good: the things that are 'final' and praiseworthy.

This is not very clear. We started from two types of good which are both 'final': choiceworthy in themselves, as ends. Will the 'merely' good man consider both types of good choiceworthy in themselves, as they in fact are? Presumably not, if we go by the way Aristotle defines the noble-and-good man. But what, then, about the latter: will he consider both types of good choiceworthy in themselves? We do not yet know.

Still the train of thought in §§ 5-6 is reasonably clear. At one extreme we have the morally bad man, who will be harmed by coming to possess natural goods. The good man, by contrast, viz. the 'merely' good one, is at least able to profit from possession of one of the types of good in question, the natural goods. But then he is perhaps in some respect lacking in relation to the other type of good? He is; for he does not consider goods of that type, which are in fact truly 'final', good *in themselves*. § § 7-10 make clearer the difference between the two types of good man.

3.2. I must paraphrase. Some people, says Aristotle, think that one ought to be virtuous, but in order to obtain natural goods. Such people are in fact morally good (*agathoi*, 1249a1) — for they profit from natural goods; but they are not noble-and-good, i.e. (we may suppose) truly morally good, since they do not value things that are noble, viz. virtue and virtuous acts, for the sake of these things themselves. It is different with people who are noble-and-good. Not only do they value things that are noble for the sake of those things themselves: goods too which are not by nature noble, but are by nature good (viz. the natural goods) are noble 'for them'. For a thing is noble if that for the sake of which the person chooses and acts is noble. And this is why natural goods are noble for the noble-and-good man. Take, by way of example, 'what is just'. What is just is noble; but it is also what accords with people's 'worth' (*axia*, a8), and the noble-and-good man is himself worthy of natural goods. Another example of the noble is 'what is proper'; but the person for whom natural goods are 'proper' is the noble-and-good man. So for the noble-and-good man the same things (viz. natural goods) are both beneficial and noble.[3] For the 'merely' good man natural goods are, it is true, beneficial, but for the noble-and-good man[4] they are also noble. For he performs many acts that are noble and involve them,[5] whereas if one believes

[3] I am doubtful about how to handle the text, but the intended sense is clearly the one that would result if the sentence read ὥστε τῷ καλῷ κἀγαθῷ τὰ αὐτὰ καὶ συμφέροντα καὶ καλά ἐστι.

[4] The MSS have τῷ δ᾿ ἀγαθῷ, which Spengel changed to τῷ δὲ // καλῷ // κἀγαθῷ καὶ καλά. I believe that both sense and principles of textual criticism favour the following correction: τῷ δ᾿ ἀγαθῷ // καὶ καλῷ // καὶ καλά.

[5] The MS reading δι᾿ αὐτά ('because of those goods') is difficult. The sense is presumably that 'by his way of handling natural goods' the noble-and-good man performs noble acts. But the use of the preposition διά remains disquieting. No proposed correction seems attractive.

that one should be virtuous just in order to obtain natural goods, one acts nobly only incidentally.

The strange claim that natural goods are noble for the noble-and-good man suggests two things. It suggests, first, that noble action does consist in handling natural goods; and the two examples show that it consists in sharing them out and in certain cases sharing at least part of them to oneself. But secondly, it also suggests that when the noble-and-good man assigns a certain amount of natural goods to himself, he does not do so just because he is the individual he is, viz. himself. Rather, he does so because he is *entitled* to the goods, due to the fact that he is the bearer of certain properties. Thus the passage unmistakably implies that noble action consists in sharing out natural goods on the basis of impersonal, objective criteria. When the noble-and-good man shares out a certain amount of goods to himself, he does so because he himself *happens* to have the properties that entitle him to the goods. This, then, is the essence of noble behaviour and noble-and-goodness: to share out natural goods on the basis of objective criteria and consequently, when one happens to share out a certain amount of the goods to oneself, to oneself *as one among others.*

3.3. If we now ask about the relationship of the 'merely' good man and the noble-and-good one respectively to the two types of 'final' good that Aristotle was operating with, we shall get the following answer. The 'merely' good man does not consider one of these two types, viz. virtue and virtuous behaviour, truly 'final' or choiceworthy in itself. He has not grasped the principle of nobility; he does not possess the rational insight that virtuous behaviour is (part of) what a man's *eudaimonia* consists in simply as the rational being that he is. For he only acts virtuously because by so doing he will himself obtain a large proportion of the only type of good that he considers 'final', natural goods.

By contrast, of course, the noble-and-good man does consider moral behaviour choiceworthy in itself. But then does he not consider *natural* goods choiceworthy in themselves, as indeed they are? The answer is undoubtedly that he does. For his acts both are and are seen by him to be concerned with natural goods, viz. with the question of how to share them out, and hence *presuppose* that such things are goods and things to be chosen for their own sake. Nor is it difficult to see why Aristotle has not made this point explicit in his definition of the noble-and-good man. For he is intent on distinguishing the noble-and-good man from the 'merely' good one. And the point of that distinction is that even when the noble-and-good man assigns a large proportion of natural goods to himself, his motive for action is not that he wants to get as many as possible of these genuinely 'final' things for himself. Rather, his sole motive for action is the consideration that that act of his is in accordance with the two principles of nobility and utility. Indeed, it is this fact that explains why for the noble-and-good man virtue and virtuous behaviour are genuinely choiceworthy *in themselves*. We may add that since the noble-and-good man's reason for action is precisely not that he will himself profit, in terms of the possession of natural goods, from performing virtuous acts, he will, as a consequence, continue to act in that way even in situations in which he will not himself profit (in the same respect) from his acts — e.g. when he decides to risk his life in order to defend his country. Here, at last, the difference between the 'merely' good man and the noble-and-good one becomes evident. But still, as I have argued, the noble-and-good man does consider natural goods choiceworthy in themselves.

3.4. So much for *EE* VIII.iii.1–10. I have claimed that in that passage Aristotle is clearly working with two of the basic ideas which I take to form part of acting nobly. First, virtuous acts consist in sharing out natural goods in some way or other. Secondly, reason tells a man that when it comes to sharing out in the proper way he himself has no special claim to the goods as against the claims of other humans. I have suggested that the second point expresses what is the essence of acting 'for the sake of the noble', and I believe that the passage we have been considering, in which Aristotle is precisely concerned to define the element of nobility in 'noble-and-goodness', makes it certain that this is his view.

4.1. I now want to consider a passage in Aristotle's discussion

in *EN* V of the virtue of justice. I have developed an account
of acting nobly which is intended to capture the element of
nobility in 'noble-and-goodness'. It is also, of course, intended
to capture what makes a state of mind a moral virtue in
general; for, as I shall argue in more detail in the next chapter,
moral virtue in general, and the individual moral virtues, are
defined by the fact that the virtuous agent acts for the sake
of the noble; and in fact, of course, though Aristotle nowhere
explicitly says so, the noble-and-goodness of *EE* VIII.iii
(but cf. also *EN* IV.iii.16, 1124a4 and X.ix.3, 1179b10) is
identical with moral virtue in general. But if this is so, then
it will be immediately clear from the details of my account
of acting nobly that according to Aristotle moral virtue
in general is basically justice, and that each individual moral
virtue is basically some form of justice. This conclusion
clearly forces us to consider what Aristotle actually says of
the relationship of the virtue of justice to moral virtue in
general: is justice, according to him, just one virtue among
the others, or is it more than that? A passage in *EN* V suggests
a fairly complex answer to this question.

The passage is *EN* V.i.7–ii.6. In this section as a whole
Aristotle has two aims. He first wants to indicate the relationship of a certain form of justice, which he calls 'comprehensive'
(*holē*) justice, to moral virtue in general. And secondly he
wants to establish the properties of a different type of
justice, which he calls 'particular' (*kata meros*) justice.

The first aim is achieved in i.12–20, on the basis of a
distinction between types of *in*justice or of *un*just man
(i.8–11): there is the unjust man who is lawless (*paranomos*,
i.8, 1129a32 and i.12, b11 ff.), and there is the unjust man
who is grasping (*pleonektēs*, i.8, 1129a32 and i.9–10, b1–10)
and unfair (*anisos*, i.8, 1129a33 and i.11, b10–11). The
former type of man is more relevant to the discussion of
comprehensive justice, the latter to the discussion of particular justice. The property of being unfair, however, is common
to both (1129b10–11), and we shall try to see how. The
second aim is achieved in ii.1–6, and Aristotle once more
starts his analysis from a consideration of *in*justice as compared with other vices.

I shall first discuss Aristotle's remarks about comprehensive justice (i.12–20) and try to resolve a certain difficulty for my thesis concerning Aristotelian moral virtue in general that seems raised by that passage. Next I shall discuss his remarks about particular justice (ii.1–6) and attempt to resolve another difficulty that seems created by that passage. The over-all aim is to work out the exact relationship to each other of Aristotelian moral virtue in general, of 'comprehensive' justice, and of 'particular' justice.

4.2. The first definition of justice that is given is based on the point that one type of unjust man is the lawless man: in one way what is just is whatever is in accordance with the law (i.12, 1129b12). Now laws (a) speak of everything (i.13, b14–15) and (b) aim at the common good (*to koinēi sympheron*, for all or the best or those in power or something similar, b15–16), hence on this conception of justice[6] things are just which 'produce or preserve *eudaimonia* and its parts for the community' (*hē politikē koinōnia*, b17–19). In this definition the talk of *eudaimonia* and its parts takes up the point (a) that laws speak of *everything*, and the talk of the community takes up the point (b) that laws aim at the *common* good.

Both points are important. If laws speak of everything and aim at *eudaimonia* and its parts, they must contain injunctions that coincide with what the moral virtues will enjoin. And if my account of the noble is correct, the fact that laws are stated to aim at the *common* good, or *eudaimonia* and its parts *for the community*, will similarly imply that the injunctions of (good) laws and of the moral virtues will coincide. In fact, Aristotle immediately goes on to say that the (good) law does command people to perform virtuous acts: those of the courageous man, those of the temperate man ('e.g. not to commit adultery nor to abuse anyone sexually', 1129b21–22), those of the good-tempered man ('e.g. not to strike another nor to speak evil of him', b22–23), etc. (i.14). It seems fair to say that my account of the noble receives some support from the fact that Aristotle here explicitly brings in virtuous behaviour in a context in which, if that account is accepted,

---

[6] This is a paraphrase of ἕνα μὲν τρόπον in b17, which takes up and makes clear the sense of πως in b12.

everything he has been saying of laws and of justice makes one *expect* that he should *also* be talking of virtuous behaviour and of moral virtue.

4.3. But then at the start of i.15 Aristotle continues as follows (1129b25-27): 'This type of justice is complete (*teleia*) virtue — though not without qualification, but in relation to others.' The latter part of this remark seems to raise a problem. Is Aristotle not here saying that justice, as described, is just one aspect, or branch, of virtue as a whole? And in that case how can I maintain that moral virtue in Aristotle *essentially* concerns one's relation to others (with respect to natural goods), and hence is essentially justice?

But notice how he continues (1129b30 ff.). The type of justice described, i.e. comprehensive justice, is complete (*teleia*) (moral) virtue in the truest sense of 'complete'; for it is an application or use (*chrēsis*) of complete virtue which is perfect (*teleia*);[7] and the use is perfect since the person who has comprehensive justice is able to use his virtue in his relations with others too — not just in relation to himself; (and that is the really difficult thing), for many people are able to use virtue in their own case, but cannot apply it towards others.

What Aristotle is saying here is that comprehensive justice is not just one branch of complete virtue but, as it were, *the* branch. It is true that he reckons with another branch, viz. one that concerns only the agent (see on this in a moment); but he is clearly saying that justice represents a branch of virtue of a special type, which is indicated by the fact that if one has it one necessarily has the other branch too, whereas the opposite does not hold. So *qua* the 'towards others'-part of moral virtue in general, justice is the *primary* element therein, as opposed to the part of moral virtue which is not 'towards others'.

---

[7] I believe, with many others, that the MS text has to be emended at 1129b 30-31. The emendation adopted by Stewart is by far the best one: καὶ τελεία μάλιστα ἀρετή, ὅτι τῆς τελείας ἀρετῆς χρῆσίς ἐστιν ‖ τελεία. ‖ τελεία δ' ἐστίν, ὅτι . . . The supposed corruption is easily explained and the emended text makes excellent sense. For other, to my mind unnecessarily complicated, suggestions see Gauthier's note ad loc.

If we understand the relation of comprehensive justice and moral virtue in general in this way, we can immediately understand the point Aristotle goes on directly to make. Rule will show the man, he says; for the ruler is right from the start concerned with others and with the community. The point is that since rule concerns others, if a man gets the chance of ruling, he cannot avoid showing whether he is virtuous, i.e. has general virtue or the state of mind that covers both aspects of goodness, or not; for if he proves virtuous in relation to others, he will necessarily be so in relation to himself too.

But does not Aristotle talk of another branch, viz. one that concerns only the agent himself? He does. When in the next chapter I come to discuss the individual virtues, we shall see that most of them do concern others — e.g. courage, the first of them. Nevertheless there is one virtue, viz. temperence, which, though it may of course concern others (as is shown by Aristotle's examples in V.i.14 paraphrased above: 'not to commit adultery or to abuse anyone sexually'), nevertheless may also be concerned with the agent's own long-term good alone. This fact might seem embarrassing for my thesis that moral virtue in Aristotle essentially concerns others; but I do not think that it is. For the similarity, in terms of a concern for 'the greater good', of so-called prudential reasoning, which concerns the agent and his personal long-term good only, and 'altruistic' reasoning, which concerns the good of others, lies at hand (and is in fact exploited elsewhere by Aristotle himself).[8] I suggest, therefore, that we take the central case of noble behaviour to be the one that concerns others, but that we do not exclude temperate behaviour from being noble, even when it concerns the agent's own (greater) good alone — though in that case it will be noble in a secondary way only.

If this construction is correct, we can make sense of Aristotle's summary (in i.19–20) of our passage. The type of

---

[8] See the fascinating passage, *Pol.* I.2, 1253a7–18, in which Aristotle argues, on the basis of the fact that man is rational, that he is an eminently social being (*politikon*): reasoned speech (*logos*) is employed to communicate to others not just, as simple 'voice' may be employed, what is pleasant or painful, but what is beneficial or harmful (prudential reasoning) *and consequently* (ὥστε καί, 1253a 15) what is just and unjust (moral, altruistic reasoning).

justice he has been considering is, he says, not just a part of
moral virtue, i.e. one virtue among the others: it is the whole
of virtue (*holē aretē*). Still although moral virtue in general
and that type of justice are one and the same state (*hē autē*),
they differ 'in being' (*to einai*), since the latter is moral virtue
in relation to others, whereas the former just is such a state
(*toiade hexis*, viz. moral virtue) without qualification. We can
now see what Aristotle means. Justice, in its comprehensive
form, is the whole of virtue, they are one and the same state,
for there is no moral virtue which is not, in some of its forms,
justice. At the same time, if there is a branch of moral virtue,
i.e. certain applications of one or more of the individual
virtues, which concern the agent alone, it will be appropriate
to distinguish (comprehensive) justice from moral virtue in
the way in which Aristotle distinguishes them; for justice,
whether comprehensive or not, will always be concerned
with others, whereas on the stated assumption moral virtue
will not. Comprehensive justice is truly identical with moral
virtue *in its primary form*, but the term 'moral virtue' also
covers the secondary form, i.e. the type of state that concerns
the agent alone.

4.4. So much for the first problem that is raised by Aristotle's remarks about justice at the beginning of *EN* V.

In chapter ii (1-6) he brings arguments for the view that,
in spite of what was said in chapter i, there is a type of
justice which is just one of the virtues and consequently has
a more restricted scope than comprehensive justice. His
account raises a new problem for my view of moral virtue.

In ii.6 Aristotle concludes, on the basis of the preceding
discussion, that 'there is a type of injustice (and consequently
of justice) which is "particular" (*en merei*) and to be contrasted with the comprehensive type' (1130a32-33). They
have the same name, since they are both concerned with
one's relation to others. Still they differ in the following
way: 'the former (viz. particular injustice) is about honour,
material goods, safety, or whatever single name there may
be to cover all those things — and because of the pleasure
one gets from gain (*kerdos*); the latter is about everything
that the good man is about' (1130b2-5).

This account of the area of particular justice and injustice
is prepared for in i.9 when Aristotle states that since the
unjust man is grasping (*pleonektēs*), he must be concerned
with good things — 'not all, but those with which good luck
(*eutychia*) and bad luck (*atychia*) have to do, viz. the things
which are always good without qualification but not always
for the individual person' (1129b2-4). Now these goods are
evidently our well-known natural goods, the goods that are
fought about by the many. Similarly the goods that are said
in ii.6 to be what particular injustice is concerned with are
the natural goods. But in the latter passage these goods are
contrasted with the goods that the good man is concerned
with. How will that be consistent with my claim that the
good man is concerned precisely with the natural goods?

4.5. We must consider exactly how Aristotle defines
particular justice, or rather injustice, in his three arguments
(in ii.2-5) for the claim that there is such a thing. It will soon
become clear that everything turns on two notions that we
have already met in ii.6 and i.9, that the unjust man acts in
particular situations because of the pleasure he gets from
gain (*kerdos*), and that he is grasping (*pleonektēs*). In a
disquisition (in *EN* V.iv.13-14) on the notion of *kerdos* and
its opposite, *zēmia* or loss, Aristotle connects *kerdos* with
being grasping: 'to have more (*pleon echein*) than one's share
is called gaining (*kerdainein*)' (V.iv.13, 1132b13-14). In the
three arguments too *kerdainein* and *pleonektein* (with deri-
vatives) are used interchangeably. We shall see, however, that
the man of particular injustice is not just a man who gets
more than his due, or 'gains' (and in both cases with respect
to natural goods); there is one more point to be mentioned.

The first and third arguments do not make that point.
According to the first (ii.2-3, 1130a16-24), when a man acts
from one of the other vices, he may well be said to act
unjustly (*adikein*), bu he is not grasping (*pleonektein*) — e.g.
if he runs away in battle because of cowardice; but when a
man is grasping (*pleonektein*), he often behaves in a grasping
way without thereby exhibiting any of the other vices; so
there must be a special vice, which is (particular) injustice.
Similarly, according to the third argument (ii.5, 1130a28-32),

whereas the rest of unjust acts are ascribed to some particular moral vice, if a man makes gain (*kerdainein*), his unjust act is ascribed to no other moral vice, but precisely to injustice.

However, the second argument (ii.4, 1130a24-28) adds to this. Here Aristotle considers the case of a man committing adultery. If he acts from sexual desire, we will say that he is profligate rather than grasping (*akolastos* rather than *pleonektēs*); if, however, he acts in order to make a gain (*tou kerdainein heneka*), we will say that he is unjust but not profligate. And the reason, says Aristotle, is evidently that he acts *with a view* to making a gain (*dia to kerdainein*.) What matters, then, is not just that there is some gain involved, but that the *motive* for acting is the one of making a gain. And this, of course, is just what is said in ii.6, 1130b4, when Aristotle states, as we saw, that the man of particular injustice acts because of the pleasure he will get from gaining.

Consider then the following reconstruction. The coward, for instance, acts unjustly but does not grasp (*pleonektein*), according to ii.2, 1130a16-17. Perhaps, however, he does grasp and does make a gain in the sense that he in fact gives to himself more than his share of the natural good that is safety. Still we should not say for that reason that he *grasps*, or *makes a gain.* For he is not motivated by the pleasure of having more than his share, the pleasure of knowing that he is 'doing better' than the others. Similarly, if a person violates another person from sexual desire, he does take more than his due of the natural good which is physical pleasure, and he is profligate. But if he performs the same act with the motive of getting more for himself of whatever natural good may be involved (other than pleasure), he is not profligate but unjust. This is evidently an extreme case, and Aristotle is right to stress, in the first and third arguments, the cases where the act that is actually done cannot in this way be referred to two different vices, but must be referred to injustice alone. Still the extreme case helps to bring out what is essential to particular injustice, viz. that the *motive* is that of making a gain in terms of natural goods, of getting more for oneself of such goods than one is in fact entitled to.

4.6. If this interpretation of particular injustice is correct, we can make the following sense of the contrast, in ii.6, between the areas of particular and of comprehensive injustice, where the latter is also the area with which the good man in general is concerned.

The man of comprehensive injustice will be concerned with a wide range of situations, the descriptions of which will mention other elements than the natural goods that will be involved. Nevertheless, because they will all involve some natural goods, comprehensive injustice too, like particular injustice, will be concerned with natural goods. But the man of comprehensive injustice will not be directly concerned with those goods in the way in which the man of particular injustice is. The coward does give himself more than his share of the natural good of safety, but he does not act with the motive of (getting the pleasure of) having more than his share of that good. He just acts as he does in order to save his life.

The man of particular injustice, on the other hand, is directly concerned about natural goods. For he acts 'because of the pleasure he will get from making a gain', viz. a gain in the amount of natural goods he obtains as compared with what others obtain. Thus understood the definition of particular injustice in ii.6, 1130b2–4 does not just make two separate points, one about the area of particular injustice and the other about the motive of the man of particular injustice. Rather, the passage makes two connected points, since the reference to the *area* should be understood in the precise sense that is made clear by the reference to the *motive* of the man of particular injustice. (One can better understand, therefore, why the remark on comprehensive injustice in ii.6, 1130b4–5 is confined to making a vague reference to the whole area with which the good man is concerned: in the case of comprehensive injustice there is not the same connection between motive and area.)

4.7. What, then, is the relationship between moral virtue and vice, comprehensive justice and injustice, and particular justice and injustice?

On the suggested reading of moral virtue in general, when the virtuous man acts for the sake of the noble, he will act with a view to sharing out natural goods in accordance with merit, i.e. justly. Thus there is a good reason why Aristotle should say that moral virtue (in general) and (comprehensive) justice are identical. But the man of particular justice will act in exactly the same way. He will be motivated by the pleasure of giving each person his share of the natural goods. There is, however, a clear difference between the virtuous man in a given area and the man of particular justice. The temperate man, for instance, will act for the sake of the noble, but in addition he is such that he *wants* to perform temperate acts *on their own*. He wants exactly the amount of food which it will be noble for him to take (this is the point of *EN* III.xii.9) — and he would feel nausea from having more. *Qua* a man of particular justice, on the other hand, a person will not want a certain amount of food. What he wants, what he finds pleasure in, is just sharing out natural goods in such a way that nobody makes unjust gains. (This, of course, is the obverse of the point Aristotle is making in V.ii.4.)

When we turn to the corresponding vices, the relationship between moral vice, comprehensive injustice, and particular injustice becomes clearer. The vicious man acts from a number of different motives. However, his acts will always go against the noble, so that he is a man of comprehensive injustice, i.e. a man who takes for himself more than his due of natural goods. But note that he does not act with that motive, as the man of particular injustice does. In the case of the vices, therefore, there is a clear difference between the vicious man and the man of particular injustice in that their motives for acting are different.

The case was not quite so clear when we compared the virtuous man in general with the man of particular justice. And it is for this reason, I believe, that in both V.i and ii Aristotle takes as his starting-point the *un*just man. Concentration on him will make clearer the difference between the man of particular injustice and the morally bad man in an area in which there is a much closer connection between moral virtue and vice and justice and injustice than might seem at first.

4.8. I conclude that the two chapters of *EN* V that I have been discussing support, rather than raise difficulties for, my general thesis concerning the sense of acting for the sake of the noble. Basically all Aristotle's virtues are forms of justice and concern a sharing out of natural goods that does not consist in taking more for oneself than one is entitled to. Such behaviour is the one that produces and preserves *eudaimonia* and its parts, not for the individual but for the community as a whole.

5. To conclude this chapter I will quote from *EN* X.viii.1, where Aristotle is talking of the degree to which a life in accordance with moral virtue and *phronēsis* may qualify as *eudaimonia*. It does so only secondarily, he says, since the acts that go into such a life are (only) human.

For just acts, courageous acts, and the rest of the acts that are in accordance with the (moral) virtues we perform *in relation to each other* (*pros allēlous prattomen*), *observing what is due to each individual* (*diatērountes to prepon hekastōi*) in commercial dealings with others (*synallagmata*), all kinds of intercourse with others (*chreiai*),[9] and all manner of actions (*praxeis pantoiai*) — and in our passions (*pathē*); and that type of behaviour seems specifically human (1178a 10-14).

The phrases I have emphasized are revealing.

[9] This rendering of χρεῖαι is suggested by the remarks of Liddell/Scott/Jones, s.v. IV, who refer to *Rhet*. I.15, 1376b13. In that passage (ἡ πρὸς ἀλλήλους χρεία τῶν ἀνθρώπων) χρεία means ὁμιλία, as Bonitz has it (s.v. χρεία): Stewart's and Ross's 'services', Rolfes's 'Notlagen', Dirlmeier's 'in der Stunde der Not' and Apostle's 'needs' will not do. Gauthier/Jolif have got it right ('relations').

3

THE VIRTUES

1. The present chapter is not intended to carry my argument forward. I want to confront the interpretation I have suggested of acting nobly with Aristotle's account of the individual moral virtues, primarily as given in *EN* III.vi–IV. This confrontation seems required if the suggested interpretation of the noble is to win approval; for the defining property of all the individual virtues, according to *EN* IV.ii.7 (1122b6–7) and i.12, 1120a23–24, is that acts that spring from them are noble and done for the sake of the noble. We should ask, therefore, whether there are any indications in Aristotle's treatment of the individual virtues of what it is for an act to be noble and to be done for the sake of the noble, and if there are, whether they fit in with the interpretation of the noble that I developed in chapter 2.

Aristotle's discussion of the individual virtues has not been very popular in modern times. It is not hard to see why. His list of virtues represents a strange mixture: if, as he seems to imply (cf. *EN* III.v.23, 1115a5), the list is intended as exhaustive, what are the ties that hold it together? Moreover, can it be of any interest to learn what type of wit, to take that only, Aristotle thought the most proper? Are we not here working with material that may be informative about the substantive moral views of a fourth-century Athenian from the upper end of the social scale, but is uninteresting to the philosopher?

A few attempts have been made recently to invest Aristotle's point that the virtues lie in a mean with philosophical interest.[1]

---

[1] I am thinking of W. F. R. Hardie's 'Aristotle's Doctrine that Virtue is a "Mean"', *PAS* 65 (1964–5), 183–204, repr. with new appendix in *Articles on Aristotle*, vol. ii, edd. J. Barnes, M. Schofield, R. Sorabji, London, 1977; J. O. Urmson, 'Aristotle's Doctrine of the Mean', *APQ* 10 (1973), 223–30; S. R. L.

In the same manner, though the following account of the virtues will leave much about them that is strange, it will attempt to remove at least some other blocks to interest.

I will stress, however, that my aim is not to provide a complete account of the virtues. Many aspects of what Aristotle says will not be touched on at all. For example, I shall not here be directly concerned with the aforementioned point, which Aristotle is so keen on making, that the virtues are mean-states between an excess and a deficiency. Nor shall I be concerned with the very important point that comes to the surface at the end of book III, when Aristotle states that the emotional or desiderative part of soul of the temperate man will agree with his reason. The point is important because it expresses the fact that the virtues (and the vices too) are states of character, and furthermore brings out what is a necessary condition for the virtuous man, and the vicious one as well, to perform *praxeis* (as they do). This whole question of the emotional content in the virtues I shall leave on one side in the present chapter.

The question I am addressing myself to is a restricted one. Keeping in mind the account of the noble that I developed in chapter 2, I will approach Aristotle's discussion of the individual virtues in the following way. In this discussion a prominent role is played by the notions of acting for the sake of the noble and acting as right reason states (*hōs ho orthos logos*), but the two notions are left completely undefined. Are there, then, indications in what Aristotle says in general of each particular virtue that tend to invest those notions with a sense that tallies with my account of the noble as given in chapter 2? Are there, to spell out the question, indications that Aristotle in fact subscribes to the twofold view of the justification of the goodness of virtuous acts that I have ascribed to him: (*i*) that such acts provide for the fullest satisfaction of needs for natural goods in the

---

Clark, *Aristotle's Man, Speculations upon Aristotelian Anthropology*, Oxford, 1975, ch. III.2; and D. F. Pears, 'Aristotle's Analysis of Courage', *Midwest Studies in Philosophy, vol. III: Studies in Ethical Theory*, University of Minnesota, Morris, 1978, 273–85. On virtue as a mean cf. also J. L. Ackrill's suggestive remarks in *Aristotle's Ethics*, Selections from Philosophers, ed. M. Warnock, London, 1973, pp. 22–3.

community of humans involved as a whole — the principle of utility; and (*ii*) that such acts are seen by the agent to be worth doing independently of how large an amount of natural goods he will himself obtain, but simply because he sees that in the sharing of natural goods he has himself no special claim to them just because he is the individual he is — the principle of nobility? Or finally, does Aristotle imply anything, in what he actually says of each individual virtue, for the question of *the objective good* of each of them?

So the question I am asking is a restricted one, and my discussion will be somewhat oblique in relation to Aristotle's own most explicit concerns. But I must also stress that I retain some doubts about the account I shall give of some of the virtues, especially those discussed in book IV. These virtues are both difficult and rather unattractive, and these properties may well be reflected in what I have to say about them. Nevertheless there is no justifiable alternative to taking them seriously. An attempt must be made to answer the question of why Aristotle discusses these particular virtues at all, and hence of what it is that makes them qualify as moral virtues, and since it is far from clear, in the case of some of the virtues, exactly what states of mind Aristotle is thinking of, one will in some cases have to discuss that question first.

2.1. The section on *courage* (*andreia*, III.vi–ix) does not yield much for the question of the objective good of the virtues. The most important passages seem to be vii.2–6, 1115b11–24; viii.9, 1116b19–23; viii.11–12 (1116b30–1117a9); and ix.4–5 (1117b7–16). (I leave on one side the discussion of 'political courage' in viii.1–3, 1116a17–29.)

The importance of the noble in connection with courage is evident. The courageous man acts for the sake of the noble and performs his acts because they are noble. There is also a clear connection between the point that he acts for the sake of the noble and the fact that he acts as reason states, as against following his passions (viii.12, 1117a8–9). Furthermore, it is clear that the influence of reason shows itself in the fact that his choices are the results of weighing certain good and bad things against each other, and that the bad things that are being weighed are naturally bad things such as wounds or the loss of the agent's life (viii.9, 1116b19-23; ix.4-5, 1117b7-16).

But there are no indications that the courageous man has an eye on the good of others or of the community as a whole; what he weighs his own losses against is just the noble (ix.4, 1117b14-15). We know, of course, from the final section of the chapter on self-love, that when the good man risks his life and sacrifices natural goods for himself, he does so for the sake of the noble or in order to obtain the noble for himself; but we also know that he acts for the sake of his friends or his country and evidently with the intention that *they* shall gain, in terms of natural goods, as a result of his own loss. There is no hint of the latter point in the section on courage itself.

2.2. There is one concept, however, in Aristotle's discussion of the individual virtues as a whole which deserves special attention, and which makes its first appearance in a passage in the section on courage. The passage is vii.2-6, 1115b11-24. It deserves more careful analysis than I shall give it here, but a few comments on it are required.

Aristotle's aim in the passage is to define the behaviour of the courageous man as opposed to that of the vicious people at either extreme. In vii.5, b17-19 he summarizes the points made in vii.2-4; and in vii.5, b19-20 and vii.6 he adds two remarks that seem intended to justify certain elements in the summary. The courageous man, according to the summary, is the man who faces, and who fears, the right things, for the right motive, in the right way, and at the right time, and who is fearless in the same way. 'For', as Aristotle adds, 'the courageous man has emotions and acts in accordance with merit (*kat' axian*) and as reason states' (1115b19-20). Now since the immediately following paragraph (§ 6) is intended to justify the point about the motive of the courageous man (he acts with the right motive, viz. for the sake of the noble), it is at least possible that the sentence I quoted is intended to justify the other half of the summary, which concerns, we may say, the actual elements of the concrete situation in which the courageous man acts.

But what would be meant by the suggestion that the courageous man acts, in relation to the concrete elements of a given situation, as these elements, and the situation as a whole, merit? It seems likely that it is a consequence of the fact that he reacts 'in accordance with merit' and as reason states, i.e. in the right *way*, that his reaction will be, as vii.3 implies, neither in the category of 'too much' (*mallon*) nor in that of 'too little' (*hētton*): they will, in fact, lie in the mean, and be 'appropriate' in the sense of proper or right. But if that is to be the consequence, the notion of *kat' axian* must evidently contain a reference to something in relation to which a given reaction to a given situation will be 'what the situation merits'. Commentators suggest that the 'appropriate' reaction is the one that exhibits the same ratio between reaction and situation as the one that exists between another situation and the appropriate reaction to *that* situation.[2] But mere consistency cannot, surely, capture the idea that the reaction which is in accordance with the merits of the situation is appropriate in the sense of proper or right. So we should perhaps forget about other situations and reactions and try instead to find elements in the initial situation itself that may be said to stand in a proper proportion in the courageous act.

It is not clear what these elements may be. But if the question is whether in response to a given situation the courageous man should remain at his post or should run away, it seems difficult to escape the conclusion that what makes his act appropriate is that there is more to be gained, in some relevant respect, when he acts in that way than if he were to act in any other way. It seems likely, in other words,

---

[2] Thus Stewart, note ad loc. Ramsauer (note ad loc.) apparently thinks that the relation of *kat' axian* may obtain just between the cause of the emotion (e.g. the fearful object) and the emotion itself (the fear). But some 'third' thing seems required in relation to which the relation between a given cause and a given reaction may be said to be appropriate. Stewart's reading at least provides that entity. Notice, however, that these 19th-century commentators at least have the merit of raising the question of the sense of *kat' axian*. Burnet just notes that *kat' axian* is 'not very different from κατὰ τὸ δέον', and Gauthier has no comment at all. Contrast with this the admirable Ramsauer's perceptive note *ad* 1115b12, in which he comments on the first appearance of *tou kalou heneka*, connects it with the appearance of *kat' axian* at b19, and indicates the importance the latter notion will take on as Aristotle proceeds.

that the notion of *kat' axian* implies the idea of a weighing
of goods, and that what makes a given reaction appropriate
is that it will bring into existence the greater mood.

But then what are the goods that will be weighed against
each other? One good will evidently be the agent's own life
and safety. And the other may be, once more, the noble. But
if I was right in suggesting that the sentence in question is
intended as justification only of the point about the *way* in
which the courageous man acts, whereas the idea that he acts
with the noble as his motive comes in only in § 6, then one
might argue that the good that is being weighed against the
risk to the agent's life and safety will not yet be the noble.
And in that case what other candidate could there be than
the gain, in terms of natural goods, on the part of people
other than the agent himself, or, in other words, on the part
of the community of humans involved as a whole?

The passage evidently does not say so, nor am I going to
base anything on the suggestion. What is important, though,
is the very existence of the notion of *kat' axian*, and the
questions it raises. Somehow the notion does seem to contain
certain implications for what it is that makes a given reaction
lie in the mean. The notion clearly deserves attention in
connection with the other virtues too.

3.1. The most relevant passages in the section on *temperance* (*sōphrosynē*, III.x–xii) are xi.8 (1119a11–20) and xii.9
(1119b15–18). I shall comment only on the first one.

In that passage Aristotle first (xi.8, 1119a11–15) describes
the temperate man negatively by contrasting him with the
man who is profligate. The temperate man neither enjoys,
when they are present, the things that the profligate man
enjoys, nor does he miss them when they are not. Thus the
emotive side of the temperate man differs from that of the
profligate one. In the lines that follow (a16–18) Aristotle
then describes more positively what the temperate man desires:
things which in addition to being pleasant are beneficial to
one's health or physical well-being, and other pleasant things
on condition that they do not go against one's health or
physical well-being or are contrary to the noble or above
one's means. For, as he continues (a18–20), if one neglects

these conditions, one loves such pleasures more than their worth (*axia*), and the temperate man is no such person but rather in accordance with right reason (*hōs ho orthos logos*).

The positive description of the temperate man clearly shows that when we move on from talking of his purely emotive side to a consideration of his reactions in terms of the notions of *axia* and right reason, the idea involved is one of relating one type of natural good, viz. bodily pleasure, to another type of natural good: health, physical well-being, and so forth.³ It is clearer here than it was in connection with courage that what makes an emotive reaction to a given situation appropriate, i.e. *kat' axian,* is the fact that that reaction places exactly the value on a given natural good that is in fact had by that good when it is compared with another natural good that is also involved in the situation.

3.2. But the passage raises some problems. I have just suggested that the notion of *axia* implies that one natural good will be weighed against another good of the same type; but the passage also suggests that in some cases what the natural good of bodily pleasure is weighed against will be the noble. And secondly, while I am arguing that morally good behaviour is morally good, viz. noble, because it results from weighing one's own good, in terms of natural goods, against the good of others, in the same terms, the passage seems to imply that only the agent's own good is involved.

I have already suggested a solution to the second problem (chapter 2, section 4.3). The type of reasoning that the temperate man is mainly represented in the passage as being engaged in is prudential reasoning, which weighs his own immediate benefit against the long-term harm or benefit he may obtain from taking or leaving the pleasant object that tempts him. But this type of reasoning is sufficiently close to altruistic reasoning, which considers also the good of others, in that they are both concerned to find the over-all good, and both reckon with the possibility that concern for that good may entail curbing the agent's immediate desires. We may say, therefore, that if there are indications that temperance is *also*

---

³ Bodily pleasure is not always included among natural goods, but cf. *EN* IX.viii.4, 1168b17 (in the chapter on self-love).

concerned with the good of others, and if there are indications that it is the latter fact that makes it a moral virtue, then Aristotle's present remarks raise no problem for my thesis, and he is free to allow prudential behaviour as one part of temperate behaviour, although as a secondary form of temperate behaviour only. So there may be a solution to the second problem.

But are there in fact any indications that temperance is also concerned with the good of others, and that it is this fact which makes it a moral virtue? Here the reference to the noble at a18 becomes relevant. For if one approaches the present passage with my account of the noble in chapter 2 in mind, one will clearly take it that this reference precisely introduces the good of others, and moreover implies that it is consideration for the good of others which renders temperance a moral virtue. But if this way of understanding Aristotle's reference to the noble in a18 is accepted, the first problem too will be solved. For in that case we may say that in saying that the agent's own immediate good is weighed against the noble, Aristotle is *also* saying that it is weighed against the good of others in terms of *natural* goods.

Clearly, I have not constructed an independent argument for my account of the noble as given in chapter 2, but I have shown that the present passage is compatible with that account, and indeed, that it makes good sense on the basis of it.

I conclude, therefore, that Aristotle's account of temperance may be seen to imply, more clearly than his account of courage, that reactions to situations are *kat' axian* and in accordance with right reason when they result from a weighing of natural goods that takes into consideration other people than oneself — or at least, as a secondary case, one's own good at other times than the present one.

4.1. The section on *generosity* (*eleutheriotēs*, IV.i) is also revealing. Generosity is concerned with the giving and taking of material goods (i.1, 1119b25) and the generous man gives and takes 'as he should' (*hōs dei, passim*). But he is more concerned with giving than with taking: i.1, 1119b25–26; i.7, 1120a9–11; i.17, 1120a34–b2. This point is presumably connected with Aristotle's claim that 'it is the nature of a generous man not to look to himself' (i.18, 1120b6). When he takes, he does so only 'as something necessary, in order that he may have something to give' (i.17, 1120b1-2).

In order to see what it is that makes generosity a good it is helpful to consider Aristotle's account of the vices in the area (i.28 ff.). They are prodigality (*asōtia*) and meanness (*aneleutheriotēs*). Prodigality consists in an excess in giving and a deficiency in taking; meanness in an excess in taking and a deficiency in giving (i.29, 1121a12-15). Prodigality is better than meanness (i.31, 1121a19-20; i.32, 1121a27-28; i.44, 1122a13-16), for a number of reasons. The most important one for my purposes is that whereas the prodigal man benefits many people, the mean one benefits none, not even himself (i.32, 1121a29-30, cf. i.44, 1122a14-15).

We may set out the various types of people in the area on a single scale. At one end of the scale we have a person (the mean one) who is a lover of material goods (*philo-chrēmatos*) and tries to get as many such goods as is possible for himself. He does not benefit others — in fact he does not even benefit himself.[4] Next comes the prodigal man, who does benefit others, and is therefore better than the mean man. In fact (i.31, 1121a25-27), since he goes to excesses in giving *and in avoiding taking*, he can hardly be said to be truly vicious (*mochthēros*). He is not immoral in character (*phaulos to ēthos*), but only foolish (*ēlithios*). Still he is not morally good; he is not generous. For though he does give and avoid taking, he does neither as he should nor well (i.31, 1121a22-23).

What, then, is it that differentiates the generous man, who is at the other end of the scale, from the prodigal one? The quick, and certainly correct, answer is that the generous man acts for the sake of the noble (see i.12-14, 1120a23-31 and i.17, b4), whereas the prodigal man does not. But the interesting thing about Aristotle's discussion of prodigality is that we learn more from that discussion about exactly what is implied in not paying due attention to the noble.

4.2. The relevant section is i.33-35, 1121a30-b7. In these

---

[4] I will not try to make sense of the latter point.

lines Aristotle is discussing a special type of prodigal man, who is not the prodigal man proper. The prodigal man proper goes to excesses in giving and avoiding taking, but the new type of prodigal man, who is in fact the normal one (*hoi polloi tōn asōtōn* in a30), is a man who both gives *and takes* excessively, and who consequently represents a mixture of prodigality and meanness (a30-32). People of that type are mistaken with respect to taking as well as to giving. For 'since they pay no attention to the noble, they take inconsiderately and from whatever source' (b1-2): they want to spend, but how and from what source is no matter to them (b2-3). That is also why their acts of giving are not (truly) generous either (b3-4). 'For they are not noble nor done for the sake of that, nor are they as they should be' (b4-5). Instead, such people give to people who ought to be without the goods, and do not give to people with moderate characters, but rather to people who procure some pleasure for them (b5-7).

Suppose the description that is here given of the faults of the acts of giving of people who exhibit the special type of prodigality is also valid for the acts of giving of the prodigal man proper. In that case we do become wiser as to what the 'foolishness' or lack of insight of that man consists in. For the point that he does not give to people of moderate character, but instead to people who ought to remain without the goods reminds one strongly of an idea we already know, viz. that only virtuous people are able to use natural goods to their own benefit (chapter 2, section 2.4). If this is the implied point, what distinguishes the prodigal man (proper) from the truly generous one is that while the former does give to others and hence (at least sometimes) benefits others, the generous man not only gives to others but also *for their benefit* and always so. For he pays attention to the noble, indeed acts for its sake; and the passage I have discussed suggests that the effect of that is that he places the goods where they will actually benefit the recipient.

I conclude that Aristotle's account of generosity contains material that throws some light on what it is to act for the sake of the noble in the area covered by that virtue; and that the light that is thrown is wholly in line with the account of the noble I developed in chapter 2.

5. *Munificence* (*megaloprepeia*, IV.ii) has close connections with generosity. Like generosity it is concerned with material goods (ii.1, 1122a19), but it differs from it in being only about actions that represent large expenditure. Thus whereas the generous man was concerned with taking as well as with giving, the munificent man is concerned with giving only, and giving on a large scale (ii.1, 1122a20-22). Aristotle defines his acts as *dapanērai* (a21). Commentators take it that *dapanē* (expenditure) is the genus of *dosis* (giving, gift), which was the term used in connection with generosity, but that Aristotle is talking of a special type of *dapanē*, viz. expenditure on a large scale.[5] It seems, however, that Aristotle's account of munificence implies that he uses *dapanē* to stand for spending on a certain scale and on occasions that are *public*, so as to concern the city as a whole.[6]

In connection with munificence there is much talk of *axia* and 'what is proper' (*to prepon*). The idea of appropriate giving is used in a number of different contexts. I shall not go into detail. But there is at least one general question we should try to answer: why is munificence a good, what is the objective point of that virtue, what is the thing that makes munificence 'appropriate'?

Consider the vices in the area (ii.20 ff.). The munificent man, of course, acts for the sake of the noble (ii.7, 1122b6-7). The vulgar man (*banausos*), by contrast, does not (he is the man who goes to excess in spending beyond what is right). Nor does the niggardly man (*mikroprepēs*), who is the man who is deficient in spending (ii.20, 1123a24-26; ii.21, a29). The former acts in order to make a display of himself, i.e. for personal gains in social prestige (ii.20, 1123a24-26). And the latter seems motivated (as Ramsauer suggests)[7] partly by the same desire, partly by his wish to keep as many as possible of his possessions for himself (cf. ii.21, 1123a27-31). By contrast the munificent man, who acts for the sake of the noble, will spend lavishly (but appropriately) — 'not on himself . . . but on what is of public interest (*eis ta koina*)'

---

[5] Thus, e.g., Ramsauer ad loc.

[6] The passages listed by Bonitz, s.v. *dapanē* support this, e.g. *Pol.* VII.10, 1330a13; III.11, 1281b3; *Rhet.* I.4, 1359b26.

[7] Note *ad* 1123a27-31.

(ii.15,1123a4-5). Here the point is certainly not just that the munificent man will spend on public *occasions*; for so will the vulgar man. Rather, the point is that when he spends on public occasions the munificent man will spend in the public *interest*, and this point is clearly important: it throws independent light on what it is to act for the sake of the noble.

But what, then, is the public interest of the expenditure of the munificent man, what is the good for the community which is brought about by his munificence? In ii.11–17 (1122b19–1123a10) Aristotle goes through the objects that the munificent man will spend on. Religious occasions and objects of direct benefit to the community (like equipping a trireme) are central (ii.11, 1122b19–23 and ii.15, b33–35). But other, more private occasions may call for munificence on condition that they in some way affect the city as a whole (ii.15). Thus even building a beautiful house may be an act of munificence: 'for this too is a *kosmos* (ornament)', viz. for the state[8] (1123a7).

The notion of *kosmos* is interesting. At the end of the chapter on munificence (ii.22) Aristotle says of the two vices in the area that they *are* vices (*kakiai*), but are not blamed because they are neither harmful for one's neighbour (*blaberai tōi pelas*) nor too unseemly (*aschēmones*). I take it that Aristotle here used 'unseemly' in a basically moral sense, i.e. as an equivalent of *aischron* or base (cf. IV.vi.7, 1126b31–35). In that case it is tempting (in spite of 'neither . . . nor') to take the first point about harming one's neighbour as stating what the moral unseemliness consists in. So vulgarity and niggardliness *are* vices (*kakiai*), but perhaps not fully so, or so vicious that they are really to be blamed; for they are not positively harmful to one's neighbour. If this is what is meant, perhaps the virtue itself, though noble and done for the sake of the noble, is not *positively* beneficial to the community either. It is, perhaps, just a *kosmos*, it adds, we may say, to the charm of the life of the community, but is not vital to its well-being in the way in which, e.g., courage is.

It is difficult to make sure how important a virtue Aristotle considers munificence to be. But it seems fair to say that

[8] Cf. Ross, who translates *kosmos* as 'public ornament'.

everything he says of the behaviour of the vicious and virtuous people in the area, and of the point of the behaviour of the latter, is well in line with and partly positively confirms my account of the noble from chapter 2.

6.1. Aristotle's account of *high-mindedness* (*megalopsychia*, IV.iii) hardly belongs among the most celebrated parts of the *Ethics*. I agree that there is much that seems odd in that account; but I also believe that it is more difficult than has often been supposed to make out exactly what Aristotle is wanting to say in the chapter.

The high-minded man is the person who judges himself worthy of high things, and who *is* worthy of them (iii.3, 1123b2). These high things are (according to iii.9-13) our well-known natural goods; 'for *axia* (worth) is said in relation to the external goods' (iii.10, 1123b17). Most important among these goods is honour (*timē*), one reason being that honour is an *athlon* or reward for the most noble things (b19-20). So the high-minded man is (mainly) concerned with honour and dishonour (b21-22).

And he is in fact worthy of honour (iii.14-16). For he is morally good, and honour is a reward (*athlon*) for virtue (iii.14-15, 1123b26-1124a1). It is important to notice here that Aristotle connects honour and virtue very closely and in the specific way of making the former a reward for the latter. He concludes: 'So high-mindedness seems to be a sort of ornament (*kosmos*) of the virtues. For it makes them greater and presupposes them. Therefore it is truly difficult to be high-minded; for it is impossible to be so without noble-and-goodness (*kalokagathia*)' (iii.16, 1124a1-4).

The idea that a good man, if he is also high-minded, will require acknowledgement by others for his goodness in terms of having natural goods, primarily honour, allotted to him soon proves more difficult than might seem at first. For the point of the two paragraphs that follow (iii.17-18) is to insist that the high-minded man does not in fact place much value on the natural goods that he will rightly claim for himself. The point was made already in iii.15, 1123b32 and is repeated emphatically at the end of iii.18, where it is connected with the idea that the high-minded man is disdainful (*hyperoptēs*, 1124a19-20). This leads to my first basic question. Why, if the high-minded man does not in fact place much value on natural goods, should he at all want to lay a claim to them? Why introduce a moral virtue that consists in deeming oneself worthy of natural goods, if these goods are not, after all, considered to be of much value?

To clarify the problem let us suppose that we lived in a society in which natural goods were the only things that were considered good. In such a society being high-minded would be claiming the highest natural goods, and especially honour, for oneself as acknowledgement of one's goodness in terms of possession of other natural goods, e.g. good birth, wealth, or power. A high-minded man would in such a society in a quite straightforward manner place a genuine value on the good that he claims as his, and there is no problem about understanding such a man. Aristotle's high-minded man, by contrast, does pose a problem, since he is represented as claiming for himself goods which he does not really consider of much value. What creates this problem is presumably that Aristotle has changed the basis for the high-minded man's claim for natural goods from possession of other such goods to the fact that he is morally good. We have moved, one might say, from an 'archaic' set-up to a more 'moral' outlook. In fact the point of iii.19-22 seems precisely to be that of comparing and contrasting the two types of basis for high valuation of oneself that I have just introduced. In these paragraphs Aristotle in effect removes the basis for claims to natural goods from possession of such goods as good birth, power, and wealth (iii.19, 1124a21-22) to possession of moral virtue.

But the problem about Aristotle's account of high-mindedness remains unsolved. I shall argue that the solution lies in seeing that Aristotle not only changes the basis for high claims from possession of natural goods to possession of moral virtue: when the Aristotelian high-minded man claims honour for himself, he does so, not because he is at all interested in honour, but as an expression of his belief that what is of genuine value is *moral virtue* — and honour is an *athlon* of virtue.

6.2. In order to see this let us consider certain aspects of Aristotle's account (in iii.35-37) of the two vices in the area: low-mindedness (*mikropsychia*) and vanity (*chaunotēs*). The low-minded man fails because he robs himself of goods that he is in fact worthy of (iii.35, 1125a19-30). Even worse, perhaps, is that he does not at all believe himself worthy of the goods (a20-21). His fault here might seem to be that he is ignorant of the worth he in fact possesses (a22-23), viz. the worth that results from being morally good. However, says Aristotle, his fault is rather that although he is clear enough about his worth, he has qualms about making the claims for himself that he knows he is entitled to make (a23-24), he is *oknēros* (a24) or lacking in self-assurance. Now why is this a fault? And why, conversely, is it a good (if one is a good man) to lay a claim to those (natural) goods that one is in fact worthy of?

Let us first consider the vice at the other extreme. The vain man is in fact ignorant of his worth, he is *ēlithios* (foolish or ignorant), as the low-minded man was not (iii.36, 1125a 27-28 and cf. iii.35, 1125a23). For although he is not worthy of honour, he believes that he is (a28-29). And the reason for this is that he believes that the true basis for a claim to honour lies in natural goods (*eutychēmata*, a30-32).

So the vain man makes large claims for himself, but he is not worthy of the things he wants to obtain since he bases his claim on the wrong sort of thing. The low-minded man, on the other hand, does not make sufficiently large claims for himself; for he has the correct basis for such claims.

But now what is interesting is that the vain man is said to be closer to the high-minded man than is the low-minded man (iii.37, 1125a32-34). Why? In one way, of course, the vain man is totally different from the high-minded man in that the former lacks, where the latter possesses, the proper basis for large claims. Apparently, however, the point where they agree is the more important one: they both have the strength to base claims on others on what they consider valuable, they both feel bound by their beliefs about what is of value. This feeling of obligation towards what one considers of value is lacking in the low-minded man. The vain man has it, albeit on a false basis. The high-minded man has it, and on the proper basis.

6.3. But then we may say, by way of solution to the difficulty I detected in Aristotle's account of high-mindedness, that when the high-minded man claims natural goods, especially honour, for himself, he does so, not because he has any particular interest in being honoured, but simply as an expression of his firm belief in the paramount value of moral virtue. He, and nobody else, values moral virtue as highly as it in fact should be valued. The low-minded man, by contrast, does not really place the value on moral virtue that it deserves. And the vain man is mistaken since, though he does place a value on certain things and does follow up his beliefs about what is of value, his beliefs are false.

So Aristotle should be seen as having taken the whole step away from an 'archaic' conception of high-mindedness. His high-minded man is worthy of natural goods because he is morally good, and he claims such goods for himself because they constitute a traditional 'reward' for what he truly values, viz. moral virtue. One can understand better, therefore, why high-mindedness is a *kosmos* or 'ornament' of the virtues, and why it presupposes and amplifies the other virtues. As I have explained high-mindedness up till now there is clearly an element of second-order attitude about it.

6.4. So much for the first main point I want to make about high-mindedness. But if this were the whole of Aristotelian high-mindedness, it would be an attitude that might be had by any person who possesses moral virtue. In fact, however, there is one more aspect to high-mindedness that has not yet been touched on, and which comes to the fore in Aristotle's much reviled portrait of the high-minded man in iii.23–34.

We have seen that the high-minded man does not really place much value on natural goods. In fact his attitude to virtuous acts themselves is not much different: ordinary, small-type specimens of virtuous activity he will not deign to engage in, and only a few exceptionally noble acts are able to catch his attention (iii.23, 1124b6–9; iii.27, b24–26). In one way it is not difficult to understand this. For if, as I have argued, moral virtue presupposes that natural goods have value (chapter 2, section 3.3), then if the high-minded man does not really place much value on such goods he cannot be bothered about (moral) acts that concern only insignificant natural goods.

But then the question arises of why it is that Aristotle construes the high-minded man as a person who places so little value on natural goods. Why, in other words, does Aristotle construe the high-minded man as a moral saint, as a person for whom moral virtue is the only thing that has value? In a way the answer is simple. For Aristotle's account of high-mindedness, as sainthood, is simply the logical outcome of his development away from the 'archaic' conception of that virtue. But the crucial question remains of what significance for the general understanding of moral virtue in Aristotle we should attach to the fact that he does develop this logical outcome in such detail. The answer I shall argue for is that we should not attach too much importance to those aspects of high-mindedness (the disdain for natural goods and the sluggishness to act unless the nobility of acting is great) which in the portrait of the high-minded man are implied to follow from the fact that he values moral virtue only.

6.5. The question I have just put concerns basically the value and role of natural goods in relation to moral virtue.[9] In an important passage in *EN* I, in which he is working towards his definition of happiness, Aristotle toys with the idea that no matter how bad a situation a person may be in as regards possession of natural goods, his moral virtue will 'shine through' and secure happiness for him — if, that is, he is 'noble (*gennadas*) and high-minded' (*EN* I.x.12, 1100b 32–33). However, Aristotle ends up (in I.x.15) by including in his definition of the person who is *eudaimōn* a reference to natural goods: such a man must, after all, be sufficiently equipped with external goods. It follows from this that the high-minded man of *EN* IV is wrong in his belief that moral virtue is the only thing that matters (viz. for happiness).

[9] The point that the question of the mutual relationship of moral virtue and natural goods is essential to the understanding of high-mindedness has been particularly emphasized by Gauthier, in his commentary (e.g. p. 274) and in his book *Magnanimité, l'idéal de la grandeur dans la philosophie païenne et dans la théologie chrétienne*, Bibliothèque thomiste, vol. 28, Paris, 1951, pp. 65–118, *passim*.

At the same time, since the passage in *EN* I does refer to that exclusive belief in moral virtue as a belief that is at least worth entertaining, the idea must have had some initial attraction to Aristotle. And one can see why, precisely because it represents the logical outcome of his development away from the 'archaic' conception of the value of natural goods.

What should be retained from *EN* I, however, is that natural goods are in fact necessary for happiness. For this fact has important repercussions for the view one should take of Aristotelian moral virtue in general and its relation to natural goods. The morally good man, as opposed to the high-minded man, does recognize the value of natural goods. And it is for this reason that he will also perform those lesser virtuous deeds that were neglected by the high-minded man. It is true, of course, as I have argued on the basis of *EE* VIII.iii.1–10 (chapter 2, sections 3.1–3.4), that the value of moral virtue does not lie simply in the fact that it is, as *Rhet.* I.9, 1366a36–37 has it, a 'capacity for procuring and preserving goods' (*dynamis poristikē agathōn kai phylaktikē*), where the goods are understood as natural goods. This view of the value of moral virtue establishes a straightforward connection between natural goods and moral virtue.[10] But it is too simple. For the value of moral virtue is the one that is captured in the principle of *nobility*. At the same time, however, it is implied in that very principle, as I have also argued, that natural goods do possess value. And this fact is neglected by the high-minded man.

We should say, therefore, that as regards the relation to natural goods of moral virtue Aristotelian moral virtue lies, in a way, in the mean between two opposed extreme views. At one extreme there is the view that the value of moral virtue lies simply in the fact that it procures natural goods; at the other extreme there is the view, in fact the one Aristotle isolates in his account of high-mindedness, that natural goods have no real value at all. In between there is the view that the value of moral virtue lies in its conformity to the principle of nobility (this point connects moral virtue with the extreme view represented by high-mindedness), but

[10] In the end, I believe, this is the line adopted by J. M. Cooper in his *Reason and Human Good in Aristotle*, Cambridge, Mass., 1975, pp. 122–7.

that this very principle presupposes the value of natural goods (this point connects moral virtue with the extreme view represented by the *Rhetoric*'s definition of moral virtue).

6.6. My account of high-mindedness has had two parts. I first attempted to develop the implications for the very understanding of high-mindedness of the fact that the high-minded man is represented as claiming goods for himself that he is after all not really interested in. And next I tried to answer the question of what significance for the general understanding of moral virtue in Aristotle we should attach to the fact that he represents the high-minded man as a moral saint. I shall argue that the virtue that Aristotle goes immediately on to discuss is closely similar to high-mindedness as regards the first main point above, but differs from it with respect to the second point.

7.1. That virtue is the one of *ambition* (*philotimia*, IV.iv). It is explicitly connected by Aristotle with high-mindedness in the way in which generosity is connected with munificence (iv.1, 1125b1-4).

Ambition is concerned with the desire for honour (iv.2, b7-8). § § 3-4 of the chapter make it clear what is good about ambition. I combine certain points in those paragraphs. In some situations being ambitious seems a good thing (so we praise it), in others it does not (and we blame it). (1) Being ambitious is a good thing if it means that one is *andrōdēs* and a lover of the noble (*philokalos*, b11-12). Translating *andrōdēs* here as 'manly' seems unilluminating. Comparison with *EN* II.ix.7, 1109b18 and *Rhet.* II.17, 1391a22 suggests that it means 'forceful in character', in the sense of 'confident in the correctness of one's own beliefs', 'self-assured'. That, then, is the good thing about ambition, and the reason that Aristotle gives (b10-11) is that by having psychic strength one will avoid the mistake of not seeking honour even for virtuous acts. (2) In some situations, however, ambition will seem a bad thing, viz. if it means that one is lacking in moderation and temperance (b12-13). This is so if one wants honour more than one should or from sources from which one should not (b8-10).

The first point above reminds one of certain elements in Aristotle's account of high-mindedness. The person who is ambitious in the right way is a lover of the noble: perhaps, then, he will not seek honour for its own sake, but merely as a 'reward' for moral virtue. And he is self-assured: perhaps the point is that he will be sufficiently convinced of the value of moral virtue to stick to that conviction. On this reading, then, ambition, like high-mindedness, will be a second-order attitude, an attitude *towards* moral virtue. Similarly the picture of the unambitious person that is also implied in the first point above will correspond to the picture of the low-minded man of the preceding chapter: his 'unmanliness' will consist in his not attaching sufficient importance to the value of noble acts.

The opposite vice in the area is the one expressed in the second point above that ambition may sometimes seem a bad thing. Why? Aristotle's two reasons were that one may seek honour (*i*) more than one should, and (*ii*) from sources from which one should not. (*i*) But can one be a lover *of the noble* to too high a degree? Perhaps, if we think of the high-minded man, the answer is positive. But ambition is precisely free of the extravagant aspects of high-mindedness. So in the area of ambition there seems no room for too high a degree of love for the noble. (*ii*) Perhaps, then, the point about the person who is wrongly ambitious is that he is not in fact a lover of the noble. Perhaps he seeks honour precisely from sources from which he ought not to seek it. Thus he might be like the vain man (of the preceding chapter) in that he believes that honour should be acquired on the basis of other things than moral virtue, e.g. on the basis of one's possession of various natural goods: good birth, power, wealth.

7.2. I have interpreted ambition on the basis of Aristotle's account of high-mindedness. The difference between the two virtues is, if we go by Aristotle's initial comparison between the two (iv.1, 1125b1–4), that ambition is free of the extravagant, saintly aspect of high-mindedness, which was its disdain for natural goods. But the two virtues go together with regard to the first main point in my discussion of high-mindedness. Neither is really concerned with honour for its own sake, but rather with honour as a reward for virtue. Both are therefore attitudes *towards* the other virtues.

It is for this reason that both high-mindedness and ambition may, after all, be said to be 'for the sake of the noble': it is not that, e.g., the ambitious man seeks honour for the sake of the noble, i.e. (the best one can make of it) *as* something noble. In fact he does not really seek honour at all, as I have argued. If a man is either high-minded or ambitious, he will have an unwaveringly positive attitude to virtuous behaviour, and it is for this reason that, when his high-mindedness or ambition is put to the test, he will act virtuously, viz. perform the acts that are enjoined by the *other* virtues, and will consequently act 'for the sake of the noble'.

8.1. The virtue of *good temper* (*praotēs*, IV.v) is perhaps the most difficult of all the Aristotelian virtues. Good temper is a mean with respect to anger (*orgē*, v.1, 1125b26). The good-tempered man will be angry when, where, and as he should, but otherwise not (v.3, 1125b31-32). Good temper lies between a deficiency, called 'inirascibility' (*aorgēsia*), and an excess, called irascibility (*chalepotēs*). But good temper is closer to inirascibility (v.1, 1125b28). Similarly the good-tempered man is not revengeful (*timōrētikos*) but rather forgiving (*syngnōmikos*, v.4, 1126a2-3).

Now revenge (*timōria*) is an element in the Aristotelian definition of anger (*orgē*). For anger is a sort of pain (*lypē*), but with the addition of the element which is in *DA* I.1 (403a30-31) called a 'desire to hit back' (*orexis antilypēseōs*). But *antilypēsis* or 'causing pain in return' is the same as revenge. So anger is pain plus the desire for revenge. The good-tempered man, then, is a man who will not very often become angry (for he is not revengeful), but will more often forgive. The latter seems to imply that he does feel pain, but without having the additional desire for revenge.

That this is in fact so is fairly clear from Aristotle's remark that the good-tempered man is a person who is unperturbed (*atarachos*) and is not led by passion but as reason dictates (v.3, 1125b33-35). Here it seems at least implied that the good-tempered man will sometimes have passions (though not fits of anger), but that he will not allow himself to act on them in ways other than those dictated by reason. A similar case may be observed in Aristotle's account of courage: the courageous man will be well aware of a risk he is running to his own life and he will be pained by the prospect of losing it, but he will nevertheless remain adamant in his decision to act in accordance with what is noble (*EN* III.ix.4). So the good-tempered man may well feel pain at certain things, but his reason will tell him to be forgiving — whereas in other cases, in fact where he should, he will be angry and will effect revenge. The question then is: when and where? Aristotle just says that 'the things (sc. that cause anger) are many and diverse' (v.2, 1125b30-31). But this is hardly sufficient.

8.2. Let us consider the two vices, taking first the deficiency, inirascibility (v.5-6). People who do not become angry when and where they should seem foolish (*ēlithioi*, v.5, 1126a5). We have met the term before: low-minded people seemed ignorant of themselves, but Aristotle corrected himself by saying that instead of being fools they should rather be taken to be lacking in self-assurance (*oknēroi*). In the same way the present passage contains two descriptions of what accounts for the lack of anger on the part of inirascible people. Such people either simply do not become aware of the thing that should have caused them to be angry (or if they are aware of it, they are at least not pained by it), or in spite of being aware of it, and pained by it too, they do not become angry because they are not the type of people to defend themselves. So they are rightly blamed, either for being simple-minded or for being 'slavish' (v.5, 1126a6-8). In view of a passage I have referred to earlier, viz. *EN* II.ix.7, 1109b17-18, it seems justifiable to take the term 'slavish' here to be one part of a pair, the other part of which is the term *andrōdēs*, self-assured. So inirascibility is a vice since it implies a failure to 'go the whole way' when there is something one feels pained at and which one in fact believes to be wrong. The good-tempered man, by contrast, will not just be pained but will feel the anger that he should feel: he has the self-confidence that is required.

In general, however, as we know, the good-tempered man is a man who will most often not feel anger, and rightly so.

For, coming now to the other vice, the state that is most opposed to good temper is the excess, viz. irascibility. 'For it is both commoner (since it is a characteristic of humans to take revenge), and people who are irascible are worse to live with' (v.12, 1126a29-31). So because good temper is the more opposed to irascibility, being good-tempered is being such that one becomes angry less often than human beings normally do.

What we have, then, is a man (the good-tempered one) who does become angry when and where he should, i.e. in situations in which not being so would be slavish, but who does not become angry as often as most human beings do. He may well be pained in situations in which most humans become angry, but he will respond to his pain by forgiveness, thus following the dictates of his reason as against the immediate passion. As a consequence he will be easier to live with than irascible people are. But this is not the criterion for the appropriateness of his state, for the inirascible man is presumably the man it is easiest to live with.

8.3. At this point I wish to make a small move. If good temper is a moral virtue, the good-tempered man must act for the sake of the noble. Now good temper is a virtue that is not directly concerned with sharing out natural goods. It is concerned with the appropriate emotional reactions (and the acts that follow on them) to things done or said by others. These 'others' must presumably be adult human beings, not just sentient beings: the latter would be sufficient for the reacting person to be able to perform *antilypēsis* (whereas one rarely becomes angry with a wall), but if one's reaction is to be dictated by reason, the central case (at least) will be the one in which the offender's reason might have been expected to dictate a different course of action. So one is reacting to the behaviour of other adults — and for the sake of the noble.

But then it becomes tempting to take the basic point of good temper to be this. The good-tempered man will feel pain and take steps to redress the balance in situations in which he is being deprived of things he values (viz. natural goods) and where the deprivation is an unjust one. In such situations he will want to take his 'revenge', not because he is himself deprived of the goods, but because the act of depriv- ation goes against the noble. Were he, like the inirascible man, just to give up redressing the (moral) wrong that he in fact believes has been done, he would prove lacking in self- assurance or confidence in the correctness of his belief in the noble.

If this interpretation is correct, good temper will be similar to ambition (*philotimia*) in that it is a virtue that ensures an appropriate emotional backing of one's belief in the noble. Similarly the vices will correspond to those connected with ambition. Thus the inirascible man will be the man who has too little confidence in the principle of nobility, whereas the irascible man will be the one who has not grasped that principle at all, and has not seen that others have rights too, which may interfere with his own immediate desires.

But good temper will not be identical with ambition since the former, but not the latter, is essentially and exclusively concerned with one's reactions to the behaviour of others.

8.4. But is the suggestion correct? One cannot feel sure. For it hangs on bringing in the noble, and there is no trace in the chapter of that concept, nor of anything that reminds one directly of it. There are, however, as I have tried to show, things in the chapter that connect good temper with the immediately preceding virtue of ambition. Moreover, if one is allowed, in spite of the fact that the ordering of the virtues is different in the *Eudemian Ethics*, to draw conclusions from their ordering in the *Nicomachean Ethics*, one may derive some support for the suggested interpretation from the fact that on that interpretation good temper is in exactly the right place: while closely connected wth ambition, it differs from it in being exclusively concerned with the reaction to other people, and consequently points forward to the mean- states that Aristotle discusses in the chapters that follow directly. For these too, as I shall show, are essentially con- cerned with one's reaction to others.

9. Let us now consider these mean-states (IV.vi–viii).

They go together in being all concerned with a 'sharing of words and deeds of certain types' (viii.12, 1128b5-6). Similarly Aristotle starts chapter vi as follows: 'In associations with others, in living with them and sharing words and deeds with them . . .' (vi.1, 1126b11-12). One main question we should try to answer is why Aristotle in this way stresses the social character of the mean-states in question. For I have argued that all the virtues must in a certain sense be social in character.

The three mean-states are intriguing, and they deserve closer analysis than I shall give them here. I shall confine myself to pointing to certain elements in Aristotle's account that imply that, in spite of the immediate impression created by him, the three mean-states are not in fact genuine Aristotelian moral virtues at all.

10. The mean-state that is discussed in IV.vi has no name of its own, but most resembles friendship (vi.4, 1126b19-20). It is, I believe, *kindness*. It differs from friendship in that it is a *general* feeling of good will towards others (vi.5). Like good temper, of the preceding chapter, it is concerned with how to react to the behaviour of others, whether to react favourably so as not to cause them pain (*apodechesthai, passim*) or unfavourably so as to cause them pain (*dyscherainein, passim*). Here the kind man strikes a note between the two extremes of being obsequious (*areskos, vi.1*), so as never to oppose anything, and being 'hard to get along with' or 'quarrelsome' (*dyskolos* and *dyseris, vi.2*), so as always to oppose everything. But it is important to see exactly how he mediates between the two positions. By himself, says Aristotle, the kind man will prefer to respond to others as they want him to, i.e. please them in response (*synēdynein*), and will take care not to offend them (vi.8, 1127a2-3). Thus his basic attitude to others is the same as that of the obsequious man. But he differs from him in that he will 'refer to' (cf. vi.6, 1126b29), i.e. take into consideration, what is noble and what is beneficial (ibid. and vi.8, 1127a5) and the greater future pleasure (a5-6), not just of the other person but with respect to himself too (vi.7, 1126b31-35). The important point here is that what the kind man will refer to when deciding how to

react to others includes all imaginable considerations: the
noble, the beneficial, and pleasure; for himself as well as for
others. It follows that if moral virtue in Aristotle is defined
as being concerned for the noble, and for that alone, kindness
will not be a genuine moral virtue. In fact Aristotle seems to
allow that a kind man will sometimes react unfavourably to
others if the opposite reaction would be *harmful*, and harmful *to himself* (vi.7, 1126b31-33). In such a case a man may
still be kind, viz. if he is *in. principle* favourably disposed
towards others. But if such a case is in fact envisaged by
Aristotle, then, clearly, kindness cannot be unequivocally
claimed to be a genuine Aristotelian moral virtue.

11. Next (IV.vii) comes the mean-state which in the
chapter itself has no name, but in *EN* II.vii.12, 1108a20
is called *truthfulness* (*alētheia*). *Alētheia* is not truthfulness
in general, but only in one's statements about the amount
of *endoxa* or reputable things one possesses (vii.2-4, 1127a
20-26). The truthful man (*ho alētheutikos*) is a mean between
the boastful man (*ho alazōn*), who makes it appear that he
possesses more than he does (vii.2, 1127a21-22), and the
self-depreciatory man (*ho eirōn*), who seeks to hide what he
does possess (vii.3, a22-23). By contrast, the truthful man
acknowledges what he has (vii.4, a23-26). But why? Aristotle
briefly suggests that he is self-reliant (*authekastos*, vii.4,
a23-24) and consequently, we may suppose, pays no attention
to the view others form of him.[11] vii.5 ff., however, suggests

---

[11] The term *authekastos* has troubled commentators and translators both here
and at *EE* III.vii.6, 1233b38-39 (the only places in the *corpus* where the term
is used). On one view (e.g. Grant, Burnet, Ross, and partly Dirlmeier) the *authekastos* in Aristotle is a man who 'calls a spade a spade'. On another view (Stewart
and Gauthier) he is 'the man who appears in his own character' (Stewart) or
'l'homme qui est "lui-meme", celui qui se montre tel qu'il est' (Gauthier, who
twice on p. 307 couples in this way being oneself and showing oneself as the
person one is). Gauthier is quite right (in his excellent note ad loc.) that Stewart's
interpretation represents an advance on the earlier one, since it makes it easier
to see the connection between the positive use of the word, which is the only one
represented in Aristotle, and the negative use, which is found, e.g., in Menander
(*Sam.* 550, Frg. 736) and Plutarch (*Mor.* 823a). The question of the sense of the
negative use is in itself difficult to settle (cf. Gomme/Sandbach *ad Sam.* 550), but
basically the sense seems to be 'self-centred' (hence, e.g., 'unforthcoming' in
Menander and 'self-willed' in Plutarch). If this is correct, Stewart's and Gauthier's
rendering of our Aristotelian passage does represent an advance, and Liddell/

a slightly different answer: for no reason; he just is such a person (vii.7, 1127b2-3). The point is made explicitly in vii.7, and it is part of the argument of vii.5-6. But if the truthful man is in this way constitutionally 'a lover of truth' (vii.8, b4), then when he speaks the truth where nothing is to be gained or lost from doing so, he will not be acting for the sake of the noble. It is true, as vii.6 makes clear, that speaking the truth is by itself noble and praiseworthy (and therefore the truthful man is himself praiseworthy), but the truthful man does not tell the truth for the sake of the noble, but simply because he 'loves' truth-telling.

That this is so is clear from two considerations. First, in the difficult § 8 Aristotle clearly starts from the case in which nothing is at stake and in which the lover of truth will speak the truth just because that is what he wants to do, and only moves on from there to the case where something is at stake and where consequently telling or not telling the truth becomes a moral question. And secondly, in his account of the vice of boastfulness (vii.10 ff.) Aristotle in the same way starts from the person who for no reason whatever claims to have more than he in fact has — in spite of the sheer futility of such a person, which Aristotle is himself quick to point to (vii.10, 1127b10-11).

The conclusion I wish to draw is that truthfulness as such will not be a genuine moral virtue if such a state is defined by concern for the noble. It is true, and important, that Aristotle (in vii.8 and vii.11 ff.) connects truthfulness with cases where a moral question is raised. But by itself

---

Scott/Jones, who for the positive sense give only 'one who calls things by their right names, downright, blunt' and quote our passage in support (thus following the first view cited above), should be corrected. I believe, however, that we should take one more step in the direction indicated by Stewart and Gauthier. A man who is *authekastos* in the good sense is not just the man who shows himself as he is: he *is* himself, in the sense that he is not in the least concerned about how he will appear to others. He is *self-reliant*. It follows, of course, that he will also show himself as he is, that he will 'appear in his own character', but this is precisely a consequence of his being what he is. It is only when this additional step has been taken, that one can fully see the connection between the positive and negative senses of the term. To be *authekastos* in the bad sense is precisely to be *too* self-reliant, *too* unconcerned about others. (The rendering by H. G. Apostle — 'the moderate man, viewing the situation as it is . . .' — is just wrong.)

truthfulness is not represented in the chapter in a way that makes it a genuine Aristotelian moral virtue.

12. Finally there is *wit* as a state of mind: *eutrapelia* (IV.viii). This mean-state too is concerned with the sharing of words and deeds of certain types (viii.12, 1128b5-6). Like kindness, it is concerned with pleasure (b7), but whereas wit has its appropriate place in the part of one's life in which one is resting from serious activity, and more specifically amusing oneself in the company of others (viii.1, 1127b33-34), kindness has its place in associations with others in the remaining, more serious part of one's life (viii.12, 1128b8-9).

It is very difficult to make out exactly what defines the mean-state in the area. But I need not go into detail. The only question that should concern us here is whether the man who jokes well acts, in some way, for the sake of the noble. The answer must surely be negative, on any interpretation of Aristotle's account of appropriate joking. For no matter how much importance one attaches to Aristotle's requirement that one should not cause pain to the object of the joke (cf. viii.3, 1128a4-7 and viii.7, a28-29), it remains the case that both the virtue and the vices in the area are concerned with one thing alone, viz. the pleasure or pain one may give to the people one is associating with in the non-serious parts of one's life. There is no mention of either of the other two motives for action, the noble and the beneficial, nor is there any real room for them.

13.1. We may therefore sum up my remarks on the three mean-states that are discussed in IV.vi-viii as follows. None of these mean-states in essentially concerned with acting for the sake of the noble. The kind man is in principle such that he will react favourably to others, but he will let that impulse be guided by a consideration for other values, one of which, but precisely just one of which, is the noble. The truthful man is a lover of truth by nature, and Aristotle starts his account of him from cases where the noble is not involved, i.e. cases where the truthful man acts as he does just because he is that sort of man. And finally there is the man of wit, who is not concerned with the noble at all. So if concern for the noble is part of the definition of a moral virtue, the three mean-states are not moral virtues.

However, there is no indication in the text that they are not. And one can well see why. For if the account of the noble I have given is correct, and if, consequently, the noble is essentially connected with one's relations with other members of the community, there will be a fairly close similarity between the genuine moral virtues and the three mean-states: the latter too are states that regulate the life of the individual in relation to that of other members of the community. But then one can also see why Aristotle makes a point of the fact that the three mean-states are such states. Whereas it is immediately clear that the genuine moral virtues (apart from temperance in one of its aspects) are social in character, if the three mean-states do not issue in acts that are for the sake of the noble, the fact that these states too are concerned with one's relation to others must be explicitly stated. One can see, then, why Aristotle included an account of the three mean-states, but one can also see why he placed that account where he did, just before his discussion (in IV.ix) of the phenomenon of shame (*aidōs*), which is explicitly stated by him not to be a proper virtue (ix.1, 1128b10-11).

13.2. Whereas in the *Nicomachean Ethics* the status of the three mean-states is, as I have argued, slightly ambiguous, in the *Eudemian Ethics* Aristotle explicitly states that they are not genuine moral virtues.

The relevant section is *EE* III.vii.1-12, 1233b16-1234a33. I shall not go into detail. The passage briefly describes a number of mean-states including the three in question and none (apart from these) that are in the *Nicomachean Ethics* stated to be (full) virtues. They are said to be mean-states 'in passions' (*pathētikai*, vii.1, 1233b18), and the point of this is expatiated on in vii.10-12: they belong in the division of passions and only 'contribute to' a certain type of virtue, viz. the one which is called natural virtue.

What is important at present is the way in which Aristotle introduces, in vii.10, his general remarks about the mean-states he has been discussing. They are mean-states and

praiseworthy, but they are not virtues, nor are the opposite
states vices; 'for they are without *prohairesis*' (1234a25). If
we compare this with what Aristotle says, in *EN* III.viii.
10-12, of one of the states of mind that are similar to, but
not identical with, courage, viz. 'spirit' or 'temper' (*thymos*),
it becomes more than likely that what he means in the
Eudemian Ethics is that the mean-states in question are not
virtues for the reason that they lack a concern for the noble.
Thus compare how he contrasts those people who act from
'spirit' with truly courageous people. (*i*) The latter act
because of the noble, and their *thymos* only aids them;
animals on the other hand (who act from *thymos*) act because
of (physical) pain (viii.11, 1116b30-32). (*ii*) Similarly the
state that issues in acts because of *thymos* seems 'only
natural' (this is the sense of *physikōtatē* in viii.12, 1117a4);
what it needs in order to be (real) courage is *prohairesis*
and the *hou heneka* (end, 1117a4-5). (*iii*) Beings (i.e. animals
and even humans) who fight because of pleasure and pain are
not courageous; 'for they do not fight because of the noble
or as reason states, but because of passion' (1117a8-9).

What is lacking, then, in the mean-states is not just an end
(*hou heneka*), but consideration for the proper end, viz. the
noble, and it is this lack that accounts for Aristotle's explicit
claim (in the *Eudemian Ethics*) that the mean-states are
not virtues.[12]

14. My aim in this chapter has been to defend, by con-
fronting it with Aristotle's discussion of the individual
virtues, the account of acting nobly that I developed in
chapter 2. I believe that there are no real difficulties for that
account in what Aristotle says of courage, temperance,
generosity, and munificence. They can all be seen to be
concerned with natural goods and (with some modification
in the case of temperance) with a sharing out of such goods

[12] There is an interesting discussion of many of the problems raised by the mean-
states in W. W. Fortenbaugh, 'Aristotle and the Questionable Mean-Dispositions',
TAPA 99 (1968), 203-31. In the latter part of the paper Fortenbaugh argues that
it is wrong for Aristotle to treat the mean-states as full virtues, as he does in the
Nicomachean Ethics (but not in the *Eudemian* one). I believe that my account of
the three mean-states shows that even in the *Nicomachean Ethics* Aristotle in
fact does not do so.

that pays no special attention to the agent's own interest in the goods. High-mindedness and ambition are, I suggested, second-order virtues, and will not, therefore, present any difficulties for my account of the noble either. Good temper did present difficulties, but I suggested a way in which they may be handled. Finally, the three mean-states seem fairly easily accounted for. It seems likely that in the *Nicomachean Ethics* too they are not considered genuine virtues, and the reason seems precisely to be that they lack the reference to the noble in the sense that I have ascribed to that notion.

15. Suppose then, that the sense of the reference to the noble is the one I developed in chapter 2. In that case we may conclude that the good man will not only perform *praxeis* (in the sense of that concept that I developed in chapter 1), but will also be able to *justify* his acts, viz. by reference to the noble. Indeed, it is because he performs his *praxeis* under the description 'doing what is noble' (with all that this implies) that he is a truly good man. For the truly good man is the noble-and-good man.

But then the question arises whether this is the only type of justification that the good man may give. What about Aristotle's notorious suggestion that the goodness of moral virtue lies in the fact that it promotes the only truly worthwhile activity, viz. the one of *theōria* or non-practical intellectual activity? In the next chapter I shall discuss how we may combine Aristotle's seemingly inconsistent remarks in various places about what type, or types, of activity go into true human happiness.

4

HUMAN GOOD

1. The question to be answered in the present chapter is the one of the roles played by moral behaviour and by non-practical intellectual activity (*theōria*) in Aristotle's account of the type of life that truly qualifies for the predicate 'human happiness'.

There are several problems that belong under this general heading.

(1) First, there is the general question whether, according to Aristotle, the truly satisfactory life consists of *theōria* alone, or whether it is a function of what he calls 'the whole of virtue', and hence includes, as an independent part, moral behaviour. In some passages he seems to be saying one thing, in others another. The question is, of course, an old one. It is of interest since the basic question that it raises is whether in his account of happiness Aristotle wanted to make room for what may be called the autonomy or intrinsic value of moral behaviour or not. I shall argue that he did, and that Aristotle everywhere considers man's happiness to be a function of the whole of virtue: in the *Eudemian Ethics* and in *EN* VI, but also in *EN* I and X.[1]

(2) But in that case a connected question arises. How, if man's happiness consists of moral behaviour as well as *theōria*, should one share one's time between the two?

---

[1] The view, now fairly generally accepted, that according to the *Eudemian Ethics*, *eudaimonia* is a function of the whole of virtue, including moral virtue, has been strongly emphasized by J. D. Monan in his *Moral Knowledge and its Methodology in Aristotle*, Oxford, 1968, pp. 126–33. I disagree, however, with crucial elements in his argument, e.g. that noble-and-goodness (in *EE* VIII.iii. 1–10) as perfect virtue includes the intellectual virtue whose exercise is the *theōria* mentioned in VIII.iii.12 ff. (ibid., pp. 128, 132). Cf. nn. 5 and 6 below. — There is a useful survey of views on how to reconcile *EN* X and I with what comes in between in J. M. Cooper, *Reason and Human Good in Aristotle*, Cambridge, Mass., 1975, pp. 149–54.

What is the 'recipe' for the good life? I shall argue that the recipe Aristotle seems to envisage runs: 'act morally well and for the rest engage in *theōria*.'

I shall try to clarify and argue for the two theses I have just formulated in the second part of this chapter (sections 6 ff.). The basic material will be certain well-known passages from *EN* I and X.

(3) But there is a further question, which though closely connected with the first one is in fact different: what is the value of moral behaviour? Aristotle seems to suggest that moral behaviour has an intrinsic value, but also that it is valuable owing to the fact that it helps to promote or make possible the (intrinsically valuable) activity of *theōria*. What is the relation between these suggestions? Does Aristotle want to maintain both, or just one of them? And are they at all compatible?

The difference between this third question and the first one is clear. Evidently, if the answer to the first question is that human happiness consists in *theōria* alone, the answer to the third one will be settled in advance: moral behaviour will not be intrinsically valuable, but valuable as a means only to furthering the activity of *theōria*. Similarly, if the answer to the first question is that human happiness consists in moral behaviour as well as *theōria*, the answer to the third question cannot be that moral behaviour has value as a means only. But in the second case some questions remain, viz. whether moral behaviour should be said to be valuable both in itself and as a means, and whether saying so is in fact possible; or, if it should be considered valuable only in itself, how the passages should be understood in which Aristotle does seem to suggest that moral behaviour is valuable as a means to the furtherance of *theōria*. It will turn out that the answer to the third question will have an important bearing on how to answer the second question above concerning the recipe for the good life.

The third question I have identified is, I believe, the really difficult one, and it is the one that raises in its sharpest form the basic question that interests me in this chapter, viz. exactly how Aristotle managed, when his other views are what they are, to maintain the genuine autonomy of moral behaviour. To this question I shall turn first (sections 2.1-5).

2.1. Let us assume, as I shall argue in the latter part of this
chapter, that Aristotle nowhere says or implies that human
happiness consists in *theōria* alone. How, then, should we
conceive of the value of moral behaviour?

One passage that throws light on this question is *EN*
VI.xii-xiii. The two chapters discuss certain problems in
connection with the two states of mind that Aristotle has
been mainly concerned with in the body of *EN* VI, viz. moral
insight (*phronēsis*) and theoretical wisdom (*sophia*). Till now
I have had little to say directly about these concepts. For
what follows I must insert the premisses that *sophia* is the
state of mind of which *theōria* is the exercise, and that
phronēsis is the cognitive counterpart of moral virtue considered as an emotive state.

The two chapters seem carefully conceived on Aristotle's
part; but he has not always taken the necessary pains to
point out exactly how the various things he says fit together.
Careful reading is required. The structure of the chapters is
this. Aristotle starts from two dilemmas (*aporiai*). The first
one concerns the utility of *phronēsis* and *sophia* respectively:
what is their use (xii.1, 1143b18), what purpose do they
serve (b21)? In xii.1-2, 1143b19-33 he develops the dilemma.
(1) '*Sophia* will not consider anything from which a man
will become *eudaimōn*, since it is not directed towards
coming into being of any kind' (b19-20). (2) *Phronēsis*, on
the other hand, does consider things from which a man will
become *eudaimōn* and *is* directed towards coming into
being of some kind (b20-21) — but then there are further
problems. (*a*) If a man is already morally good, one may
wonder how he will become better able to act by acquiring
phronēsis. For the latter is a state of knowing 'about things
just and noble and good for man' (b22-23), and the good
man (*anēr agathos*) already performs such things. The problem is here to understand how *phronēsis* may do what we *a
priori* want it to do, viz. serve a purpose in connection with
the man who is already morally good (b21-28). (*b*) If, then,
phronēsis serves no such purpose, perhaps it will be of help
to *make* a man morally good? This suggestion is problematic

too. For, first, the consequence will be that *phronēsis* is not, after all, of any use to a man who is already morally good. And secondly, just as one need not be a doctor in order to become healthy, it seems likely that one need not either be *phronimos* in order to become morally good (b28-33).

In xii.3, 1143b33-35 Aristotle then formulates the second dilemma, which is concerned with the mutual relationship of *phronēsis* and *sophia*. It would be odd, he says, if *phronēsis* 'being inferior to *sophia* is nevertheless in authority over it', but it seems that it must be so; 'for in any area an art that produces something rules over and issues commands to that thing.'

In xii.3, 1143b35 Aristotle starts (b35-36) his discussion of the two dilemmas. The first problem he attempts to solve in xii.4-xiii.7 (1144a1-1145a6). He first provides three arguments (xii.4, 5, and 6, 1144a6-9), that I shall come back to in a moment, adds a note (xii.6, 1144a9-11) relevant to these arguments, and then embarks (in xii.7) on a major attempt to show how *phronēsis* will serve a purpose even in connection with the man who already is morally good. This passage, which takes up the problem that was raised in xii.1, 1143b21-28, goes as far as xiii.6, 1144b32, or, including the note-like lines that follow, xiii.6, 1145a2. I shall discuss it in detail later (chapter 8, sections 2.1-3). In xiii.7 (1145a2-6) Aristotle recapitulates two of the small arguments he gave earlier, viz. those of xii.4 and 6, but only in so far as they are concerned with the utility of *phronēsis* (not, that is, with that of *sophia*).

Finally, in xiii.8 (1145a6-11), he turns to solve the second problem of the mutual relationship of *phronēsis* and *sophia*.

2.2. I now want to discuss the two arguments of xii.4-5 to the effect that *phronēsis* and *sophia* are useful. I shall try to show that Aristotle provides his answer to his question by working on the very notion of use or utility. And I shall try to bring out what follows from his answer for our underlying question about the value of moral behaviour.

Aristotle's first point (xii.4) is that even if *phronēsis* and *sophia* do not produce (*poiein*) anything, they will be choice-worthy in themselves since they are the virtues of their

respective parts of soul. It is not initially clear that this is a
very good point to make. For why are they the virtues of
their respective parts of soul? What is important, however,
is that this first argument reveals that at the start of the
chapter Aristotle construed the problem of the utility of
phronēsis and *sophia* as the question of their utility in terms
of producing something that is worth having, and moreover
producing it in what I shall call the 'poietic' sense of the
term. And if we go back to his original formulation of the
problem, in xii.1, 1143b18-21, it does look as if the utility
of *phronēsis* and *sophia* that he is looking for is utility of
a 'poietic' type: *sophia* ought to consider things from which
a man will 'become' (*estai*) *eudaimōn*, but unfortunately it
is not concerned with 'coming into being' (*genesis*) of any
kind; *phronēsis*, on the other hand, does both things — but
then there are additional difficulties. In the first argument,
then, Aristotle is correcting this way of understanding the
problem: *phronēsis* and *sophia* may be 'useful' even though
they do not actually produce anything.

2.3. This development of the initial formulation of the
problem is continued in the second argument (xii.5). Here
Aristotle takes up the term 'produce' (*poiein*) and suggests
that in addition to the strict 'poietic' sense that he was
operating with both in his original formulation of the problem
and in his first attempt at a solution, there may be a different
sense of 'producing', in terms of which one may, after all,
speak of a 'productive' utility of *phronēsis* and *sophia*. The
argument makes clear what that sense is and at the same time
provides an answer to the question of the value of moral
behaviour.

The argument runs (1144a3-6):

Furthermore, they [sc. *phronēsis* and *sophia*] in fact (*kai*) do produce
something, not (however) as the art of medicine (produces) health, but
as health does — in that way *sophia* (produces) *eudaimonia*; for being
part of the whole of virtue it [sc. *sophia*] makes (produces, *poiei*) (a
man) *eudaimōn* by being possessed or rather (*kai*) by being exercised.

Important as this argument is, it is extremely condensed
and has accordingly been extensively commented on. I
believe, however, that what I shall extract from it cannot be

seriously questioned, and I shall therefore refrain from detailed textual exegesis.[2]

It seems certain that Aristotle is introducing in this argument a sense of 'producing' that is to be contrasted with the 'poietic' one. Moreover, the new sense is the one that is involved when the statement *'sophia* produces *eudaimonia'* is taken to mean that *sophia* (or rather, as Aristotle says, its exercise) is one thing that *eudaimonia consists in* — and this, apparently, is the sense Aristotle intends to bring out, and to contrast with the 'poietic' one, when he states that *sophia* produces something, viz. as it turns out *eudaimonia*, not as the art of medicine produces health (the 'poietic' sense), but as health does, i.e. as health *produces health.*[3] In view of the specific way in which Aristotle here relates the new sense of 'producing' to the concept of *eudaimonia*, we may call that sense its 'practical' sense; and we may conclude that he is explicitly contrasting that 'practical' sense with the 'poietic' one.

But it also seems certain that Aristotle wants to contrast the 'productive' utility of *phronēsis* and *sophia* as follows. Whereas *sophia* is useful in being productive of *eudaimonia* in the 'practical' sense only, *phronēsis* is useful on two counts.

---

[2] A. J. P. Kenny, for one, obtains the same information from the passage in his book on *The Aristotelian Ethics*, Oxford, 1978, pp. 209-10.

[3] This is the traditional way (in modern times) of supplementing the sentence (Ramsauer: *hygieian*, Stewart: *to hygiainein*, Burnet, Dirlmeier). It does not matter whether one supplements *hygieian* or *to hygiainein*. In both cases the idea will be that the 'principle of health' produces, as formal cause, a healthy state (Stewart). We start from the notion of a healthy state, i.e. the state of which 'health' is predicated and which will manifest itself in healthy activity. We then say that *sophia* produces *eudaimonia* in the way in which health, the formal principle of a healthy state, produces that state: health is what makes the healthy state what it is, and in the same way *sophia* is what makes the 'eudaimonic' state what it is. Recently a different interpretation has been gaining ground. Ross translated 'but as health produces health', but added a note: 'i.e. as health, as an inner state, produces the activities which we know as constituting health.' This is reflected by H. G. Apostle, who translates 'but as health (as a habit produces a healthy activity)'. And A. J. P. Kenny, who cites Ross with approval, takes the idea to be that health produces, causally (as he says), the activities of a healthy body (*The Aristotelian Ethics*, p. 210). However, there is a clear difference between saying that health produces the healthy state and saying that it produces, even causally, the activities that spring from such a state. And I believe that the traditional interpretation is supported by my account of Aristotle's use of the notion of *eudaimonia* and by the smoothness of everything he says in the chapter, right from the start, if he is taken to be working with only two senses of 'produce'.

Like *sophia* it produces *eudaimonia* in the 'practical' sense; it it an independent part of the whole of virtue (a function of which is *eudaimonia*) and consequently, like *sophia*, makes a man *eudaimōn* by being exercised. But unlike *sophia* it is also useful by being productive of *eudaimonia* in the 'poietic' sense. I take it, then, that the passage implies that there are two answers to the question of the value of *phronēsis* and consequently of moral behaviour.

But the second answer is unclear. For on my interpretation of Aristotle's use of the concept of *eudaimonia* it simply does not make sense to say that *phronēsis* produces *eudaimonia* in the 'poietic' sense of the term. If *phronēsis* is to be productive in that sense, it must be productive of some other thing, which may then in its turn be claimed to be productive of *eudaimonia* in the 'practical' sense, i.e. to be one thing that *eudaimonia* consists in.

Now one might suggest that what *phronēsis* produces in the 'poietic' sense is moral behaviour; and the third argument (xii.6, 1144a6-9) might be used in support. But this suggestion will not catch the strong 'poietic' sense of 'producing' that we are working with. And in fact there is a strong argument to show that what Aristotle has in mind is the idea that *phronēsis* produces *eudaimonia* (in the 'poietic' sense) by producing, not moral behaviour, but *sophia*, which in its turn is one thing that *eudaimonia* consists in. For on this interpretation one can see why Aristotle should formulate as his second dilemma in the chapters we are discussing precisely a problem that turns on the premiss that *phronēsis* produces *sophia*: *phronēsis* is less valuable than *sophia*, but produces it — but then will it not be in authority over it and consequently more valuable than *sophia*? And one can see the point of Aristotle's resolution of this dilemma in xiii.8: what produces something is not necessarily in authority over it, as the relationship of medicine to health shows; the former does not use the latter but 'sees to it' that it comes into being; similarly *phronēsis* issues orders for the sake of *sophia*, not to it. There can be no doubt, then, that Aristotle does wish to say in the two chapters that *phronēsis* produces *sophia* in the 'poietic' sense of the term, i.e. as medicine produces health.

I shall come back later to the question of what is meant by saying that *phronēsis* produces *sophia* in the 'poetic' sense. The conclusion, for the moment, is that according to *EN* VI.xii–xiii *phronēsis* and moral behaviour have value in two ways. They have value of a 'practical' type, since the exercise of *phronēsis*, which is identical with moral behaviour, is one thing that *eudaimonia* consists in. And they have value of a 'poietic' type, since they produce *sophia*.

3. But I believe that initially this dual account of the value of *phronēsis* and moral behaviour should be found problematic. In the end, as I shall argue, it is not, but some reformulation will be required.

According to the passage we have considered *phronēsis* and moral behaviour have value of the 'practical' type and also of the 'poietic' type. And in fact, though the concepts of *praxis* and *poiēsis*, as I have defined them, are mutually exclusive, one and the same act may clearly, when viewed from different viewpoints, be considered a case of *praxis* and also one of *poiēsis*. In the case of moral acts, however, considered as the exercise of *phronēsis*, there is the difficulty that these acts (so considered) are *defined* as *praxeis*, as is clear from Aristotle's definition of *phronēsis* (in *EN* VI.v.1–6). It follows that these acts cannot, under that description, be said to have a 'poietic' value, either in general or in the specific sense that they help to produce *sophia*. Correspondingly, *phronēsis* cannot strictly be said to have a 'poietic' value at all. But we have just seen that in *EN* VI.xii–xiii Aristotle more or less explicitly says that it has just such a value.

So the dual account in VI.xii–xiii of the value of *phronēsis* and moral behaviour raises a problem when confronted with Aristotle's claim that *phronēsis* is essentially 'practical' in the strict sense. And the difficulty is an important one. For if it is genuine, the very fact of its existence shows that in the concept of *praxis* Aristotle had the conceptual means to maintain the intrinsic, autonomous value of moral behaviour, and that he wanted to use the concept to that effect. On the other hand, there is no trace in *EN* VI.xii–xiii that Aristotle is at all aware of the difficulty.

I shall now consider the final chapter of the *Eudemian*

Ethics and try to show that in this passage Aristotle confronts the difficulty directly and introduces the distinction that is required to resolve it. Following that I shall return briefly to *EN* VI.xii–xiii and explain the precise sense in which Aristotle after all may say that *phronēsis* has 'poietic' value.

4. The contrast that Aristotle draws in *EE* VIII.iii.1–10 between the man who is 'merely' good and the noble-and-good man is a contrast between a man who performs acts, which are in fact morally good, as *poiēseis*, viz. in order to obtain natural goods for himself, and a man who performs such acts as *praxeis*, viz. because they conform to the principle of nobility. Aristotle implies that one and the same type of act may often be seen as valuable on both counts, but he insists that what makes an act noble and hence a genuine case of moral behaviour is that it is performed as a *praxis*: 'the person who believes that one should possess the virtues for the sake of external goods acts nobly only incidentally (*kata symbebēkos*)' (iii.10, 1249a14–16).

Now in the rest of the chapter (iii.12–17) Aristotle asks, as is well known, for a standard for the value of a certain type of act, and finds it in 'contemplation of God' (*tou theou theōria*), which I take to be equivalent to *theōria* as non-practical intellectual activity in general.[4] But what type of act? Commentators have recently stressed that Aristotle describes the acts as, in effect, takings (*haireseis*) of natural goods (iii.12, 1249a24–25) and have concluded that he is not talking of the standard of moral acts at all.[5] But this must be false. For he goes immediately on (in iii.13) to contrast the present search for a standard with his

---

[4] For a suggestive discussion of the relationship of *theōria* as 'contemplation of God' and as 'exercise of theoretical knowledge in general' see J. Ritter, 'Die Lehre vom Ursprung und Sinn der Theorie bei Aristoteles', *Veröffentlichungen der Arbeitsgemeinschaft für Forschung des Landes Nordrhein-Westfalen, Geisteswissenschaften*, Heft 1, Köln and Opladen, 1953, 32–54. Also in Ritter, *Metaphysik und Politik, Studien zu Aristoteles und Hegel*, Frankfurt am Main, 1977.

[5] J. D. Monan, *Moral Knowledge and its Methodology in Aristotle*, pp. 129–32; W. J. Verdenius, 'Human Reason and God in the *Eudemian Ethics*', in *Untersuchungen zur Eudemischen Ethik*, edd. P. Moraux and D. Harlfinger, Peripatoi, vol. i, Berlin, 1971, 285–97, pp. 295–6; J. L. Ackrill, 'Aristotle on *Eudaimonia*', *PBA* 60 (1974), 339–59, pp. 355–6; J. M. Cooper, *Reason and Human Good in Aristotle*, pp. 137–41.

repeated earlier, vague remark that one should act 'as reason states'. The reference to earlier remarks can only be aimed at remarks made in the discussion of the individual moral virtues; hence the standard Aristotle is looking for will also be a standard for moral virtue.[6]

Why, then, should he first describe the acts as takings of natural goods and insist on that description when, at the end of the passage, he comes out with his standard (iii.16, 1249b16–21)? By now the answer should be clear. *Theōria* cannot be the standard of moral acts *considered as moral acts*, i.e. as they are considered by the noble-and-good man. For so considered they have no standard outside themselves, but are valuable in themselves, just because they conform to the principle of nobility. But just as the acts of the merely good man and those of the noble-and-good man were materially the same, so moral acts may also be viewed as takings of natural goods; and in that guise they do have a standard outside themselves, *theōria*. I have not spelt out what the sense of the latter claim may be. iii.17 contains a hint, according to which the idea would be that for a man to be able to engage unhindered in *theōria*, a certain amount of goods must be present to the non-rational part of his soul, which is the seat of his emotions and desires: certain needs must be fulfilled. Be that as it may, the important point is that in *EE* VIII.iii, as opposed to *EN* VI.xii–xiii, Aristotle quite clearly implies that the 'poietic' value of moral acts, i.e. the fact that they tend to promote *theōria*, does not belong to them as moral acts, but as takings of natural goods.

We may conclude, if we are to go by the account of *EE* VIII.iii, that the dual account of the value of moral behaviour that is contained in *EN* VI.xii–xiii does create a difficulty; and furthermore, that what lies behind that difficulty is Aristotle's insistence on the autonomy of moral behaviour.

[6] A. J. P. Kenny too, in *The Aristotelian Ethics*, stresses that Aristotle is in iii.12 ff. talking of the standard of moral acts. But his arguments (pp. 182–3) differ from mine. I particularly disagree with one of them, viz. the suggestion that Aristotle himself says, in iii.17, 1249b24, that he has just, i.e., as Kenny takes it, in iii.12–17, been giving the standard of noble-and-goodness. In iii.17, 1249b24–25, as I see it, Aristotle summarizes the whole of VIII.iii by saying that he has said what the definition (*horos*) of noble-and-goodness is, viz. *in iii.1–10*, and what the aim (*skopos*) of natural goods is, viz. *in iii.12–17*. To my mind Kenny's assumption vitiates his whole account of *EE* VIII.iii (pp. 181–3, 206–8).

5. Are we, then, allowed to transfer the difficulty as well as its resolution from the *Eudemian* to the *Nicomachean* passage? It is of course true that in the *Eudemian* passage Aristotle's clarity about the merely accidental connection between moral behaviour and *theōria* is due to the fact that he has just been engaged in defining the element of nobility in noble-and-goodness. In the *Nicomachean* passage, by contrast, and in *EN* VI as a whole, he does not work seriously with the concept of the noble. Still it seems clear that the *Eudemian* role of that concept, as maintaining the autonomy of moral behaviour, is being played, in *EN* VI, by the concept of *praxis*. And as I interpreted the two arguments of *EN* VI.xii.4 and 5, the latter concept, and its difference from that of *poiēsis*, is present in *EN* VI.xii–xiii itself. So it seems that we ought to detect a difficulty in the *Nicomachean* passage too.

And the *Eudemian* resolution of it will follow suit. When Aristotle implies that *phronēsis* has (also) value due to the fact that it produces *sophia*, he must be taken to mean that *from a different viewpoint from that of phronēsis itself, phronēsis* and its exercise may be said to be valuable as helping to produce *sophia*. This other viewpoint we may term an 'objective' one and contrast it with the 'subjective' one of *phronēsis* itself and of the man who is *phronimos* (in so far as he is just that). The idea will be that there is a viewpoint which provides a comprehensive account of the good for man that will mention all the valuable types of human activity and will consider the relationship between them. According to this viewpoint, which is in fact not much different from Aristotle's own viewpoint in writing the *Ethics* as a piece of *theoretical* inquiry, i.e. as philosophy, *phronēsis* and its exercise will have value both of a 'practical' type and of a 'poietic' type in relation to the exercise of *theōria*. But this viewpoint is to be contrasted with the more restricted one of *phronēsis* itself, which is the one that renders the acts enjoined by *phronēsis* genuine *praxeis*. And according to the latter viewpoint, moral acts have no 'poietic' value; they are considered valuable just because acting in that way is taken to be one thing that *eudaimonia* consists in.

6. I have taken pains over *EN* VI.xii–xiii in connection
with the question of the value of moral behaviour. It was
assumed that Aristotle nowhere states or implies that human
happiness consists in *theōria* alone; in *EN* VI.xii–xiii and *EE*
VIII.iii, at least, he clearly does not. In the latter part of this
chapter I shall try to show that he does not either in passages
in which he is normally taken to do so. And I shall try to
show how, if *phronēsis* and *sophia* are each independently
valuable, we should arbitrate between the claim of each part
of soul to the effect that we must act in accordance with
that part: what, in other words, is the recipe for the good
life? My discussion of the two issues will be based, in the
main, on *EN* X.vi–viii.

7.1. First, however, I mention a few passages from *EN* I.
In some of them Aristotle does seem to want to say that
sophia is the only thing that goes into *eudaimonia*. In others
he switches back and forth between that view and the rival
view that *eudaimonia* consists in the exercise of what in *EN*
VI.xii.5 was called the whole of virtue. If Aristotle is seriously
entertaining both views, the problem of reconciling them
becomes acute.

Aristotle concludes his *ergon*-argument of I.vii.9 ff. as
follows (vii.15, 1098a16–18): '. . . it follows that human
good is an activity of the soul in accordance with virtue,
but if the virtues are more than one, in accordance with
the best and most final (*kata tēn aristēn kai teleiotatēn*).'
The reference here to the best and most final virtue has
traditionally been taken as a reference to *sophia*. I believe
that this is correct. Recently, however, it has been argued
(by J. L. Ackrill) that what Aristotle has in mind is not
sophia, but full or total virtue as something that includes
all (relevant) virtues.[7] For (*i*) there is no warrant in the
preceding argument for restricting *eudaimonia* to being
the exercise of *sophia* alone; (*ii*) in the *Eudemian Ethics*
(II.i.9, 1219a38–39) Aristotle concludes in a more or less
similar way that *eudaimonia* is the activity of a complete
life in accordance with complete virtue (*kat' aretēn teleian*),

---

[7] J. L. Acrill, 'Aristotle on *Eudaimonia*', pp. 352-3.

and the context shows that by 'complete virtue' he means all relevant virtues; and (*iii*) the remark about the best and most final virtue points back to Aristotle's suggestion in *EN* I.vii.3, 1097a28-30 that if there is only one final end, the good that is sought will be that one, whereas if there are more than one, the *most* final of them will be the good that is sought — and then, as we know, Ackrill takes the most final end to be an inclusive end.

None of these arguments is, I believe, conclusive. The reference to vii.3 is of little help since in that passage, as I have tried to show, Aristotle's talk of the most final end is designed to introduce the concept of the totally indeterminate 'eudaimonic' state as against, in the later passage, the virtue or virtues whose exercise falls under that state. And while the points made in the two former arguments are no doubt correct, this does not, of course, prove that Aristotle is not thinking of *sophia* when he talks of the best and most final virtue.

Ackrill further refers to two passages in *EN* I (ix.10, 1100a4; xiii.1, 1102a6) where Aristotle is talking of complete virtue (*aretē teleia*) and is probably thinking of 'the whole of virtue'. But first, there is a clear difference between 'complete virtue' and 'the best and *most* final (or complete) virtue'; and secondly, there is a further relevant passage in *EN* I that seems to settle the question: viii.14, 1099a29-31. Here Aristotle has been showing (viii.10 ff.) that moral acts are pleasant, and he has added (viii.13) that they are also good and noble (the well-known triad). In viii.14, then, he summarizes his remarks by saying that *eudaimonia* is best, noblest, and most pleasant: the three predicates to together and together belong to the best activities. 'Such activities, *or the one of them which is best*, we claim to be *eudaimonia*' (1099a29-31). In view of what precedes Aristotle must be mainly thinking of moral acts as the 'activities . . . we claim to be *eudaimonia*'. But then he includes, and with absolutely no warrant in the preceding argument, a reference to a single, best type of activity, which can hardly be any other than the exercise of *sophia*. This seems incontrovertible evidence that Aristotle is in fact prepared to suggest, with no warrant in the preceding argument, that only one type of activity, the best one (viz. the exercise of *sophia*), is what constitutes *eudaimonia*.[8] Furthermore, the similarity between this passage and vii.15 is so close that we may take it that in vii.15 Aristotle is in fact hinting, as the traditional view has it, that human happiness consists in activity of the soul in accordance with the virtue of non-practical reason, and in such activity alone.[9]

7.2. On the other hand, it is equally clear that throughout much of *EN* I Aristotle is talking as if the exercise of moral virtue will be an independent part of *eudaimonia*, as he does, for example, in the passage that leads up to the lines I have just been discussing. And in general, while in the chapters that follow his definition of *eudaimonia* as given in vii.15 some of the things he says may fit equally well a conception of *eudaimonia* as exercise of *sophia* alone and a conception of it as including the exercise of moral virtue, other things are definitely tailored to a conception of the latter sort — as when, in ix.9, he remarks that there is a good reason why human beings alone may be said to be *eudaimones* since they alone may be good and capable of moral behaviour. Similarly when in *EN* I.xiii he introduces the subsequent books of the work with the remark that 'since *eudaimonia* is some sort of psychic activity in accordance with complete virtue (*kat' aretēn teleian*), one must discuss virtue, for by doing so one will perhaps get a better view of *eudaimonia* too' (1102a5-7), the 'virtue' whose discussion he is announcing is not *sophia* alone, as the rest of the work proves.

7.3. So *EN* I unmistakably hints at two opposed views of what *eudaimonia* consists in. In some passages Aristotle clearly implies that just one thing, the exercise of *sophia*, goes into human *eudaimonia*. In others he seems prepared to accept the view that *eudaimonia* is a function of the whole of virtue, including moral virtue. The two views are inconsistent.

---

[8] Cf., for a similar move, *EN* VII.xiii.2, 1153b10-11.

[9] The same criticism of Ackrill has been advanced by A. J. P. Kenny (*The Aristotelian Ethics*, pp. 204-5), but on different grounds. And cf. J. M. Cooper's arguments (*Reason and Human Good in Aristotle*, p. 100 n. 1) against a view similar to Ackrill's.

How could Aristotle subscribe to both?

For an answer to this question, as well as the question of the recipe for the good life, we should turn to *EN* X.vi–viii.

8.1. In *EN* X.vi–viii Aristotle at last reaches the stage where he is prepared to state what, according to him, *eudaimonia* consists in. He shows by a couple of references (vi.1, 1176a32–33; vii.2, 1177a19) that he is aware of taking up the inquiry from the stage it had reached at the end of *EN* I, and first reintroduces, from I.vii, two points about *eudaimonia*, viz. that it is not a *hexis* but an *energeia*, and that it is something chosen for its own sake (X.vi.2, 1176a33–b6). His aim is to reject the suggestion that since 'amusements' are activities and are chosen for their own sake it is they that should be taken to be what *eudaimonia* consists in (vi.3–7).

Next, in vii–viii, he distinguishes between two sorts of activity that may make up *eudaimonia* and two sorts of human life that may be taken to be the *eudaimōn* one. On the one hand there is the activity of the highest human faculty, reason or *nous*, which when engaged in during a complete life is perfect *eudaimonia* (*teleia eudaimonia*, vii.1, 1177a12–18; vii.7, b24–26), and the life that consists in this sort of activity (*ho kata ton noun bios*, vii.9, 1178a6–7) is the most *eudaimōn* one (*eudaimonestatos*, ibid.). On the other hand there are the activity and the life in accordance with the rest of virtue (*ho kata tēn allēn aretēn*, sc. *bios*, viii.1, 1178a9), i.e. *phronēsis* and moral virtue, which is *eudaimōn* in a secondary way only (*deuterōs*, sc. *eudaimōn*, ibid.).

8.2. It is important to see exactly what Aristotle is doing here. He is contrasting two types of life and, correspondingly, two types of people, viz. the people who live the two types of life. But he is, I believe, doing so in the abstract.[10] He is no doubt talking of two types of human being. Thus several times (e.g. vii.4, 1177a28–29; viii.4, 1178a25–27) he mentions the fact that both the person who lives a life of perfect

---

[10] In pursuing the question about what types of people Aristotle is contrasting I have been influenced by J. M. Cooper's discussion, *Reason and Human Good in Aristotle*, pp. 160–7. Our answers differ, however.

eudaimonia, i.e. the wise man (*sophos*), and the person who lives the life which is only secondarily *eudaimōn*, the morally good man (*spoudaios*), will require some of the bare necessities of life (a healthy body, food, etc., viii.9, 1178b33–35) in order to engage in their specific activities. But when these basic human demands have been fulfilled, the two types of people are sharply contrasted as being engaged in different activities and in those activities alone. The wise man is a human being and consequently has a need for the necessities of life, but otherwise he is identified as a man who engages in nothing but *theōria*. And the morally good man, while also in need of certain basic goods, is different from the wise man in being identified as a man who does nothing but act morally well.

But of course such people are fictions. No human being will be able to engage in *theōria* alone — as Aristotle himself points out in a passage to which I shall return. And while it might be possible for somebody to do nothing but engage in the life of a politician, we shall see that it would hardly be possible for anyone to do nothing but act morally well — and it is this kind of life, which is a different thing from the life of a politician, that Aristotle describes as secondarily *eudaimōn*.

That Aristotle does in fact intend to contrast abstract types of people is clear from what he says of their respective identities as human beings. Thus the wise man will be living a life that is 'too high for man; for it is not in so far as he is a man that he will live so, but in so far as something divine is present in him' (vii.8, 1177b26–28). And this divine something is different from the compound (*syntheton*) that is man (b28–29), i.e. from man as mind and body, and its activity is 'separate' from the activity of that compound (viii.3, 1178a22). The important point here is Aristotle's employment of the terminology of 'in so far as' (*hēi*). This shows that when he talks of the wise man, he is talking, it is true, of some man, but viewed only from the perspective of a conception of man as possessing something divine in him and to the exclusion of all other perspectives, apart from the one according to which man, any kind of man, has a need for certain basic necessities of life.

Similarly, I believe, when he talks of the morally good man, he is talking of some man, but viewed from the perspective of a conception of man as a compound, and once more to the exclusion of all other perspectives, apart from the one mentioned above. This seems indicated by his use of the word 'human' (*anthrōpikos*) of the activities and virtues that go into the life that is *eudaimōn* in a secondary way (viii.1, 1178a10, 14; viii.3, a21). The predicate *anthrōpikos* does not here just mean 'human' but 'only too human'; the term is used of behaviour which falls short of a certain ideal because it reflects how human beings in fact, regrettably, are. Thus Aristotle is contruing the life in accordance with 'the rest of virtue' as a pointedly 'low' one. But since human beings are capable of non-practical thought in addition, it seems that he means to be talking only of the good life for a type of man who has not fully realized all man's potentialites or, to put it the other way round, for man as he really is, but only in so far as he is a compound and displays those all too human virtues that go precisely with the compound (viii.3, 1178a20-21).

This deserves to be emphasized. Aristotle is talking of two kinds of life and of two types of people, and he is making use of that philosophical tool of his which finds expression in the word *hēi* or 'in so far as' to ground his talk of the two kinds of life and people in two different conceptions of human identity. According to one conception man is *nous* (vii.9, 1178a2, 7). And it is in so far as this conception is operative that he will live the life in accordance with *nous* and will be the person who is called the wise man. Hence this person and this life are fictions that have been cut out, abstracted, from the concepts of real, full, human beings and the life they lead. According to another conception man is man (vii.8, 1177b27; viii.6, 1178b5), i.e. is a compound of such a kind that *nous* is 'above' him, is divine in comparison with him (*theion ho nous pros ton anthrōpon*, vii.8, 1177b30) or different from him (b28-29), and its activity is 'separate' from his (viii.3, 1178a22). And it is in so far as this conception of man is operative that he will live the life in accordance with 'the rest of virtue' and will be the person I called the morally good man. Hence this person too and this life are fictions that have been abstracted from the concepts of real, full, human beings and the life they lead.

This cannot be too strongly emphasized. For it means that Aristotle has said nothing till now that answers the question of what *eudaimonia* consists in for man *as he in fact is*, viz. a compound of body and mind who has *also* the capacity for non-practical thought. What Aristotle has been doing is to grade the two types of life he has been concerned with and the two types of activity that correspond, both of which will go into *eudaimonia* for man as he really is. And he has, most importantly as we shall see, based his grading on two different views of man's identity. But he has not yet said what the best life will be like for man as he is.

8.3. I shall now try to suggest an answer to this question. In so doing I shall bring out, as I have promised, what, according to Aristotle, the recipe for the good life will be. My discussion will remain based on the assumption that human happiness, according to Aristotle, is a function of the whole of virtue. I have not yet argued completely for that assumption, and I shall return later to the question of how Aristotle may hold that view, as implied, e.g., in *EN* VI.xii–xiii, and at the same time, as seemed indicated by certain passages in *EN* I, toy with the idea that *eudaimonia* consists in the exercise of *sophia* alone. For the moment, however, I will emphasize that my reading of *EN* X.vii–viii has shown that that passage is neutral with respect to that question, as it is with respect to the question of what the recipe will be like.

8.4. So first the question about the recipe for the good life.

I believe that Aristotle himself indicates, in a curiously offhand way, his awareness that this is a question that has not been answered by distinguishing and contrasting, as he does in *EN* X.vii–viii, two abstract types of person. Thus in viii.6 (1178b3–7) he concludes in the following way one of those remarks about the bodily needs of the wise and the morally good man that are so strangely scattered throughout the two chapters:

The wise man (*ho theōrōn*) has no need for any such things [viz. external goods] — with a view to his activity, that is; in fact, they are so to say hindrances — with a view to *theōria*, that is; but in so far as he is a man and lives together with others he chooses to act in accordance with (moral) virtue; hence he will need such things in order to live a human life.

Here Aristotle evidently shows himself aware that in addition to living 'in so far as something divine is present in him' the wise man will also live 'in so far as he is a man'; and it is his recognition of this obvious fact that creates the whole of the present problem, i.e. the problem of how *theōria* and moral behaviour should be *combined* in the best human life, the best life for man as he in fact is.

Aristotle himself says very little in answer to this question. This may seem strange, but it is a fact that goes well with a similar attitude of his in the *De Anima* and in the *Metaphysics*. There too he does not attempt in any sustained manner to relate reason as something which is separate from the body to the other mental faculties, which are forms of matter, nor to relate the highest substance (*ousia*), viz. God or pure act, to 'normal' substance, which is form in matter. Nevertheless, the question of how moral action and *theōria* are to be combined in the best human life seems so central to the whole of Aristotle's endeavour in ethics that we ought to be able to construct some kind of answer.

It should, however, be emphasized that when we engage in an attempt to obtain that answer, we go beyond what Aristotle is explicitly concerned with in X.vii-viii. His own intention is to *contrast* two abstract types of life and people and to bring out two different conceptions of human identity on which to ground the two abstract types. But what we want to see is how the various activities that are involved will *combine* in the best life for man as he in fact is, viz. a compound of mind and body with the capacity for non-practical thought. The reason why Aristotle himself does not go into this is not, I believe, that he could not give an answer: he may have been too rapt with the pleasure of bringing out as sharply as possible the ideal of a life totally filled with activity of that supreme part of man, *nous*; or he may have thought that the answer would be easy to give once he had brought out explicitly the difference in value between the activity of *theōria* and that of moral behaviour.

8.5. How, then, do *theōria* and moral action combine in the best life for man as he in fact is? Here I believe we shall be helped if, recalling that in *EN* VI.xii–xiii Aristotle was prepared to consider *phronēsis* valuable both in itself and as a means to the exercise of *sophia*, we for the moment think of the exercise of *phronēsis*, i.e. of moral acts, as valuable in the latter way and in that way only. This is not a view of the value of *phronēsis* and moral acts that is contained in VI.xii–xiii, and it is not a view that is consistent with taking the value of moral acts to be only incidentally their capacity to promote the exercise of *sophia*. But it is the view that Aristotle will have to adopt if he in fact takes seriously the suggestion that he seems to be hinting at in *EN* I, that the exercise of *sophia* is the only thing that goes into *eudaimonia*.

We have, then, a hypothetical view of the good for man according to which man's *eudaimonia as* a compound of body and mind which possesses the capacity for non-practical thought lies in the exercise of that capacity alone, whereas the virtues of the compound are valuable as means only. According to this view the role of moral behaviour will be exactly like the role of external goods in relation to the 'pure' wise man of *EN* X.vii–viii, who, since he was after all conceived of as a human being, was in need of certain necessities of life in order to be able to engage in his specific activity. Similarly, since we have now allowed him not just a body but the whole compound of body and mind, he will be in need, not only of the barest necessities of life, but also of acting morally well. Here we need not ask once more how moral behaviour may be thought to contribute to the exercise of *sophia*. The important point is just that on the hypothetical view it is thought to do so, indeed that it is considered a necessary condition for the successful exercise of *sophia*.

It follows from this that moral behaviour, in the role it has in the hypothetical view, and generally when it is considered valuable as a means to the exercise of *sophia*, must be *limited*, in the very mundane sense that a man cannot normally be expected to have to spend on it all the time that he has at his disposal. If moral behaviour is a necessary means and if the hypothetical view is a view of what human *eudaimonia* consists in, then it would seem perverse and distinctly un-Aristotelian to imply that the situation of humans is such that normally they will have no chance of reaching the goal to which the activity that they engage in is a means.

But if moral behaviour is limited in this way, then on the basis of Aristotle's implication that the exercise of *sophia* is the most worthwhile activity, a view that follows from his rating the abstract 'life of *theōria*' as perfectly and most *eudaimōn*, we may ascribe to him the view that the best life for man as he is is the life of a man who has the barest necessities of life, acts morally well, *and for the rest engages in theōria.*

The point I am trying to make is that there may be thought to be a difference between moral behaviour and *theōria* with respect to 'finitude'. *Theōria* is an activity that is unlimited in the sense that the more it is done the better. Not so, at least not necessarily so, with moral behaviour. It may be that moral behaviour is limited in such a way that, normally at least, when morals have had their due, there is room for activity of a different kind, e.g. amusing oneself (*EN* X.vi) — or engaging in *theōria*. If so, when Aristotle praises *theōria*, he is exhorting people to spend their 'surplus time' on that kind of activity rather than on any other, and he is bringing arguments to show that that kind of activity is in fact the best one that a human being may engage in.

If this interpretation is correct, the recipe for the good life that he is giving will not be 'maximize *theōria*, and for the rest act well',[11] but 'do what you can to maximize *theōria*, i.e. act well and for the rest engage in *theōria*.'

One may feel that there is a certain downgrading of *theōria* here. But this is not so. We took as our starting-point the view that the only genuinely valuable type of activity is that of *theōria* and that moral behaviour is valuable only as a means to that end. This is not changed by the fact that our recipe for life includes a command to act well. That this

---

[11] This is the formula discussed by J. L. Ackrill, 'Aristotle on *Eudaimonia*', pp. 357–8.

command has to be included is only due to something which, according to the view from which we started, is a regrettable fact, viz. that man is not reason alone, but also a compound of body and mind, which accordingly must have its due if a person is to be able to engage in the only valuable activity, the one of *theōria*. Such, then, is the recipe for the good life if one takes that life to consist in the exercise of *sophia* alone and takes moral acts to be valuable as means only.

8.6. Suppose, then, that we leave the hypothetical view and consider a view of the good life which incorporates the other account of the value of *phronēsis* and moral behaviour that was contained in *EN* VI.xii–xiii, viz. the account according to which *phronēsis* and moral behaviour are valuable as an independent part of *eudaimonia*. On the new view, then, the good life will consist in the exercise of *sophia* and the exercise of *phronēsis*, and both types of exercise will be independent parts of *eudaimonia*. What will the recipe for the good life look like in this case?

I believe there are two answers to this question. One answer will account for the normal cases, in which *phronēsis* and moral behaviour may at the same time, though, as I have argued, only incidentally, be said to have value both in themselves and because they are a means to the promotion of the exercise of *sophia*. As long as there is identity, though only coincidentally, of truly moral acts, which are independently valuable, and moral acts as means to the promotion of the exercise of *sophia*, the recipe I gave for the hypothetical view of the good life I discussed a moment ago will apply to the new view too. Thus even when moral behaviour is considered valuable in itself, the recipe will in some cases be 'act well and for the rest engage in *theōria*'.

8.7. But the crucial case is clearly the one in which the material coincidence of morally good acts and acts which as acquisitions of natural goods promote *theōria* is disrupted. In *EE* VIII.iii.1–10 Aristotle implied that acts that are genuinely morally good, i.e. noble, are normally materially identical with acts that bring natural goods to the agent — otherwise his conception of the 'merely good man' will not make sense.

Similarly he clearly implied, in the second half of the chapter, that there is often a relation of material identity between noble acts and acts which as takings of natural goods have *theōria* as their standard — otherwise his description, in iii.12, 13, and 16, of the type of act he is considering will not make sense either. But if the account I have given of nobility, an account that was partly based on *EE* VIII.iii.1-10 itself, is correct, then it is easy to see that noble acts and acts which as takings of natural goods have *theōria* as their standard may very well come into conflict with each other. For whereas the latter will only reflect the personal interests of the agent, the former will take into consideration the interests of all people involved, with the consequence that the agent will often choose acts that are not conducive to his personal exercise of *sophia*. It is easy to think of examples: for instance a person may find himself in a situation in which courage requires him to remain at his post at the risk of losing his life. I believe, however, that Aristotle's injunction in this type of case will be the same as the one we have already encountered: 'act well and for the rest engage in *theōria*.'

Consider the passage X.viii.6 quoted earlier. Aristotle is arguing (from viii.4) that the wise man requires a smaller amount of external goods than the morally good man, and he concludes his discussion (in viii.6) by remarking that though the wise man has no need of external goods with a view to the exercise of his specific activity, *theōria*, he needs them with a view to living a human life (*pros to anthrōpeuesthai*); for 'in so far as he is a human being and lives with others, he chooses to act in accordance with virtue.' Now this fact, that the wise man is a man and lives with others, is most important. For if this is so, and if the wise man sees that it is so (and he must), then the insight of his reason that when there are natural goods to be shared he cannot justifiably act for his personal advantage, will be binding on him. If he sees himself as living with others, he cannot justifiably neglect the claim on his behaviour that is made by this fact — not even if the personal advantage that he may obtain by neglecting that claim is the one of engaging in that supremely valuable activity, *theōria*. It is true that it would be better for himself, considered as the only inhabitant of the world, to further his chances of engaging in *theōria*, since that type of activity is the truly satisfying one. But the point is precisely that no man *is* the only inhabitant of the world. It is part of his definition that he lives with others.

Here, then, Aristotle is once more basing a view of the good life for man on a certain view of his identity. Man does not 'live the life of an eremite' (*bion monōtēn zēn*, *EN* I.vii.6, 1097b9), as Aristotle points out in the middle of that crucial passage on *eudaimonia*, and hence the self-sufficient will not apply to 'himself alone . . . but also to his parents, his children, his wife, and generally to his friends and fellow citizens; for by nature man is a social being (*physei politikon ho anthrōpos*)' (1097b9-11). The importance of this cannot be overstated. When Aristotle comes to decide what the good life is for man as he is, the fact cannot be neglected that man is a social being. This fact lies at the base of the principle of nobility, according to which no matter what personal advantage in terms of the possession of natural goods one may get from going against the principle, the criterion to be applied for deciding what to do is the greatest good of the community as a whole of which one is a member. If that criterion is applied, the effect will in practice always be that one should forsake one's personal advantage. It follows that moral behaviour has a stronger claim on man than the demand that he should engage in *theōria*. And the basic reason lies in a fact about man's identity.

It is of course true that when Aristotle confronts directly the value of *theōria* with that of moral behaviour, the former type of activity comes out as the only one that is truly choice-worthy in itself (*EN* X.vii.1-5). Moral behaviour, says Aristotle (vii.6, 1177b12-15), is not self-contained (it is *ascholos*); it aims, of course, at being social activity for its own sake (i.e. at being truly moral activity: acting nobly), but in addition it also aims[12] at procuring power and honour or at least *eudaimonia* for the agent and his fellow citizens — and that is something different from the activity itself. This remark does not go against the point that noble behaviour is valuable in itself. When Aristotle claims that *theōria* alone is valuable in

---

[12] The preceding two lines constitute an attempt to capture the sense of παρ' αὐτὸ τὸ πολιτεύεσθαι περιποιουμένη . . .

itself, he is fixing on a special aspect of moral behaviour: in addition to being intrinsically valuable, i.e. to having the value that it has for the person who sees and subscribes to the principle of nobility, moral behaviour is valuable in extrinsic terms in that it brings natural goods; and it does the latter either in the way that it brings power or honour to the moral agent himself or that it brings about the best state (with respect to the possession of natural goods) of the community as a whole. Aristotle is entitled, therefore, to his claim concerning *theōria*. But still moral behaviour has a stronger claim on man just because he is the type of being that he is. There is no downgrading of the value of *theōria* here. It is the supreme activity, the only one that is really worth our aspirations. But since man is the kind of being that he is, it is a regrettable fact that other claims on him take precedence over the claim of his (non-practical) *nous*. Since he is a man and consequently lives with others, he will choose to act in accordance with (moral) virtue in preference to everything else.

8.8. But, it may be asked, if this is Aristotle's view what is the point of arguing, as he does in X.vii–viii, that *theōria* is the most worthwhile activity for human beings to engage in? The answer is easy to find. For the view that Aristotle is arguing for has direct practical consequences. The recipe we ended up with did after all recommend people to engage in *theōria*. And by arguing as he does in X.vii–viii Aristotle becomes able to make the point that though the life that follows his recipe is indeed the best life for human beings as they are, still it is only second-best compared to the type of life, consisting of pure *theōria*, that seems within reach of human beings — but in fact is not. In X.vii–viii Aristotle at last comes to grips with the question of what the being *is* whose happiness he is trying to define.

8.9. This leads to the second problem I wanted to discuss on the basis of *EN* X.vii–viii. Does Aristotle want to say both that human happiness consists in the exercise of *sophia* alone and that it consists in the exercise of *sophia* as well as the exercise of *phronēsis*, and if he does, how can he? Both views seemed hinted at or implied in different passages in *EN* I;

are they both Aristotle's considered views, and in that case how will he reconcile the apparent inconsistency between them?

My answer is simple: Aristotle unqualifiedly accepted only the second view, that human happiness consists in the exercise of *sophia* and *phronēsis* (plus the presence of a certain amount of natural goods).

I have already claimed that *EN* X.vii-viii does not go against this suggestion. There, as we saw, Aristotle is talking of two abstract types of life and two abstract types of person, but not of man as he is nor of the best life for man as he is. In that case when he states that perfect *eudaimonia* is a life in accordance with *nous*, he is not saying that the best life for humans as they are is a life of exercise of *sophia* alone.

But X.vii-viii may also teach us what Aristotle means when he hints, in *EN* I, that the best life for humans *as they are* does consist in the exercise of *sophia* alone. In *EN* I Aristotle is in fact talking of the best life for man as he is, i.e. as a being with the third type of identity I have introduced, a compound of body and mind with a capacity for non-practical thought. This is clear, e.g., from the way the *ergon* argument develops (I.vii.10-16) and from I.xiii as a whole. In X.vii-viii, by contrast, he is contrasting two views of man's identity which are only partial views of man. But then since one of these views identifies man with what is, according to Aristotle, highest in him, it is tempting for Aristotle, even in *EN* I, i.e. even where he is discussing the good life for man as he in fact is, to imply that that life will consist in the activity that expresses man's 'highest' identity or his nature, *if only* he were identical with what is in fact just the highest element in him.

We have seen that in *EN* X Aristotle operates with different views of man's identity while at the same time implying (at viii.6, 1178b3-7) that only one of them is the correct one. When in *EN* I he hints that human happiness consists in the exercise of *sophia* alone, he must be drawing on what is in fact one of the partial views. But if I am right in saying that he is talking in *EN* I of the good life for man as he in fact is and that in *EN* X he is aware of introducing what are only partial views of man's identity, then we should understand his hints in *EN* I that man's happiness consists in the exercise of *sophia* alone as a suggestion of what man's happiness would be like if only he were, as he is not, identical with his *nous*. This, then, is the qualification that Aristotle will want to add when he claims human happiness to consist in the exercise of *sophia* alone.

9. If this interpretation is correct, Aristotle nowhere unqualifiedly asserts, or hints, that human happiness consists in *theōria* alone. In *EE* VIII.iii and *EN* VI.xii–xiii he implies the opposite, in *EN* X.vi–viii he implies nothing in either direction, and his hints in *EN* I should be taken as carrying an important qualification with them.

The last suggestion is the most controversial one. But it is recommended, if by nothing else, by the existence of what seems a regular Aristotelian thought-pattern: whenever he finds himself with a group of things that play a certain role in a certain context, he has a tendency to concentrate on the most distinguished member of the group.

Compare the line of thought in *EN* IV.iii.9–10, the chapter on high-mindedness. Aristotle is concerned to define the area of that virtue. He starts as follows: 'If, then, the high-minded man considers himself worthy of great things . . . and above all (*kai malista*) of the greatest things, he will above all (*malista*) be concerned with a *single* thing' (iii.9, 1123b15–17). Why, among things that are great, will the high-minded man be 'above all' concerned with the greatest things, and why will he even be 'above all' concerned with a *single* thing? Aristotle provides no answer. He just continues as follows. The relevant type of thing is external goods, and the greatest such good is honour; so the high-minded man is concerned with honours and dishonours (iii.10, b17–22). Now it soon becomes clear (in iii.17–18, 1124a4–20) that the high-minded man is in fact also concerned with goods other than honour. Apparently, however, Aristotle wants to concentrate on the most distinguished type of external good: that, I believe, is the only way to make sense of the strange argument of iii.9 quoted above.

In a similar way, I believe, when in *EN* I he from time to time hints at the single component view of human happiness,

Aristotle is giving in to a tendency on his part to concentrate on the most distinguished member of a given group. At the same time he is also pointing forward, as it is normally taken, to the claim in *EN* X that a life in accordance with (non-practical) *nous* is perfect *eudaimonia*, but since the latter claim should be understood in the way I have suggested, in pointing forward to *EN* X he is precisely not implying that *eudaimonia* for man as he in fact is will consist in *theōria* alone.

10. Let me summarize.

I have attempted to show that Aristotle's view of the value of natural goods, moral behaviour, and *theōria* in relation to *eudaimonia* is as follows. Moral behaviour is valuable in itself as an independent part of *eudaimonia*, but it may also be considered valuable, though only coincidentally, as a means to *theōria*, due to the fact that moral behaviour will often coincide materially with acts that bring a certain amount of natural goods to the agent, the result being the promotion of *theōria*. Furthermore, when it comes to weighing the claims of moral behaviour and those of *theōria* against each other, the former take precedence over the latter owing to certain facts about the type of being that man is. And finally, though Aristotle clearly considers *theōria* the most worthwhile type of activity that a human being may engage in, he nowhere unqualifiedly implies that man's happiness consists in that type of activity alone.

PART II

INTRODUCTION

I have discussed Aristotle's views on the good for man (chapters 1 and 4). The basic texts were, significantly, passages at the start and end of the two ethical treatises or at important transitional points within them: *EN* I, *EE* VIII.iii.12 ff., *EN* VI.xii-xiii (end of the discussion of the virtues of desire and thought), *EN* X.vi-viii. I have argued that Aristotle nowhere neglects the value of moral behaviour as an independent part of the good for man, either when he relates it to the concept of *eudaimonia* or in his answer to the question of what human happiness in fact consists in. In chapters 2 and 3, I attempted to bring out the specifically moral element in moral behaviour. Here the basic texts were a chapter in the treatise on friendship (*EN* IX.viii), Aristotle's account of noble-and-goodness (*EE* VIII.iii.1-10), and his discussion of the individual virtues in *EN* III.v-V.

I now want to concentrate on moral goodness as a state of mind, i.e. on moral virtue. In part I of this book I have already been much concerned with the question of how the morally good man *sees* things, in connection with the notions of *eudaimonia* and *praxis* and with that of the noble. In the present part I shall take this concern about the state of mind of the virtuous man further by introducing the other basic element in moral virtue, viz. that of *wanting*. The main question I shall be concerned with is the one of the roles played in the different types of moral virtue that Aristotle is working with in *EN* II and VI by the faculties of the human psyche that are relevant to moral virtue.

In taking that question as basic I am following Aristotle's own lead. For in *EN* I.xiii he introduces the general topic of books II-VI, which is that of the human virtues, the exercise of which may be thought to constitute *eudaimonia* (cf. I.xiii.1), in terms of a theory of the psychic faculties of man and spends much time on defining the relationship between the two relevant faculties, viz. those of 'the desiderative part' (*to epithymētikon kai holōs orektikon*, xiii.18, 1102b30) and reason.

However, I do not intend to discuss for its own sake the question of how the various psychic faculties interact in moral virtue. Rather, my aim is to bring out the point of Aristotle's complex view of the psychic components of full moral virtue. Full moral virtue, i.e. the state of mind that is at the end of *EN* VI called 'genuine virtue' (*kyria aretē*), contains both a rational cognitive element, viz. *phronēsis*, and a desiderative element, which is 'virtue of character' (*ēthikē aretē*). I first want to show that in two respects the desiderative state is the more important. It provides the element of desire which secures that the person will perform those acts which he believes should be done (no matter how he has arrived at that belief) *as praxeis*, i.e. just because they are the acts they are and with no view to the goodness of any 'extrinsic' results they may be taken to bring. And it also provides the detailed knowledge of what, in the actual situations, a person should do. In so doing it makes *phronēsis*, which is itself knowledge of what to do, or at least a rational state that enables a man to *discover* what to do, a conceptualization of knowledge which is already there.

However, though I conclude that the desiderative element is in these ways the more important component of *kyria aretē*, my whole aim in discussing these matters is to answer the question 'What, then, is brought into play by its other component, *phronēsis*?' What is the element that *phronēsis adds* to (non-rational) moral virtue, thereby helping to make up 'genuine virtue'? My answer will be that *phronēsis* provides the element that I take to constitute the second main point of Aristotle's ethical theory. The first main point is that moral acts are done for the sake of the noble in the sense of this phrase that I have argued for in chapters 2 and 3. The second main point is that for an act to be a moral act it must be a *praxis*, it must directly reflect the agent's view of what *eudaimonia* consists in. I have already stated, in chapter 4, that moral acts, as the exercise of *phronēsis*, are *praxeis*. But my aim in part II is to show that the very point of *phronēsis* lies precisely in the fact that it is the possession of *phronēsis* which makes a man perform acts, which by themselves will be the right ones, *as praxeis*. The two respects in which the desiderative state is the more important element in *kyria aretē* both point to this view of the basic moral insight that Aristotle tries to capture in his notion of *phronēsis*. Thus we shall see that *phronēsis* may, in a certain sense to be specified, be regarded as a conceptualization of the element of desire that is provided by virtue of character. And I have already suggested that *phronēsis* is a conceptualization of the knowledge of what to do which is also part of virtue of character. Thus the basic point of *phronēsis* should be taken to be that of *rationalizing* a non-rational emotive and cognitive state, of bringing a person's immediate responses to situations under the concept of *eudaimonia*. But then the possession of *phronēsis* will make a man perform his acts as *praxeis*, as I have explained the term. And if this is indeed the basic point of *phronēsis*, then we may conclude that it *is* a main doctrine in Aristotle's ethical theory that acts, to be moral, must be *praxeis*.

In the final chapter of this part of the book (chapter 9) I shall try to show that this view of the point of *phronēsis* connects closely with Aristotle's account of human responsibility.

THE PSYCHOLOGY:
PASSIONS AND REASON

1. In the first part of this chapter I intend to discuss two questions. In *EN* II.i Aristotle starts his discussion of moral virtue (*ēthikē aretē*) by making the point that it comes about as a result of habituation (*ethismos*). No moral virtue comes to be present in us by nature (*physei*, i.2, 1103a19), or against nature (*para physin*, i.3, a24): we are by nature 'such as to receive them', but are 'perfected' by habituation (a25-26). Acquiring moral virtues by habituation includes performing the very same acts which we shall perform when the virtues have been acquired. Therefore the acts that we perform before acquiring the virtues should be of a certain type, viz. good (i.4-8). Now the two questions I intend to discuss concern moral virtue, or generally a moral *hexis* (state of mind), as something that results from habituation. What psychic faculties are involved in habituation and consequently in the *hexis* that results from it? And what is the special property of a *hexis* which is *ēthikē* or a state of *character*?

In the second part of the chapter I shall try to specify the mark of rationality in Aristotle in order to deepen the account I shall give of the type of moral virtue that results from habituation (*ethistē ēthikē aretē*).

2. I recapitulate certain relevant elements of Aristotle's moral psychology.

A moral *hexis* is one of three things that may be mentioned to characterize a person's character (*ēthos*): states (*hexeis*), capacities (*dynameis*), passions (*pathē*) — thus *EE* II.ii. The same passage contains a definition of *ēthos* (II.ii.2, 1220b5-6). The text is damaged but the idea is clear. *Ēthos* is a 'quality' (*poiotēs*) of the part of soul which is non-rational but capable of following reason. It is clear what this part of soul is from Aristotle's division of the soul as given elsewhere, in *EN* I.xiii.9-19 and *EE* II.i.15-20. I shall present this division rapidly, relying mainly on the *Nicomachean Ethics*. The *Eudemian Ethics* is in substantial agreement, but less clear.

The rationale for the division is the extent to which any given part of soul involves reason. One part is totally non-rational (*alogon*), viz. the part which is termed the vegetative part (*to phytikon*, *EN* I.xiii.11, 1102a32-33 and xiii.18, b29) or the nutritive part (*to threptikon*, xiii.14, b11) and is stated to be responsible for the functions of nutrition, growth, etc. Another part, the appetitive and generally desiderative part (*to epithymētikon kai holōs orektikon*, xiii.18, b30), is described in two ways, either as non-rational but sharing somehow in reason (*metechein logou*) since it is capable of *obeying* reason (xiii.15, b13-14; xiii.17, b25-26; xiii.18, b28-31), or as rational (*logon echon*) but in a secondary way only, viz. as being capable of *listening* to reason (xiii.19, 1103a1-3). Thirdly, there is the part which is through and through rational, viz. in the primary sense and in itself (*kyriōs kai en hautōi*, ibid.).

There can be no doubt that it is an idle question whether one should say of the desiderative part that it belongs to the non-rational part of soul but with certain qualifications (this is the picture in *EN* I.xiii.9-18), or that it belongs to the rational part but with certain other qualifications (this is what happens in the first part of xiii.19). The former description is the official one, as *EN* I.xiii itself bears witness, and it is the one used in the definition of *ēthos* that I referred to. We may conclude, then, that *ēthos* is a 'quality' of the desiderative part.

But now two questions arise. If *ēthos* is just one 'quality' of the desiderative part, what is the special property of being 'ethical', of belonging to character, i.e. the property that differentiates that 'quality'? And what *is* the *orektikon* or the desiderative part of soul? I shall discuss the latter question first and come back to the former later (sections 4.1-4.2).

3.1. What is the *orektikon* and what is *orexis* (desire),

which is its exercise? The question is not silly. In *EN* I.xiii.
15-16 Aristotle most carefully argues for introducing this part
of soul, and in modern philosophy of action the definition of
desire and the question of its role in the explanation of action
are matters for debate. It is no doubt true that Aristotle often
operates with the *orektikon* as just one more independent
part of soul (compare the way he introduces his discussion
of it in *DA* III.9), but since he seems to have an account of
orexis that makes clearer the relation of desire to the other
parts of soul and the role that it plays, it is worth discussing
the concept. As a result of my discussion we shall also know
more about the various elements in a state of character
(*ēthikē hexis*).

3.2. There is one psychic part which Aristotle does not
mention in his psychological sketch in *EN* I.xiii, viz. the
perceptual part (the *aisthētikon*). This may seem surprising,
since after all he does mention another part which, like the
perceptual one, is common to rational and non-rational
beings, viz. the nutritive part. Several reasons for the omission
may be given. But one is presumably that Aristotle in a way
has mentioned the perceptual part. For that part and the
desiderative part are one and the same part in a particularly
strong sense. Aristotle makes this point in *EE* II.i.14, 1219b33
and more directly in *DA* III.7, 431a13-14. For my discussion
of *orexis* I need as a premiss an interpretation of certain
points about perception that I have put forward elsewhere.[1]
I shall therefore turn briefly to Aristotle's account of perception.

Perception implies awareness. In the paper referred to I
suggest that Aristotle made this point by talking of 'perceptive
predication' and of *phantasia*. Any act of perception, be it
special, common, or incidental perception, may be represented as involving an implicit act of predicating 'something
of something' (*ti kata tinos*), a 'saying in one's heart' that is
propositional in form; and any act of perception involves a
phantasia, which is precisely the name of the perception in

---

[1] In 'Begrebet *phantasia* hos Aristoteles', *Museum Tusculanum* (Copenhagen),
34-5 (1979), 31-71.

so far as the latter involves the act of predication.[2] A similar account should be given of all non-veridical perceptual experiences (hallucination, dream, illusion, etc.). A careful reading of Aristotle's chapter in the *De Anima* on *phantasia* (III.3) and his account of dreaming in the *De Insomniis* will show that when he represents perception and other perceptual experiences in terms of predication, his aim is to express the element of awareness or immediate belief about the world of particulars which forms part of any such type of experience. Similarly it will show that what ties together his various remarks about *phantasia* in those texts is his wish to give expression to the same concept of perceptual awareness. In what follows I shall make use of this point about perception for the analysis of *orexis*.[3]

3.3. *DA* III.7, 431a8–14 runs (in Hamlyn's translation):

Perceiving, then, is like mere assertion and thought; when something is pleasant or painful, (the soul) pursues or avoids it, as it were asserting or denying it; and to feel pleasure or pain is to be active with the perceptive mean towards the good or bad as such. Avoidance and desire, as actual, are the same thing, and that which can desire and that which can avoid are not different either from each other or from that which can perceive; but what it is for them to be such is different.

The topic of this passage is feeling pleasure (*hēdesthai*) and feeling pain (*lypeisthai*). In *EN* II.v, where Aristotle argues that moral virtue is a *hexis* (and neither a capacity nor a passion), he gives the following account of passions (*pathē*). 'By passions I mean appetite (*epithymia*), anger,

---

[2] Thus my interpretation of *phantasia* differs fundamentally from the one recently proposed by M. Schofield, according to whom *phantasia* comes into play primarily in cases in which there is scepticism, caution, or non-committal, i.e. some degree of *doubt*, about the veridical character of a perceptual experience. See Schofield, 'Aristotle on the Imagination', in *Aristotle on Mind and the Senses*, edd. G. E. R. Lloyd and G. E. L. Owen, Cambridge, 1978, 99–140. Also in *Articles on Aristotle*, vol. iv, edd. J. Barnes, M. Schofield, R. Sorabji, London, 1979.

[3] My account of *phantasia* in its relation to desire should be compared with that of M. C. Nussbaum in her edition of the *De Motu Animalium*, Princeton, 1978, Essay 5: The Role of *Phantasia* in Aristotle's Explanation of Action (pp. 221–69). Nussbaum's book appeared after I had reached my own view of *phantasia* and its relation to desire. The similarities of the two accounts is striking. Both connect *phantasia* with 'awareness' and with 'seeing as' and assign to *phantasia*, in connection with action, the role of presenting an object to the faculty of desire. But the differences are equally striking. Whereas Nussbaum starts from

fear, confidence, envy, joy, friendly feeling, hatred, longing, emulation, pity, *and in general the feelings that are forms of (hepetai) pleasure or pain*' (v.2, 1105b21-23). I take it that in the quoted passage from the *De Anima* his topic is precisely passions. We shall see later that in that case he will not be talking of all kinds of *orexis*. Still a look at the quoted list of passions will show that if I am right about the passage from the *De Anima*, in that passage Aristotle will be talking of at least one type of what we should call *desire*, viz. the type instantiated by appetite (*epithymia*). He will also be talking of what we should call *emotions*, as instantiated (e.g.) by pity (*eleos*). If Aristotle is talking in the passage from the *De Anima* of passions, he will be talking of (at least) one type of desire and of emotions.

Let us first consider the second and third sentences of that passage. In the first sentence Aristotle has been talking of perception proper: it is like simply saying (*phanai*) and grasping (*noein*). He now concentrates on the case in which something is pleasant or painful. But is the new situation just that 'there is' something which is either pleasant or painful? The third sentence suggests that it is rather that there is something which is considered either pleasant or painful. For in that sentence Aristotle defines feeling pleased or pained as 'being active with the perceptive mean' towards the good or bad as such, i.e. not as having some factual property or other, but precisely *as* good (or pleasant) or bad (or painful). And in fact the grammatical subject of the second sentence is

---

phantasia in connection with desire and action and only later turns to consideration of *phantasia* in connection with perception and thought, I start from the other end (thus following Aristotle's own procedure in the *De Anima*). Whereas Nussbaum believes that the 'official' passage on *phantasia* (*DA* III.3) is basically incoherent, since it vacillates between an 'image view' of *phantasia* and a use of the concept that connects it with *phainesthai* and 'seeing as', and takes Aristotle, e.g. in the *De Insomniis*, to connect *phantasia* more or less unequivocally with the justly criticized 'image view', I argue, in the paper referred to, for a unitary account of *phantasia* that connects it with *phainesthai* and 'seeing as' and is to be found in the *De Insomniis* as well as in *DA* III.3. Finally there is the difference that Nussbaum dismisses as 'clearly false' (p. 223) the view that *phantasia* is a kind of propositional judgement, whereas I make much of that view and in fact take it to be identical with the 'seeing as' view. It is, perhaps, in consequence of the last difference that Nussbaum refers only once (p. 222 n.1), and very obliquely too, to *DA* III.7, 431a8-14, of which I make so much (below, sections 3.3 ff.).

'the soul'. We may therefore take the first part of the second
sentence to mean 'when the soul takes the thing to be either
pleasant or painful . . .'. And if we want a verb to govern
'pleasant or painful' we may introduce some form of saying
(*phanai*).[4] So here too there is a suggestion of an implicit
act of predication, the predicates being 'pleasant' or 'painful'.
It may well be that this idea of an act of predication is
contained in the words 'as it were asserting or denying it'
(*hoion kataphasa ē apophasa*) in the latter part of the second
sentence, but the fact that these participles go with '(the
soul) pursues and avoids it' shows that the idea of an implicit
act of predication is not all that is contained in those participles. I shall come back in a moment to the question of what
more is involved.

3.4. Now, however, if Aristotle is working with the idea of
an act of predication in his account of feeling pleased or
pained, it is likely that he is introducing that idea in order to
account for the intentionality of passions, for the fact that
having a passion implies an awareness of something as pleasant
or painful. If this is correct, we should also expect him to
introduce the concept of *phantasia* in connection with
passions. For in his analysis of perception *phantasia* went
together with implicit predication as ways of capturing the
element of awareness in that concept.

In fact, of course, Aristotle does talk of *phantasia* in
connection with desire.

DA III.10, 433b27-29 runs (Hamlyn): 'In general, therefore, as we have said, in so far as the animal is capable of
desire so far is it capable of moving itself; and it is not cable
of desire without imagination.'

What is this *phantasia* without which no animal will have
orexeis? Consideration of what immediately follows will help
us find the answer (III.10, 433b29-30 and III.11, 434a5-10):

---

[4] Cf. 7 lines further on: τῇ . . . διανοητικῇ ψυχῇ . . . ὅταν δὲ ἀγαθὸν ἢ κακὸν
φήσῃ ἢ ἀποφήσῃ, φεύγει ἢ διώκει (431a14-16); or 431b8-9: καὶ ὅταν εἴπῃ (sc.
τὸ νοητικόν) ὡς ἐκεῖ τὸ ἡδὺ ἢ λυπηρόν, ἐνταῦθα φεύγει ἢ διώκει; or, finally, *EN*
VII.vi.1, 1149a34-b1: ἡ δ' ἐπιθυμία, ἐὰν μόνον εἴπῃ ὅτι ἡδὺ ὁ λόγος ἢ ἡ αἴσθησις,
ὁρμᾷ πρὸς τὴν ἀπόλαυσιν.

But all *phantasia* is either calculative (*logistikē*) or perceptual (*aisthētikē*). The latter, then, other animals too will have a share in. . . . Now perceptual *phantasia*, as was said, is found in other animals too, but deliberative (*bouleutikē*) *phantasia* is found in calculative animals (only); for finding an answer to the question whether one should do this or that is already a task for calculation, and the alternatives must be measured by a single standard (for people pursue the greater good), so that they will be capable of combining several *phantasmata* into one.

According to this passage a deliberative *phantasia* seems to be a belief which results from calculation (or deliberation) and may be expressed in a statement of the form 'this should be done'. But then a perceptual *phantasia* is likely to be a belief that may be expressed in a statement of the same form, but which is the direct result of perception. In fact, a passage in the *Eudemian Ethics* to which I shall come back later in this chapter strongly supports the suggestion that the *phantasia* without which no animal will have *orexeis* is a (rationally based or non-rational) *belief* that something should be done. The passage is *EE* II.x.18, 1226b21-25: 'This is why decision (*prohairesis*) is found neither in animals nor in man at every age or in every condition; for no more is deliberation or the grasp of "why"; but nothing hinders that many (animals) form a belief (*doxazein*) whether something should or should not be done: to do so through deliberation is beyond their reach.'

So Aristotle does talk of *phantasia* in connection with desire. But is this what we were looking for? We were looking for passages on *phantasia* to be connected with Aristotle's talk of implicit acts of predication in the analysis of feeling pleased or pained in *DA* III.7, 431a. But there, I claimed, he is talking of *passions* (*pathē*), whereas in *DA* III.10-11, 433b-434a he is talking of *orexeis*. However, the problem is solved before it becomes serious. Passions are expressions of a man's *ēthos* and the latter is a 'quality' of his *orektikon*. So if there will be *phantasiai* in connection with *orexeis* in general, there will be too in connection with passions. In the latter case the propositional content of a *phantasia* will not be 'this should be done'. It will be 'this is pleasant' or 'this is painful' for non-practical passions like pity, i.e. for 'pure' emotions, and 'this (referring, e.g., to a peach) is pleasant' plus 'this (referring to the act of taking the peach) should be done' for practical passions like appetite (*epithymia*). But the difference does nothing to invalidate my claim that a *phantasia* will be involved in connection with passions no less than with *orexeis*. In fact the connection with *action* of Aristotle's three types of value (the pleasant, the beneficial, and the noble, and their counterparts the painful, the harmful, and the base), which are values that are relevant to passions too, is so close that in one passage (*EN* II.iii.7, 1104b30-32) he may introduce these values as 'things pertaining to takings' (*ta eis tas haireseis*) and 'things pertaining to avoidance' (*ta eis tas phygas*) respectively or, in Ross's simpler but precisely correct translation, the 'three objects of choice and three of avoidance'. So passions, even 'pure', non-practical emotions, are in some way all so closely connected with action that they will necessarily belong under *orexeis*.

We may conclude, then, that having *orexeis* in general and having passions in particular includes having a *phantasia*. We also know that having a passion involves predicating 'in one's heart' and it is likely that the same goes for having an *orexis*. The important point, the one I have wanted to make, is that any type of desire presupposes what I shall call an evaluative cognitive state on the part of the person who has the desire.[5]

However, there is more to having an *orexis*. When we have seen what, we shall be clearer on the sense in which the *phantasia* or cognitive state is 'presupposed' by the desire.

3.5. We must go back to the analysis of passions in *DA* III.7, 431a8 ff.

___

[5] The scholar who has most strongly emphasized the cognitive element in passions is W. W. Fortenbaugh, in a series of articles the most important of which are 'Aristotle's Conception of Moral Virtue and Its Perceptive Role', *TAPA* 95 (1964), 71-81; 'Aristotle: Emotion and Moral Virtue', *Arethusa*, 2 (1969), 163-85; 'Aristotle: Animals, Emotion, and Moral Virtue', *Arethusa*, 4 (1971), 137-65. In his book *Aristotle on Emotion*, London, 1975, Fortenbaugh attempts to show the importance of his idea for Aristotle's doctrine on rhetoric, poetics, ethics, and politics. Fortenbaugh's point about passion is, however, totally different from mine, since he uses the term cognition to stand for *rational* states of knowledge only (hence, e.g., his claim that animals cannot have passions, cf. 'Aristotle: Animals, Emotion, and Moral Virtue' pp. 137-8). Nor does he reach his point by the same route as I have reached mine.

We saw that in that passage Aristotle is talking of two things: of perception and, in connection with having a passion, of evaluative predication. There is, however, a third topic. In a12-14 Aristotle states that actual avoidance (*phygē*) and desire (*orexis*) are identical though different in being, and similarly with the faculty of avoidance (*to pheuktikon*), that of desire (*to orektikon*), and that of perception (*to aisthētikon*). This point is introduced (a12) by the particles καὶ . . . δέ, where the former particle denotes 'that something is added, the latter that what is added is distinct from what precedes' (J. D. Denniston).[6] In addition, then, to perception proper and evaluative predication Aristotle is also talking in the passage of avoidance and desire.

The fact that Aristotle couples avoidance with desire, instead of, e.g., pursuit, shows that he is not talking of the actual performance of certain types of act, but of certain psychic entities that 'correspond' to such actual performance. He is in fact talking of desire-to-get and desire-to-avoid. But then we can see that already in the second sentence of the passage under consideration Aristotle has been talking of this third topic, viz. when he states that the soul pursues or avoids (*diōkei ē pheugei*) what is considers pleasant or painful.

This points to the way in which we should understand the relation of the element of desire that is apparently part of a passion and the evaluative predication that we have also seen to be so. For in the second sentence Aristotle describes the soul's pursuit and avoidance, i.e. the desire, as 'a sort of assertion (*kataphasis*) or denial (*apophasis*)'. *Kataphasis* and *apophasis* are not just 'proposition in the affirmative' and 'proposition in the negative', but precisely 'assertion that something is' and 'assertion that something is not'. So 'psychic pursuit and avoidance', or the desire to get and the desire to avoid, are assertions and denials, and moreover, we may suppose, assertions of the propositions we have also seen to be part of desire and of passions.

This reading is supported by a few lines that introduce a very important passage in the *Ethics*: *EN* VI.ii.2, 1139a21 ff. Here, in lines a21-22, Aristotle states that 'what assertion

<hr>

[6] Denniston, *The Greek Particles*, Oxford, 1959[2], p. 199.

(*kataphasis*) and denial (*apophasis*) are in thought (*en dianoiai*), pursuit (*diōxis*) and avoidance (*phygē*) are in desire (*en orexei*)', and then goes on to draw certain conclusions from that point. The point is simple. Just as in thought assertion and denial contain two elements, one being the propositional content of the thought and the other being the element of assertion of that content, so full desire contains an element of assertion (that is the explicit point of the quoted lines) and in addition, since there must be something to be asserted, some propositional content that will be expressed in evaluative terms.

3.6. What, then, is desire in Aristotle? The answer is twofold. Full desire, e.g. *epithymia*, contains an element of awareness of the desired object as pleasant and as to be taken. This element Aristotle tries to capture by talking of evaluative predication and of *phantasia*. But it also contains an element of 'bare' psychic pursuit or avoidance, which is described by Aristotle as a sort of assertion of the propositional content of th predication and the *phantasia*. This element is the one that is specifically provided by the faculty of the *orektikon*. In actual fact, of course, it will always be combined with the element of awareness, which is provided by the faculty of the *phantastikon* (or that of reason, where the *phantasia* is a *bouleutikē phantasia*). Still we may now give the following account of *orexis* according to Aristotle, i.e. of 'bare' desire, as the element that is specifically provided by the *orektikon*. Such desire is an assertion of evaluative propositions entertained by the soul. It is, therefore, what accounts for the behavioural efficacy of man's evaluative beliefs. That, of course, is precisely how Aristotle introduces *orexis* and *to orektikon* in *DA* III.9: we have discussed those faculties that perform the 'critical' task of the soul; we must now discuss what part of soul is responsible for movement in place (432a15-19). And that is how he summarizes at the end of *DA* III.10: 'In general, then, . . . it is *qua* capable of *orexis* that an animal is able to move itself' (433b27-28). But we now know more precisely what that element of *orexis* is, and we know more precisely why Aristotle immediately continues by saying that *orexis* 'presupposes' *phantasia*.

4.1. So much for *orexis* and *to orektikon*. It will be remembered that my over-all aim in the present chapter is to decide what psychic faculties are at work when a person is being habituated and as a result acquires a habituated ethical state. Before turning to this question we should attempt to define the property of being 'ethical' (*ēthikē*). We saw that *ēthos* is a 'quality' of the *orektikon*: what quality? Similarly we have been discussing (on the basis of *DA* III.7, 431a8–14) passions, which are ethical entities, and (on the basis of *DA* III.10–11, 433b–434a) *orexeis* in general as including passions: what is the specific difference of passions as against *orexeis* in general?

In *DA* III.10–11 Aristotle operates with rational desires, i.e. with desires that include a rational (deliberative or calculative) *phantasia*, and with non-rational, perceptual desires, i.e. with desires that include a perceptual *phantasia*. Passions too may be found in either guise. I cannot here argue fully for that claim, since the argument relies on premisses that have not yet been introduced. But in outline the argument runs as follows. Passions are the exercise of moral capacities or of moral *hexeis*; some moral *hexeis* contain a rational component, others do not; passions, then, may be rational or non-rational.

The specific difference of passions in relation to *orexeis* in general lies elsewhere, viz. in the distinction between *poiēsis* and *praxis*. The *orexeis* of *DA* III.10–11, 433b–434a will include desires that are rational and 'poietic' by being desires for means, in the proper sense, to independently desired ends. Such desires will in fact be identical with 'poietic' decisions (*prohaireseis*) as described, e.g., in *EN* III.iii (on *prohairesis*). Passions, on the other hand, are exclusively 'practical' (as opposed to 'poietic').

4.2. Let us consider two specimens from Aristotle's list of passions, appetite (*epithymia*) and pity (*eleos*). I have already hinted how the analysis of passions that we saw to be contained in *DA* III.7, 431a8–14 will run for these two passions. Appetite, e.g. for a peach, contains both a predication, that (having or eating) a peach is something pleasant, and an assertion of that proposition: a psychic 'bare' pursuit of the thing (or state of affairs) of which 'being pleasant' is predicated. Again, pity of somebody for something contains both the predication that 'that thing's having occurred to him is something painful', and its assertion: a psychic 'bare' avoidance of the state of affairs of which 'being painful' is predicated.

Apart from this similarity, however, the analysis of appetite and pity will differ in that where the analysis I have given captures everything that goes into pity, this is not so for appetite. Appetite does not consist in the emotive element only; it is a form of *desire*, and consequently also contains an attitude towards acting. In a way pity does too. If I feel pity for somebody, then even if I cannot do anything to alleviate his pain, it will remain the case that if I had been present when the painful thing happened and if I had been able to do something to prevent it from happening, I would have had at least some desire to do what I could to prevent the misery from occurring. Appetite, however, is even more directly connected with action. It has an emotive element, but it also contains a specifically desiderative one. This too may be analysed in accordance with the pattern I have suggested. Thus we may say that appetite also contains a predication that 'making the pleasant thing (some state of affairs or event) obtain is a good' and a psychic assertion of that predication: a psychic 'bare' pursuit of the act that is stated to be choiceworthy. Thus appetite for a peach will contain the predication that 'taking or getting the peach is a good thing', and a desiderative assertion of the predication. (Some confirmation of the more complex analysis I have suggested of those passions which, like appetite, are desires is provided by what Aristotle says in various places of the passion of anger (*orgē*). In some places he defines anger simply as a pain (*lypē*) that one has suffered some slight or injustice (e.g. in *EN* IV.v.10, 1126a21-22, together with V.viii.10, 1135b28-29), while elsewhere he defines it as a *desire* (*orexis*) for revenge, *combined* with such pain (*Rhet.* II.2, 1378a30). Anger, then, is another passion that contains both the emotive and the desiderative aspects.)

4.3. But now let us consider the evaluative beliefs we have

been operating with: 'this thing or state of affairs or event is pleasant or painful or, in general (cf. *DA* III.7, 431a12), good or bad' and 'making the thing obtain or cease to exist is a good'. Good, or bad, for what purpose? It seems immediately clear that an emotive evaluative belief like the first one mentioned will not contain any reference to some purpose that explains why the thing, state of affairs, or event is considered either good or bad. Thus in the case of pity I do not for some ulterior purpose believe it a bad thing that something has happened to somebody, as long as I am simply feeling pity. And similarly with appetite for a peach, which includes also the desiderative belief. As long as I am simply moved by the prospect of having or eating the peach, and hence desire to get it, I do not wish to have it for any ulterior purpose — and this simple wish for it, and the consequent desire to get it, is all that goes into the 'passion' of appetite. It is of course true that in the case of appetite one of the elements in that passion, the desire to get the peach, 'has a purpose', viz. that of having or eating it. But this does not mean that there is an ulterior purpose behind the passion as a whole, and for two reasons. The first is that what constitutes the purpose, having or eating the peach, is the intentional object of the emotive element that is part of the passion itself, and this element has no ulterior purpose, so that the passion as a whole has none either. The second reason is that, as I tried to show in chapter 1, an act has an ulterior purpose in the sense which turns it into a *poiēsis* only if the act-*result* is pursued for some further purpose, and in the case of appetite for a peach, as just that, it is not.

I believe that this point about the lack of an ulterior purpose will prove valid even when applied to passions like anger or fear (*phobos*), where the analysis of the emotive and desiderative aspects is more complex. And I therefore suggest that with a number of reservations we may think of passions, any type of Aristotelian 'passion' (*pathos*), as a 'practical' (as opposed to 'poietic') phenomenon. I mention two reservations. First, whereas *praxeis* and *poiēseis* are of course acts, it is only in connection with some passions, viz. those that contain a desiderative element, that we must talk of acts and hence of something which may qualify as a *praxis*. Secondly, while only acts which are justified *rationally* will be either *praxeis* or *poiēseis*, passions, as I suggested, are not necessarily rational. Some are, but many are not, e.g. those of animals, children, and adults in various deranged moods. Thus defining passions as a 'practical' phenomenon is only a heuristic device.

But it is, I believe, a helpful one. For we can now see how passions differ from *orexeis* in general: passions are 'practical', but not all *orexeis* are. And if passions are 'ethical' (*ēthika*), as they are, and are what the two elements that characterize a person's *ēthos*, viz. capacities and *hexeis*, issue in, then we can also see what 'quality' of the *orektikon ēthos* is. It is the 'practical' part of a person's *orektikon*.

5. I have discussed Aristotle's account of *orexis* and *to orektikon* and the question of what differentiates *ēthos* as a 'quality' of the *orektikon*. We may now return to the habituated moral virtue from which we started and try to answer the question of what faculties are involved in such a state.

First, of course, a moral virtue that results from habituation will be a *hexis* of the *orektikon* in its guise as issuing in 'practical' *orexeis*, i.e. passions. But secondly, it will also be a cognitive state, since what it issues in, the passions, contain a cognitive element. That, of course, is the point I tried to establish when I discussed Aristotle's account of *orexis*.

But then what critical faculty, or faculties, will be responsible for the cognitive element? In other words, will the cognitive element in the passions in which an habituated moral virtue issues be represented by *phantasiai* which are perceptual (*aisthētikai*) or by *phantasiai* that are deliberative (*bouleutikai*) and calculative (*logistikai*)? The answer is not difficult to find. For children may undergo habituation and may consequently acquire a habituated moral virtue (*EN* II.i.8). And since children do not possess reason (*EE* II.x.18–19), we must say that the critical faculty that is responsible for the cognitive element in a habituated moral virtue (and the passions in which it issues) is the combined faculty ·of the perceptual part (*to aisthētikon*) and *to phantastikon*; the evaluative beliefs that will be involved are *perceptual phantasiai*.

This result is an important one. We shall see why, when in chapters 6-7 we turn from the question of what faculties are at work when a habituated moral virtue is being formed, to the question of why precisely those faculties, and no others, are involved. First, however, in order to see what a habituated moral virtue is *not*, viz. a rational cognitive state issuing in deliberative or calculative *phantasiai*, we must discuss exactly how Aristotle distinguishes reason from perception.

6. When considering Aristotle's psychology one should always keep in mind the distinction between faculties and the states or occurrences which are the faculty 'at work', its exercise. Aristotle himself does not always distinguish explicitly between the two. Thus at *An. Post.* II.19, 99b35-37 he says: 'For they (sc. all animals) have an inborn critical ability, which people call perception (*aisthēsis*). Now when perception (*aisthēsis*) is present, in some animals there comes to be a retention of the percept, in others not.' Here the one word *aisthēsis* is first used of the perceptual faculty and then of an occurrence of perception.

The faculties Aristotle is normally working with in connection with the phenomenon of having beliefs are perception (*aisthēsis*), *phantasia*, and reason (*nous*). This is an exhaustive list of the 'critical' faculties in Aristotelian psychology, and these are the three critical faculties that are distinguished in *DA* II and III.

The most important of the critical states or occurrences that Aristotle discusses are these: perception (*aisthēsis*), *apatē* (illusion, hallucination), dream (*enhypnion*), memory (*mnēmē*), experience (*empeiria*), belief (*doxa*), productive art (*technē*), moral insight (*phronēsis*), scientific knowledge (*epistēmē*), insight (*nous*, as a state or occurrence), wisdom (*sophia*). The relationship between these states or occurrences and the three faculties is this. Perception is an exercise of the faculties of perception and of *phantasia*. *Apatē*, dream, and memory are exercises of the faculty of *phantasia*.[7] Belief, productive art, moral insight, scientific knowledge, insight, and wisdom are exercises of the faculty of reason.

[7] I argue for the claims made in this and the previous sentences in the paper referred to in n.1.

The latter point, which is the important one in the present
context, is clear from *EN* VI.iii.1 when the passage is taken in
context. The context consists of i.4-ii, especially i.5-7 and
the two lines that immediately precede iii.1, viz. ii.6, 1139b
12-13. Aristotle wishes to discuss the virtues of thought
(*dianoia*, i.4). He divides the rational part (*to logon echon*)
into two parts (i.5-6), and states that he is trying to find the
best state (*aretē*) of each and that this state will be relative
to the characteristic product (*ergon*) of each part (i.7).
Having then (in ii) discussed the product of one of the parts,
viz. the 'practical and rational one' (ii.3, 1139a29-30), he
concludes, in the two lines that immediately precede iii.1,
that the product of both *noetic* parts is truth and that
consequently by finding those states in accordance with
which each part will be in possession of truth we shall find
the best state of each part. And then, in iii.1, he musters
five things 'in virtue of which the soul possesses truth when
asserting and denying': productive art, scientific knowledge,
moral insight, wisdom, and insight; and he adds that he has
not included 'grasp' (*hypolēpsis*) and belief (*doxa*) since
they admit of falsity. There can be no doubt that the five
states mentioned, and in addition the two that are not
included among necessarily true states, are actualizations of
the two rational parts, and it is equally certain that the
two parts of the rational part, the two 'noetic' parts of ii.6,
1139b12, are divisions of the faculty of *nous*.

We should note that Aristotle here mentions one state
as rational which I did not include in my list of rational
states or occurrences, *hypolēpsis*. The reason for the difference is that in spite of the present passage Aristotle does not
consider *hypolēpsis* as just one rational state among others.
Rather, it is a generic term for all the rational states. This is
clear e.g. from a passage in *DA* III.3 (on *phantasia*). Aristotle
has been contrasting *phantasia* with, on the one hand, perception and, on the other hand, thought (*dianoia*) and
has been using the term *hypolēpsis* as a synonym for *dianoia*
(427b14-16). He then produces two arguments in support
of the distinction between *phantasia* and *hypolēpsis* (427b
16-24) and concludes the section with the following paren-
thetical note: 'Within *hypolēpsis* itself there are also differences

— scientific knowledge, belief, moral insight, and their opposites; the difference between them is the topic of another discussion' (427b24-26). The task, therefore, of defining the difference between perception and reason will be fulfilled if we succeed in defining *hypolēpsis*.

7.1. There is one state on my initial list which has not yet been assigned to any of the three faculties: *empeiria* (experience). It seems likely that consideration of that state will make the defining property of rational states in general clearer. For *empeiria* seems intended by Aristotle to provide a sort of bridge of the gap between perception and *phantasia* on the one hand and *hypolēpsis* and reason on the other.

Material for an understanding of *empeiria* is found in *Metaph.* Alpha 1 and *An. Post.* II.19. The passages are well known, but I must single out some points in them.

All animals possess the faculty of perception (*Metaph.* 980a27-28, *Anal.* 99b34-35). From perception memory is produced in some animals, in others not (*Metaph.* 980a28-29, *Anal.* 99b36-37). The next step is described in the *Metaphysics* (980b25-29) in an interesting way: 'Animals other than man live by *phantasia* and memory (in *empeiria* they have only a small share); but the human race lives both by *technē* and by reasoning (*logismoi*). Now from memory *empeiria* is produced in men . . .'. The main contrast here[8] is the one between other animals, which live by *phantasia* and memory, and humans, who live by *technē* and reasoning, and it would therefore be natural for Aristotle to go on directly to talk of *technē* and reasoning. However, he inserts a remark about *empeiria* between the two things being contrasted: 'as for *empeiria*, they [sc. the other animals] have only a small share in it.' So they do share in *empeiria*? Perhaps not after all. For having stated that humans live by *technē* and reasoning Aristotle asserts that *empeiria* arises from memory *for humans*. So *empeiria* seems to be specifically human and the little that other animals share in it verges on nothing. In fact, after a short description (980b29-981a1) of *empeiria*, to which I shall come back in a moment, Aristotle

---

[8] Cf. in b25-26 the plural τὰ μὲν and in b27 the *singular* τὸ δὲ.

states that '*empeiria* seems to be virtually the same thing as scientific knowledge (*epistēmē*) and *technē*', but hastens to correct this over-statement by claiming the correct account to be that '*epistēmē* and *technē* come to be present, *for humans, because of (dia) empeiria*'.

It is amusing to try to follow Aristotle's thought in the way I have paraphrased it. He clearly wishes to say both that *empeiria* has some affinity with *phantasia* and memory, and hence would seem to belong on the side of 'other animals', and that it is special to humans, but nevertheless is different from what is specifically characteristic of them, viz. *technē*, *epistēmē*, reasoning. The message he intends to convey is, I believe, that *empeiria* is found in humans alone, but that its definition will only mention states or capacities that are found in other animals too.

7.2. What, then is *empeiria*? *Empeiria* is 'experience', but this is not very clear. Aristotle describes it in the following ways. 'For many memories of the same thing make up the "power" of a single *empeiria* (*mias empeirias dynamin apotelousin*)' (*Metaph.* 980b29-981a1). 'From (*ek*) the repeated memory of the same (thing) *empeiria* comes about (*ginetai*); for memories that are many in number are (*estin*) a single *empeiria*' (*Anal.* 100a4-6). What is the point of the 'many memories' (*pollai mnēmai*) that are mentioned in both accounts? One might think that *empeiria* is experience in the sense of a state which, whatever else we may say of it, is the result of an accumulation, for which memory is responsible, of observations of one and the same phenomenon (*to auto pragma*), e.g. that some illness is best cured in a certain way. According to this interpretation the two quoted accounts of *empeiria* say nothing of what kind of state *empeiria* is, but only that for it to arise memory is a necessary condition since *empeiria* is the result of an accumulation of particular observations. This interpretation would account for the idea of *empeiria*'s arising *from* (*ek*) memory.

It would not, however, account for the point that the 'many cases of memory' *are* (*estin, Anal.* 100a6) a single state of *empeiria*. Nor would it make clear exactly how *empeiria* differs from *technē* and *epistēmē*. I believe that

Aristotle has a more precise conception of *empeiria* in mind. As a clue we may take the example he gives of *empeiria* a few lines further on in the *Metaphysics* (981a7-9): 'For to have a grasp (*hypolēpsis*) that for Kallias, when he suffered from that illness, that (treatment) was beneficial and for Socrates and for many individuals in the same way, is a matter of *empeiria*.' According to these lines it is a matter of *empeiria* to have a *hypolēpsis* (I shall return to the use of this term later) the content of which is that when Kallias suffered from this or that illness (as indicated e.g. by certain symptoms), this or that remedy helped to cure him; when Socrates suffered from the same illness (i.e. had the same symptoms), he was cured by the same remedy; etc. If we go by this example, we may say that *empeiria* is a mental state that a person is in when, at something which may in some recognizable sense be called 'the same time', he has more than one actual memory of different, but relevantly identical past particular events. That, at least, seems the best way to make sense of Aristotle's statement that 'memories that are many in number *are* a single *empeiria*'. And we shall see that if *empeiria* is understood in that way, it will in fact bridge the gap between perception and reason in a very precise sense. *Empeiria*, then, is not just experience in some vague sense. It involves actual memory, indeed *is* the connected memory of a number of past particular events.

7.3. But there is more to be said of *empeiria*, which we may bring out by considering what Aristotle says in the two chapters about *technē* and its relation to *empeiria*.

Technē is stated to arise from *empeiria* in the following way (*Metaph.* 981a5-7, cf. *Anal.* 100a6-8): '*Technē* arises when a single universal grasp (*mia katholou hypolēpsis*) of similar things arises from "many thoughts of *empeiria*" (*ek pollōn tēs empeirias ennoēmatōn*).' And corresponding to the quoted example of *empeiria* the following example of *technē* is given (*Metaph.* 981a10-12): 'But (to have a grasp) that for all such people, defined according to a single type, when they suffer from that illness, (that treatment) was (or is) beneficial . . . , is a matter of *technē*.'

What Aristotle mans by the 'many thoughts of *empeiria*'

in his account of the way in which *technē* arises from *empeiria* is not, I think, 'many cases of *empeiria*' but 'many "thoughts" as part of a single state of *empeiria*'. The idea is that when there is *empeiria* consisting of a sufficiently large number of memories (the 'thoughts') of one and the same phenomenon as present in earlier situations, there may arise a single universal *hypolēpsis* 'concerning' (*peri*) all those individual cases. This *hypolēpsis* is universal and 'concerns' those cases in the sense that it is a grasp of the one universal of which the particular cases are tokens (cf. *Anal.* 100a7-8: 'the one thing apart from the many, which, whatever it is, is present in them all as one and the same thing'). I shall come back to this notion of a grasp of some universal in a moment. At present I wish to suggest that if *technē* is a grasp of the universal and if *technē* arises from *empeiria* in the way described, then we should ascribe to the man who has only *empeiria* an *implicit* 'grasp of the universal'. This man does see the similarity between the particular events he remembers as part of his *empeiria*. Indeed, if these cases are not cases of the same thing (*to auto pragma*), his connected memory of them is not *empeiria*. It is true that he has no *explicit* grasp of the one and the same thing in them all that makes them similar, but he does see that they are similar to each other; hence we are entitled to ascribe to him an *implicit* grasp of the universal which is that one and the same thing.

But it is very important to see that this implicit grasp of the universal, of what makes the particular cases similar, is not itself *empeiria*. *Empeiria* is the actual memory of a number of similar particular cases, and the implicit grasp of the universal I have ascribed to the man of *empeiria* is a state that is introduced in order to account for that actual memory. In fact the implicit grasp of the universal of the type I have introduced is not only to be found in the man of *empeiria*. If somebody has experience in our sense of the term, if, that is, he reacts in the same manner to relevantly identical situations, e.g. by believing that certain acts, which are in fact similar, should be done in each of those situations, then we must ascribe to him too an implicit grasp of the universal. But this person will not necessarily have *empeiria* in the Aristotelian sense. He may well 'see' those situations in the same way without at the same time remembering any specific examples of the relevant type of situation. Experience, as something I show myself to have e.g. when I am driving my car, involves an implicit grasp of universals which accounts for my reacting in relevantly identical situations in the same way. But it neither involves an explicit grasp of those universals nor even that actual memory of particular cases which is Aristotelian *empeiria*.

So far, then, we may say that *empeiria* is a state of actual memory of a number of relevantly identical particular cases, and that the state must be accounted for in terms of an implicit grasp of the universal which makes the cases identical.

8. By contrast, *technē* involves, in my terminology, an explicit grasp of a universal. I have not yet shown the precise position of *empeiria* in relation to the three critical faculties. First I shall try to clarify the distinction I have introduced between an implicit and an explicit grasp of the universal in order to bring out what Aristotle means when he talks of *technē* as a grasp or knowledge *of* the universal. I wish to claim that in bringing out his meaning here I shall make explicit the precise point where reason differs from perception.

Let us distinguish between three different ways of being related to some universal. One may (*i*) grasp it implicitly, (*ii*) grasp it explicitly, or (*iii*) think of it. (*iii*) is an uninteresting relation: Aristotle will certainly never have made it a necessary condition of possessing e.g. a *technē* that the technician should actually think of or rehearse the universal propositions the grasp of which defines a *technē* − either always, or even when he makes use of some universal proposition by applying it in practice.

We may try to bring out the specific sense of an explicit grasp of the universal (*ii*), which is the one that defines *technē* versus *empeiria*, by suggesting that a technician who applies his knowledge in practice, although he need not actually rehearse the universal that he grasps, must nevertheless be immediately able, if asked why he decided to do what he did, to produce a sentence that is universal in form and states that in situations of a certain type, viz. the type of which the particular situation is a token, acts of a certain type should be performed (with a view to the aim of the *technē* in question). We may take the presence of this ability as a sign that the person in question has the explicit grasp of the universal. He need not rehearse the universal when he is using it, but in order for us to be entitled to ascribe to him this explicit grasp he must be *immediately able* to rehearse it and hence produce a sentence that makes it explicit.

The man who has only *empeiria*, however, does not have this ability. We may ask him why he proceeded to try that cure on Kallias, and he may well give an answer to the question why. Thus he may have *a* reason to give. But even though the cure he advocates may also be the correct one, he does not know why, he is not able to give the correct reason for his act, which is that the particular cases he refers us to are all tokens of some type. And it is a sign of this lack of knowledge on his part that he is unable to produce a sentence that states what the type is. We have seen reason to ascribe to him an *implicit* grasp of the universal, which accounts for his seeing the similarly between all those particular cases that are in fact similar to each other. The difference is only that he is not immediately able to 'bring it to consciousness', he has not the full rational grasp of those particular cases whose similarity he sees.

9.1. In order to bring out more clearly this distinction between an implicit and an explicit grasp of the universal I shall discuss in more detail an interesting passage in the *Eudemian Ethics*, II.x.18-19, 1226b21-30.

We must consider the context of the two paragraphs. In x.16-17 Aristotle is arguing towards a definition of decision (*prohairesis*), in the following way. He starts by mentioning two properties of deliberation (*bouleusis*), (*i*) that *bouleusis* is not about the end but that the end is settled (*keitai*), and (*ii*) that *bouleusis* goes on until one has hit upon something one can oneself do. He then starts his argument about decision (x.17, 1226b13) by stating that *prohairesis* presupposes deliberation; and having repeated the two properties of deliberation (b15-16), in the reverse order, he concludes that *prohairesis* is deliberative desire for things in one's power.

In this definition the mention of 'things in one's power' refers back to the second property of deliberation (*ii*), but apparently, and rather oddly, there is no mention in the definition of the first property. Aristotle might have added to this definition: 'and for the means to some end', but he does not. There is, however, a reason for this, viz. that this property is precisely the one treated in x.18-19.

Having produced his definition Aristotle makes a paren-thetical remark (x.17, b17-19) about the relation between deliberation and *prohairesis* (the former is a necessary, but not a sufficient, condition of the latter) and adds a brief explanation (b19-20) of the sense he attaches to the term 'deliberative' in the definition. A desire is deliberative if its starting-point (*archē*) and cause (*aitia*) is deliberation, i.e. (*kai*) if one desires *because of* (*dia*) deliberation. And then (b21) he embarks on the argument of § § 18-19.

His aim here is to show both that and why *prohairesis* is found neither in other animals nor in human beings in childhood, during illness, and the like. This claim is introduced as a corollary of the preceding remarks (cf. b21 *dio*). The connection seems to be the following one. Aristotle has just defined deliberative desire as a desire that has deliberation as its starting-point and cause and 'because of what' (*dia ti*). He now concentrates on the idea that deliberation itself has a cause and a 'because of what', and tries to show how it follows from this that *prohairesis* is a specifically rational phenomenon. The corollary, then, is triggered off by the immediately preceding remarks about the causal relation between deliberation and desire, but at the same time it is evidently the case that Aristotle is going back to the first property of deliberation, viz. that it has a settled end. In fact he himself makes that clear by concluding the argument of § § 18-19 in the following way (b29-30): 'So that beings for whom no aim (*skopos*) is settled (*keitai*) are not deliberative.'

9.2. Let us consider Aristotle's argument in detail. The passage runs (b21-30):

This is why *prohairesis* is found neither in animals nor in man at every age or in every condition; for no more is deliberation or the grasp of 'why'; but nothing hinders that many (animals) form a belief (*doxazein*) whether something should or should not be done: to do so through deliberation is beyond their reach. For the deliberative part of soul is the one which considers (*theōrein*) some cause (*aitia tis*). For the that-for-the-sake-of-which (*hē hou heneka*) is one of the causes. (For the why is cause, and that-for-the-sake-of-which something is or arises, that thing we state to be causing (*aition*); thus of walking getting one's money (is causing), if the man walks for the sake of that.)[9] So that beings for whom no aim is settled are not deliberative.

The central point here is that in order to have the ability to deliberate and consequently to believe through deliberation that something is or is not to be done one must have *a grasp of 'why'* (*hypolēpsis tou dia ti*). But how are we to understand this? Is Aristotle suggesting that no animal or child may act for an end? That would be a very strange suggestion. A child may certainly have a grasp of something that he wants to bring about and may take steps to reach that end.

In fact Aristotle's remark about the deliberative part of soul suggests that he is making a different claim. The deliberative part of soul is able to consider some cause (*theōrētikon aitias tinos*). What Aristotle means by 'some cause' here is not 'any given thing that explains', but 'one of the (four) explanatory concepts (causes)'. He is not saying that in order to be able to deliberate one must be able to 'consider' or keep clearly in mind e.g. 'getting one's money', where this is one's aim in going for a walk. He is saying that in order to be able to deliberate one must be able to grasp, to use the same example, the *concept* that would be employed in explaining one's going for a walk, viz. the concept of an end. That this is so is certain in view of the explanatory sentence he appends: 'for the (cause of) that-for-the-sake-of-which (*hē hou heneka*, sc. *aitia*) is one of the causes.' This sentence can, I believe, only mean that the that-for-the-sake-of-which

---

[9] The words in parenthesis seem to contain an argument for the claim that the cause of *hou heneka* is in fact a cause (*aitia*), but it is difficult to see exactly how the argument goes. The best I can produce is this. Aristotle first states, not that the why *in general* is cause, but that any particular thing that we state to be the thing that answers the question 'Why?' is the *cause* we shall want to mention in that context. He then states that the *thing* which in any given context is the thing for the sake of which some other thing either is or arises is 'causing' (*aition*), i.e. that it is the *thing* that answers the question 'Why?' (Therefore, the *thing* which is the thing for the sake of which some other thing either is or arises is the *cause* we shall want to mention in that context. And therefore, the that-for-the-sake-of-which *in general* is one of the causes.)

is one of the well-known Aristotelian 'causes', viz. the final cause. It is 'the final cause', then, or the concept of an end, that the soul must be able to consider if it is to be capable of deliberation. And when Aristotle said earlier in the passage that one must have a grasp of 'why' (*to dia ti*) in order to be able to deliberate, his point was that one must have the grasp of 'explanation', of the *concept* of why. It is not sufficient that one has a grasp of something which, in the particular case, instantiates the why: one must have knowledge of that concept itself.

But how are we to understand the idea of a grasp of the concept of explanation? Let us consider an example. A child will, I have suggested, be able to act for an end, but will not possess the concept of explanation. 'Why are you fetching that stick?' 'I want to get that ball on the roof.' This would be a normal type of answer for a child. The child may also say, 'In order to get that ball on the roof'. But if we then exclaim, 'Ah, your fetching the stick is a *means* to getting the ball?', we may well expect that our remark will not seem very informative to the child. Why not? Because children do not possess the conceptual machinery that is required to classify acts of theirs as means. They do not possess a grasp of the explanatory means-end relationship as such, in the abstract, and consequently are not able to see any particular act as instantiating any item in that relationship. They can act for an end, and they can also explain why they do what they do, but they cannot say, 'This is the *means* to the *end* of . . .', where the emphasis on 'means' and 'end' serves to give the following meaning to the sentence: 'there is such a thing as the means-end relationship, and this act instantiates the concept of means, etc.'

10. It will, I hope, be clear that this way of understanding the grasp of 'why' which is a necessary condition for deliberation is exactly parallel to the way I suggested we should understand the idea of the grasp of the universal which defines a *technē* in relation to *empeiria*. In both cases we may take it as a sign that a person has the grasp involved, that he is immediately able to formulate a sentence that is universal in form. The technician will formulate a sentence that

mentions a certain type of situation and a certain type of act. The person who is able to deliberate will produce a sentence that introduces a certain type of relationship, viz. the means-end one. In both cases it is a sign of their having an explicit grasp of some universal that they may immediately formulate a sentence mentioning that universal.

But in the context of different types of grasp it will also be true that there are some persons, e.g. children, who do not possess that explicit universal grasp which accounts for people's being able to produce a sentence of the required form, but to whom we will nevertheless wish to ascribe an *implicit* grasp of the universal. We saw this in the context of *technē*, but it will also hold in the context of *bouleusis*. Children may not deliberate, but they do possess an implicit grasp of the relationship (the means-end one), an explicit grasp of which is a necessary condition for the ability to deliberate. What they lack is not the ability to act for ends (and for this ability to be there we must ascribe to them an implicit grasp of the means-end relationship), but the ability to make 'rationally transparent' those particular cases in which they apply their implicit grasp of that relationship.

But here too, of course, it is not a necessary condition of people's having an explicit grasp of the means-end relationship that they actually think of or rehearse in internal monologue the abstract content of that relationship.

We may suggest, then, that all the states or occurrences that belong under *hypolēpsis* as a generic term will involve somewhere in their definition a reference to an explicit grasp of some concept or universal proposition in the sense of 'explicit grasp' that I have introduced.

11. Let us now return to *empeiria*. The question that was left hanging was the one of the exact position of *empeiria* in relation to the three critical faculties. Now, after my discussion of the technical grasp of the universal, in which I tried to bring out what the mark of a rational *hypolēpsis* in Aristotle is, we may conclude that *empeiria* is not a state for which reason is responsible: nowhere in the analysis of *empeiria* is there any implication of an explicit grasp of some universal. But Aristotle still claims that *empeiria* is found in

humans alone, and presumably 'not at every age or in every condition' (to quote, once more, *EE* III.x.18, 1226b21-22), but only in sane adults. *Empeiria*, then, is found only where there is also rationality.

I believe that the reason for this is that *empeiria*, though in itself entirely non-rational, is considered by Aristotle as the last step before the coming into existence of the explicit universal grasp, which *is* rational. And I think this is reflected in two elements in the definition of the concept: (*i*) that it is an *actual* memory, and (*ii*) that it is the *connected*, actual memory of a number of cases. *Empeiria* is 'bringing the many into one', which is the last step before the grasp *of* 'the one' (*ii*); and it is an 'explicit' awareness, because actual memory, of certain particulars in a way that is, if not identical with, at least similar to the way in which the resulting grasp of the universal is an explicit one (*i*). One can see, therefore, why *empeiria*, though in itself non-rational, is found in rational beings only, as we concluded from Aristotle's ambiguous remarks in *Metaph.* Alpha 1, 980b25 ff. And it is, I believe, a reflection of this close connection between *empeiria* and *technē* that Aristotle may say, in the passage in the *Metaphysics* on the two concepts that I have been discussing, that it is a matter of *empeiria* to have a *grasp* (*hypolēpsis*) that Kallias was cured in that way, Socrates in the same way, etc. He has just explained how *technē*, which he paraphrases as a universal grasp (*katholou hypolēpsis*), arises from 'the many thoughts of *empeiria*', and he then feels free to use the same term in connection with *empeiria* — almost paradoxically, but in order to bring out the close connection between *empeiria* and *technē*.

But now it is most important that it is elements in the actual definition of *empeiria* that explain why *empeiria* is only found in rational beings. The close connection between *empeiria* and rational knowledge is not due to the fact that in order to account for the state of *empeiria* we will want to introduce the concept of an implicit grasp of some universal. This grasp is, as we saw, not specific to *empeiria*; hence it cannot be the element that accounts for the special connection between *empeiria* and rational knowledge. But from this it follows that 'experience' in our sense of the word not only is not a rational phenomenon, but is not even very closely connected with rational states. Experience, then, or the implicit grasp of the universal, is totally non-rational (in Aristotle's sense of rationality), and if we ask what critical faculty is responsible for it, the answer we shall get is: perception and *phantasia*.

12. We must consider this function of, basically, the faculty of perception in slightly more detail.

In a few, but important, passages Aristotle states that perception, though of course responsible for an awareness of some particular object, nevertheless when grasping that object is also grasping something universal. Thus in *An. Post.* I.31, 87b28–33 he says:

Nor is it possible to 'understand' (*episthasthai*) by perception. For though perception is admittedly of a 'some kind' (*to toionde*) and not of a 'this (whatever it is)' (*tode ti*), it is necessary that one actually perceives a 'this (whatever it is)' and somewhere and now. But it is impossible to *perceive* the universal and what is in all cases (*to epi pasin*); for that is no 'this (whatever it is)', nor (is it) now; otherwise it would not be universal, for we say that (it is) that which is always and everywhere (that) is universal.

I believe that Aristotle's point in claiming that perception grasps not just a 'this (whatever it is)', but a 'some kind' should be distinguished from the one I have been making, viz. that it is the faculty of perception which is responsible for the implicit universal grasp of experience; but the two points are clearly connected. What Aristotle means in the quoted passage is presumably that perception is awareness of some particular *as* of some kind, e.g. red or moving. But he is, I suppose, thinking only of the specific objects of perception, and perhaps only of objects of special perception (like colour) and objects of common perception (like movement). One could at least understand him as saying that the capacity for perception itself, which is an inborn capacity that we have from birth without acquiring it in practice (*EN* II.i.4), is an ability to be aware of and discriminate between particulars, an ability of which one may also say that it involves or is based on a universal grasp, viz. of the perceptual qualities, red, moving, etc. The ability to discriminate between red things and white things is there from the start, and red and white are universals. But this universal grasp, which lies at the base of perception simply as an ability to be aware of and discriminate between particulars, is different from the implicit grasp of a universal that I have been talking of. Where the former is a constituent of the capacity for perception itself, the latter is a state of the capacity for (or faculty of) perception that is not necessarily present just because a being has the capacity for perception: it is acquired or learned at a later stage in life. Where the former type of universal grasp, while certainly a state, is not a state *of* the perceptual capacity, the latter type of universal grasp is: any particular version of this grasp or state may or may not be there without this affecting the perceptual capacity itself.

As examples of such a state, then, I would mention the implicit grasp of experience that accounts for actual perceptions of situations *as* of some kind and the type of grasp of the means-end relationship that will sometimes operate in the behaviour of children. And I would suggest that were we to discuss Aristotle's remark that the perceptual grasp is of a 'some kind', rather than of a 'this (whatever it is)', in connection with *incidental* perception, then the grasp of the universal which we should introduce to account for any particular perception, e.g. of a peach, should also be understood as an acquired state *of* the perceptual capacity, not a state that constitutes capacity in the way in which the universal grasp that lies behind perceptions of red and moving does so.

I wish to claim, then, that the faculty of perception may be invoked not only in connection with perception proper (special, common, and incidental), but also in connection with beliefs about particular situations, or perceptual *phantasiai*, that spring from a state which contains an implicit grasp of some universal connection and which has been acquired from experience. Furthermore, I suggest that we should understand the grasp that accounts for *incidental* perception in the way we should understand the implicit universal grasp of experience. Both are states which, like the states that account for perception of particulars as red and moving, account for perceptions as of some kind, but unlike those former states they are not intrinsic parts of the

inborn capacity for and faculty of perception, but are acquired
states of that faculty.

13. Let me sum up the results of this discussion. I have
tried to work out four different types of 'critical' grasp.
(*i*) First, and at the lowest level, there is the grasp that
constitutes the faculty of perception, the universal grasp of
the perceptible qualities of special and common perception,
e.g. red and moving. (*ii*) Next comes the implicit grasp of
some universal which is a state of the perceptual faculty and
which accounts for perceptions of the objects of incidental
perception, for unreflected reactions in particular situations
due to experience, for the use in particular situations of the
idea of the mean-end relationship, and the like. (*iii*) Thirdly
comes the explicit and connected memory of a number of
particular cases which is Aristotelian *empeiria*. (*iv*) And
fourthly, and at the highest level, comes the explicit grasp
of the universal which is the mark of Aristotelian rationality.

14. Let us go back to the habituated moral virtue from
which we started. If the account I have given of *empeiria*
and a rational *hypolēpsis* is correct, it will follow from what
Aristotle says of habituation that the cognitive grasp which is
part of a habituated moral state will belong at the second of
the four levels I have distinguished. At the same time, however,
it will be clear from my discussion that placing the cognitive
grasp at that level will not at all turn habituation into a
'mindless' process.[10] On the contrary, many highly developed
cognitive states belong at that level. In addition to those
discussed we might mention the skill of the brilliant musical
performer, e.g. the virtuoso on the cithara (*EN* II.i.6). Such
skill is certainly highly developed; in fact, if we may draw
on the way in which Aristotle contrasts *empeiria* and *technē*
in *Metaph*. Alpha 1, the artist who has learned by practising
may perform just as well as the 'technician' in the area (if
there is such a person). The difference is just that the former

[10] Fear of this is, I believe, what accounts for the attempt of some commentators to connect habituation with the use of reason. Cf., e.g., R. Sorabji, 'Aristotle
on the Role of Intellect in Virtue', *PAS* 74 (1973-4), 107-129, esp. pp. 107
and 124-8.

only knows 'the that' (*to hoti*), not 'the why' (*to dihoti*, *Metaph.* 981a29); he does not 'possess a rational account' (*logon echein*), does not 'know the explanation' (*tēn aitian gnōrizein*, 981b6, cf. a30), he does not know (*eidenai*, 981b7). Aristotle's conception of rationality is an exclusive one, and just for that reason excludes cognitive states which in other respects must be rated highly.

6
MORAL INSIGHT
AND DESIRE

1. The preceding chapter has provided a set of premises that I shall make use of in this and the next chapter. The basic question that I want to answer in both chapters is why Aristotle states that moral virtue is acquired by habituation. Habituation is a non-rational process that results in a desiderative state (of the *orektikon*) and a non-rational cognitive state (of the faculty of perception). But why is moral virtue acquired by a non-rational process: what is the rationale behind that claim? I shall discuss the question in a slightly different form: why is the presence of a (good) non-rational moral state a necessary condition for the 'intellectual', i.e. rational, virtue of moral insight, *phronēsis*, to be there?

A few remarks will clarify the content of this question. First, when I talk of a non-rational moral state, I am thinking of either a habituated moral state or of the type of state that Aristotle calls a natural moral state (*physikē ēthikē hexis*). For the latter concept I provisionally refer to *EN* VI.xiii.1-2 and VII.viii.4 (and cf. *EE* III.vii.10-12). We may note in passsing that there is no incongruity between Aristotle's use of the concept of a natural moral state or virtue and his point (in *EN* II.i.2-3) that no moral virtue is present in us by nature (*physei*). Moral virtue is not inborn, in the sense of being always and unchangeably present, as e.g. the capacity for perception is. It may, of course, be present from birth, but it is capable of being changed in other directions. Secondly, my question presupposes that the presence of a non-rational moral state is in fact a necessary condition for *phronēsis* to be there. But this has not been shown. I shall therefore attempt to show both that and why this is so. Thirdly, *phronēsis* is, as we already know, a rational state and consequently a cognitive state, a state whose point is the possession of truth. A non-rational moral state, on the other hand, is both a cognitive state (of the faculty of perception) and a desiderative state (of the *orektikon*). Consquently I need to do two things. I need to show that the rational cognitive state of *phronēsis* presupposes the non-rational *cognitive* state of non-rational moral virtue, and why it does so. I also need to show that the rational cognitive state of *phronēsis* presupposes the *desiderative* state of non-rational moral virtue, why it does, and in what sense of the word 'presuppose'. In the present chapter I shall attempt the latter task, and only in the next chapter turn to the former.

When we bring in *phronēsis*, we move from *EN* II (and III-V) to *EN* VI. I now propose to consider in detail an important passage near the beginning of that book: VI.ii. The passage is extremely difficult and it is necessary to consider certain points in some detail. But I shall use it for wider purposes: to show that *phronēsis* presupposes a certain desiderative state and how it does so (sections 2.1-2.7); to show why it does (sections 3.1-3.2); and to show that *phronēsis* 'presupposes' a certain desiderative state in the sense that such a state must be there *independently* of the cognitive grasp that is *phronēsis* (section 4). In the latter half of the chapter (sections 5 ff.) I shall then try to show, on the basis of other passages, why it is that a desiderative state is presupposed by *phronēsis* in this particular way.

2.1. The context and purpose of VI.ii is this. Following his programme as sketched in *EN* I.xiii.1, Aristotle turns in VI.i.4 from the moral virtues to those of thought: what are they? Thought itself has two parts (i.5-6), the scientific (*epistēmonikon*) and the calculative (*logistikon*). The virtue of either will be found by discovering the proper 'work' of either, i.e. what they are designed to produce. Then follows the crucial passage (ii.1-5, with 6, 1139b5-11 as an appended note), and Aristotle concludes (ii.6, b12-13) that the work of both rational parts is truth, and that correspondingly the virtues he is looking for will be the states in which each part is in possession of truth. In iii ff. he then considers what these states may be.

Against this background one would expect the purpose of

ii.1-5 to be that of showing that the work of each rational part is truth. But what actually happens in the passage differs from this in a number of respects. First, Aristotle almost exclusively concentrates on the 'work' of the calculative part. Secondly, his purpose in the passage seems to be that of showing that that work is truth of a special type, viz. practical truth. But thirdly, the passage seems even more clearly designed to show what follows from this for the understanding of what psychic entities are involved when that work is produced. And here the most basic purpose of the passage seems to be to show that in the production of that work *two* faculties, viz. those of thought and desire, *work together*. Thus while it is clear that ii.1-5 (or 6) as a whole fulfils its purpose in Aristotle's over-all design, it is also evident that he has chosen to bring out in the passage more explicitly and in a more concentrated form than almost anywhere else in *EN* VI certain facts about practical thought.

2.2. In ii.1 Aristotle seems to mention two candidates for what may be the proper 'work' of the two rational parts of soul: *praxis* and truth. In fact, however, it is more likely, considering how the chapter actually develops, that '*praxis* and truth' is intended as a provisional account of the work of the calculative part only. Thus we might say that in ii.2-3, 1139a21-31 Aristotle takes up one part of this account, the suggestion that the work is truth, whereas in ii.4-5 he takes up the other part, the suggestion that the work is *praxis*. I believe, however, that what he wants to say in the two sections is the same.

I translate ii.2-3, 1139a21-31:

What affirmation and denial are in thought, pursuit and avoidance are in desire. So that since moral virtue is a state that issues in *prohaireseis* and *prohairesis* is deliberative desire, the thought must, for these reasons, be true and the desire right if the *prohairesis* is to be good, and what the one asserts and the other pursues must be the same. This (type of) thought and truth, then, is practical; but of thought which is theoretical and not practical (nor, of course, 'poietic') goodness and badness are truth and falsity respectively (for this is the work of any rational part); but of the practical, rational part the work is truth corresponding to right desire.

Aristotle is trying to bring out, on the assumption that the work of the calculative part is truth, how it differs from that of the scientific part: the former is truth of a special type, viz. practical truth or truth corresponding to right desire. But he is also going into detail about the psychic state that is responsible for practical truth. Let us ask: what is practical 'thought' (*logos* and *dianoia*, a24-26) about, and how should we understand the relation of the 'correspondence' of (practical) truth to right desire?

First, however, we should make it clear that the practical 'thought' and truth that Aristotle is talking of in the passage are in fact the reasoning and truth that is part of and results from *phronēsis*. *Phronēsis* is not mentioned in the chapter, and for good reasons in view of Aristotle's strategy from i.4 onwards. Still it is certain, on the basis of *EN* VI.v, and v.8 in particular, that in whatever he is saying of practical rationality in chapter ii Aristotle is in fact talking of *phronēsis*.

What, then, will this reasoning and truth be about? The crucial lines are a22-26. It is normally taken that the 'thought' (*logos*) of a24 represents the rational element in a *prohairesis*, i.e. in what is commonly, and quite rightly, taken to be a decision to perform some particular act in some particular situation, and a decision that has been reached by deliberation. So the 'thought' would be the one that expresses a particular decision to act, together with the one involved in the process of deliberation that leads to that decision. I believe, however, that the 'thought' is implied to contain more. For the normal interpretation, according to which Aristotle is in a24–26 talking of the relationship of thought and desire in a *prohairesis* only, completely neglects the fact that he starts, in a22, not from *prohairesis*, which he might well have done, but from moral virtue. We should take it therefore that in a24-26 he is talking of the relationship of thought and desire *in moral virtue in general*, and that the special case of *prohairesis*, which is the particular decision that moral virtue issues in, is introduced for argumentative purposes only: in the case of *prohairesis* the mutually supporting coexistence of thought and desire that we must reckon with in connection with moral virtue too is particularly clear. So the thought of a24-25 will in fact be the proposition that expresses a *prohairesis* and the reasoning process (deliberation) by which that proposition is reached; but corresponding to the fact that moral virtue is a *hexis*, i.e. a settled state, it will also include *universal* propositions that express what *types* of act moral virtue consists in.

2.3. I have already concluded that moral virtue, as introduced in a22, like the *prohaireseis* in which it issues, will contain a rational element as well as a desiderative one. That rational element, furthermore, is *phronēsis*, although Aristotle does not say so in so many words in the passage. *Phronēsis*, therefore, is the cognitive element in moral virtue of the type introduced in a22, the type that will at the end of the book (VI.xiii) be called *genuine virtue* (*kyria aretē*) as against natural (*physikē*) and (we may suppose) habituated (*ethistē*) virtue. But what, then, is the relationship, in moral virtue of that type, of its two elements, the rational, cognitive one and the desiderative one? Or what, in other words, is the relation of correspondence that holds, according to a30-31, between truth, as the 'work' of *phronēsis*, and the 'corresponding' right desire?

The way in which Aristotle starts the whole section, in a21-22, and the fact that what he goes on to say from there is represented as something that follows from his first remark (cf. *hōste*, 'so that', in a22)[1] suggest that, with my discussion in chapter 5 of Aristotle's account of desire (*orexis*) in mind, we should answer the question as follows. Thought and desire 'correspond' in moral virtue in the sense that desire, as 'bare' desire, provides the element of assertion, and thought the intentional element, both of which are required for there to be a genuine state of desire.

2.4. I retain, then, from these remarks on ii.2-3, 1139a21-31 (*i*) that *phronēsis*, as the cognitive element in moral virtue, includes a grasp of universal propositions that state what

---

[1] The conclusion that Aristotle is driving towards is solely the point made in a25-26 that what thought asserts and what desire pursues is the same. The point made in a24 (that the thought must be true and the desire right) is a subsidiary one only. We may try to capture the semantic point of the pair μέν (a24) – καί (a25) by translating: 'so that since . . . , it will follow that, while the thought must of course be true and the desire right if the *prohairesis* (and the moral state) is to be good, what the one asserts and the other pursues must be the same.'

types of .act moral virtue consists in, and the ability to reach,
by deliberation based on that grasp, particular decisions on
how to act in particular situations; and (*ii*) that *phronēsis*,
as the cognitive element in a genuine state of desire, presupposes a state of desire, viz. the state of 'pure' or 'bare',
non-intentional desire.

2.5. The next two paragraphs run (ii.4-5):

Now of *praxis* the originator is *prohairesis* — as efficient but not as final
cause — but of *prohairesis* it is desire and thought for an end. That is
why *prohairesis* presupposes both reason and thought (*nous* and *dianoia*)
and a moral state (*ēthikē hexis*). For *eupraxia* and its opposite presuppose thought (*dianoia*) and character (*ēthos*). But thought by itself
moves nothing, only thought that is for an end and practical. For that
type of thought is in authority over 'poietic' thought too. For everybody who produces produces for the sake of some end, and the result
that is produced (*to poiēton*) is not an end without qualification — that
thing [sc. the *poiēton*] is (good) relative to some other thing and (the
result) of some particular (process); rather, it is the result of *praxis*
(*to prakton*) that is an end without qualification — for the *eupraxia*
that it [sc. the *praxis*] is, is the end — and the desire [viz. the one that
guides even the *poiēsis*] is for this [viz. the *prakton*]. That is why
prohairesis is either desiderative thought (*orektikos nous*) or rational
desire (*orexis dianoētikē*); and such an originator is man.

In this section Aristotle is discussing the 'work' which is
praxis and which was mentioned, alongside truth, in a18.
In §§ 2-3, 1139a21-31 he was concerned with the work
that is truth, but he now takes up again[2] *praxis* and tries to
show what psychic elements are involved when that work
is the result. I have argued that in his discussion of truth in
the preceding section Aristotle was thinking of the truth of
universal propositions as well as particular ones. In the present
section we should expect him to be talking of the particular
case only, since his topic is *praxis* and, as its psychic counterpart, *prohairesis*. In fact, however, I believe that his account
of what produces *prohairesis* and *praxis* implies the more
comprehensive view that I took to be contained in the preceding section, and indeed that §§ 4-5 presuppose §§ 2-3.

[2] Cf. οὖν (a31). Commentators have found fault with the text of ii.2-5. Thus
Greenwood suggests (pp. 174-5) that 1139a31 ff. should be read directly after
a20, and Gauthier adds (p. 444) that a21-31 may be a misplaced note. I believe
that my account constitutes a defence of the traditional text. Cf. also Stewart's
salutary dismissal of attempts at rearranging the text (II, p. 26).

2.6. There are three considerations.

(*a*) The originator of *praxis*, according to 1139a31, is *prohairesis* — as efficient but not as final cause. Why should Aristotle make the latter point here? It is at least a reasonable guess that he is here implicitly contrasting *prohairesis* as the efficient cause of action, or the initiator in particular situations of particular acts, with those more universal elements in a *praxis* whose existence I suggested was implied in § § 2-3. For the universal grasp of types of act to be done in certain types of situation which if true is part of practical truth may precisely be considered to express the end, i.e. the final cause, of the given *praxis*: the *praxis* is good *because* it instantiates the *type* of. act that is grasped. No doubt, as it clear from what follows, Aristotle also has in mind another final cause of *praxis*, viz. *eupraxia*. But we should precisely say that the universal grasp of types of act to be done expresses what the indeterminate state of *eupraxia* consists in.

(*b*) The originator of *prohairesis* is desire and thought for an end, and Aristotle takes this fact to imply that *prohairesis* presupposes both reason and thought and a moral state (*ēthikē hexis*). But why a moral *state*? The reason seems to be that *prohairesis* is considered as the concrete actualization of a general state (*hexis*), as it was in ii.2-3.

(*c*) In 1139a34 Aristotle gives the following reason why *prohairesis* requires both reason and thought and a moral state: *eupraxia* requires both. (Instead of *ēthikē hexis* Aristotle just says *ēthos*, but this hardly matters.) This point is developed in a35-b4. Thought does not by itself move anything (and the thought that is involved in *prohairesis* does move), only thought which is for an end, in fact strictly 'practical' thought; for that type of thought is the originator of 'poietic' thought too. I have already discussed (in chapter 1, section 9.3) the sense of the latter point: any piece of 'poietic' thought, which is of course also for an end and hence moves, will in the final outcome imply a piece of strictly 'practical' thought that introduces the concept of *eupraxia*.

But then we can see why *prohairesis* requires both thought *and character* (*ēthos*). Aristotle is talking of the *prohairesis* that orginates a *praxis*, not a *poiēsis*. Now the originator of both types of *prohairesis* is desire and thought for an end.

But there is a difference as far as the desire is concerned. Where what the *prohairesis* originates is a *poiēsis*, the desire is wholly derivative: there is a desire for some other thing, viz. the end of the act, and the desire for the act is wholly derived, via the thought that is 'for an end', from the desire for that other thing. When, however, the end or what the thought is 'for' is *eupraxia*, when, that is, the act is a *praxis*, we must use a different model since *eupraxia* is no such thing that a desire for it may ground the desire for something else. However, Aristotle does wish to talk of the type of thought that originates a 'practical' *prohairesis* as being 'for some end'. In chapter 1 I suggested that this may be taken to mean that the act that is originated by such a *prohairesis* is claimed, by means of the phrase 'for the sake of *eupraxia*', to fall under that indeterminate state. I now suggest that in the present passage Aristotle wishes to introduce something determinate as that-for-the-sake-of-which a *praxis* is done, something, that is, that may be a proper object of desire and that may therefore ground the desire for the particular act which is a *praxis*, in a manner that corresponds to the way in which the desire for an act which is a *poiēsis* is grounded in a desire for the end of the act. That determinate thing is the universal type of act that we saw to be grasped when there is truth in connection with moral virtue. This is a proper object of desire and something that may ground the desire for the particular act that instantiates the type. And at the same time, of course, it is an end of the *praxis*-act which does not render that act a case of *poiēsis*. That this is Aristotle's idea is, I believe, implied by his two claims that ('practical') *prohairesis* requires reason and thought *and* a moral *state*, and that *eupraxia*, which is the final cause of *prohairesis*, itself presupposes thought and *character*. But this, of course, is something a reader can only be expected to see on the basis of § § 2-3.

I conclude that § § 4-5 presuppose § § 2-3 and that Aristotle's discussion in both § § 2-3 and 4-5 contains the same doctrine on the co-operation of thought and desire in the production of the 'work' of the calculative part of soul.

2.7. Summarizing we may say that *EN* VI.ii contains the

following picture of the connection between some of the basic concepts in Aristotle's ethical theory. When there is moral virtue, there is a certain grasp of true universal propositions that state what types of act should be done in what types of situation. There is also the realization that the universal propositions that are grasped express what the indeterminate state of *eupraxia* consists in. This grasp and realization expresses truth. The state that contains the grasp is *phronēsis* and the faculty that is responsible for the grasp is the rational one. However, the truth that is grasped is practical: when there is moral virtue, there also is a certain desiderative state, a state of the desiderative faculty. This state provides the element of assertion of the truth that is grasped by *phronēsis*. Furthermore, if we move from the level of universal rationally grasped propositions and settled ethical states, a moral virtue is a state that issues in *prohaireseis* and hence in *praxeis*, both of which are particular things. It follows that when there is a moral virtue, there will be a desire for particular acts which is an actualization of the ethical *state*, and there will be, to correspond, a rational judgement that particular acts are to be done, which is related by thought 'for an end' to the universal grasp and the concept of *eupraxia*.

These were my more general conclusions. I have already made more specific use of the passage in support of my initial claim that *phronēsis* presupposes a certain desiderative state, suggesting that it does so in the sense that *phronēsis* is the intentional element in a full state of desire (moral virtue), which includes, as the asserting element, a state of 'bare' desire. But I shall make further use of the passage for the specific question that concerns me in this chapter, of the relationship between *phronēsis* and desire.

3.1. For now the question arises why *phronēsis*, which is a state of a rational, cognitive part of soul, is the intentional element in a state of *desire* and why, for that very reason, it presupposes a state of 'bare' desire. The answer that is implied in the passage is that *phronēsis*, as the type of thought Aristotle is discussing in the passage, is a cognitive state that is practical in the sense of actually leading to action — and action, according to Aristotle, requires desire. But the crucial question is clearly why *phronēsis* is *necessarily* practical in that sense. Could one not have the rational grasp that is *phronēsis* without it being the case that that grasp is part of moral virtue? Must that grasp be practical in the sense of actually leading to action? The passage implies that it must and that *phronēsis* is always and only a part of moral virtue. So why is that?

3.2. Here we must take into account a point in ii.2-3, 1139a21-31 that I have not yet mentioned. The type of truth discussed here by Aristotle is practical, not just in the sense that it issues in action (and necessarily so), but also in the sense that the acts in which it issues are *praxeis* proper. This is clear from the sentence (a27-29) that follows immediately on the one in which Aristotle has been talking of the type of thought and truth which is practical (a26-27). For here he again talks of practical thought and contrasts it with both theoretical *and* 'poietic' thought. He writes τῆς δὲ θεωρητικῆς διανοίας καὶ μὴ πρακτικῆς μηδὲ ποιητικῆς which we may translate as follows: 'but of thought which is theoretical and not practical (nor, for that matter, 'poietic') ...' The exact wording of this sentence proves that in the preceding sentence he was not thinking of practical thought and truth as something that includes both strictly 'practical' and 'poietic' thought and truth. Rather, he was thinking of strictly 'practical' thought and truth alone. Nor is it difficult to see why; for in the lines that precede he had after all only been talking of thought and truth in connection with moral virtue, and as we know 'moral' and 'ethical' implies 'practical'.

But now if the acts are *praxeis* proper, then the propositions that will be true must have the form 'in this type of situation this type of act should be done — for its own sake or for the sake of *eupraxia*' or 'in this type of situation one should do what is (e.g.) just — for its own sake or for the sake of *eupraxia*' or 'in this type of situation one should do what is noble — for its own sake or for the sake of *eupraxia*'. Such propositions contain evaluative terms that are unconditional. By contrast the evaluative terms that go into propositions that codify *poiēseis* are conditional. What such propositions say is that *if* one wants to bring about a certain thing, *then* certain other things should be done. 'Practical' propositions are not conditional in this way, for here the condition is necessarily fulfilled: nobody will not want to do what he considers choiceworthy for its own sake or for the sake of *eupraxia*. But furthermore, the propositions that express practical truth evidently are not just entertained. If there is truth, if the propositions are 'grasped', they will be asserted. But then it will follow that when a (strictly) 'practical' proposition is truly had (and not just entertained), it will necessarily be acted on, it will necessarily be practical in the sense of issuing in action. For how can one say, and mean, that in a certain type of situation a certain type of act should unconditionally be done without acting accordingly when one finds oneself in a situation of that type?

The reason, then, why the truth that is grasped by *phonēsis* is necessarily practical in the sense of leading to action and hence necessarily presupposes a certain desiderative state is that it is 'practical' truth — and, of course, truth that is asserted.

If this is correct, one can see the profound reason why Aristotle makes his initial point about the identity of rational assertion and denial, on the one hand, and desiderative pursuit and avoidance on the other. If the truth that Aristotle wants to describe as the 'work' of *phronēsis* is strictly 'practical', then if it is asserted, as it must be, it must be acted on; but if it is to be acted on, desire must be there. The presence of desire, then, is required for there to be truth proper of the type that is involved; *for desire provides the asserting element.* So seeing of the type that goes into *phronēesis* necessarily requires a certain desiderative state.

4. But I want to go further. *Phronēsis* necessarily requires a certain desiderative state; but why is this so important a point to make? Suppose it were possible by reasoned argument of some kind, e.g. by following an Aristotelian course in ethics, to acquire universal but wholly specific propositions that state what *eupraxia* consists in. Suppose nothing prevented an Aristotelian course in ethics from leading to a wholly determinate grasp of the good. We know that the

propositions that constitute that grasp will only be genuinely acquired if there is a corresponding desire. Acquiring means coming to possess; hence for the propositions to be acquired they must be asserted, not just entertained; but it is desire that provides the asserting element. But now might it not be the case that if a person comes to *entertain*, by reasoned argument e.g. of the kind that is exhibited in the *Ethics*, those propositions which when backed by desire are part of *phronēsis*, the very fact of his entertaining those propositions as a result of reasoned argument of various types will *generate* the desire to back up his grasp of the propositions and turn that grasp into a proper, asserted grasp?

Aristotle's answer to this question is emphatically negative. In a moment I shall turn to passages from *EN* X and I that show this. Meanwhile let us note that if this were his idea, the point he will be making in *EN* VI.ii will not be a very intersting one — but it looks as if it should be an interesting one. It is not interesting to say that for there to be a rational grasp in the area of moral virtue there must be desire — but that is no problem, for if the grasp is properly backed by argument, desire will come into existence. On the other hand, it is interesting to say that for there to be a rational grasp in the area of moral virtue there must be a corresponding desire which has come to be there *independently* of the rational grasp. This, I take it, is the point Aristotle wishes to make.

Note here that whereas I have argued that *phronēsis* pre-supposes a state of *bare* desire, such a state is an abstraction in the sense that it will necessarily always be combined with the cognitive state (be it rational or non-rational) which provides the intentional element that is asserted by the state of 'bare' desire. The type of desiderative state which must be independently present for *phronēsis* to be there will therefore be a genuine desiderative state which *includes* a cognitive state (and in fact a non-rational one). But the reason why such a genuine desiderative state must be present (and independently so) is that it contains the state of 'bare' desire, which, as I have just suggested, must have come into existence independently of the rational grasp that is *phronēsis*, and is required to turn that grasp into a truly asserted one.

There are two ways in which a desiderative state may be present independently of any rational grasp. It may have been there before the process that led to the presence of that grasp ever started, no matter how we should define its starting-point — e.g. if the desiderative state was already there from birth. Or it may only come to be present at the same time as the rational grasp is being acquired, but still in a way that is independent of the rational grasp. This is what happens e.g. when a person is being habituated. Habituation concerns both seeing and wanting, and if the person who is being habituated is a rational being (a child who is growing up or an adult), the non-rational seeing that is the immediate result of habituation may easily be transformed into a rational grasp. But the point is that though the person comes to see and to want by the same process, his coming to want is not engendered by his coming to see.

I conclude that the desiderative state that is presupposed by *phronēsis* must be there independently of the grasp that is part of *phronēsis*.

5. But why is this so? Why, to return to the formulation of the beginning of this chapter, is it the case that if moral virtue is not already there, it will have to be acquired by the non-rational process of habituation? The answer will evidently lie in a certain view of the relationship of reason to desire. For the grasp that is part of *phronēsis* is a rational one, whereas the process by which the desire may be acquired (if it is not present at birth) is the non-rational one of habituation. In the remainder of this chapter I shall introduce and discuss some texts that show what Aristotle's view of that relationship was.

6.1. We may start by asking in what ways rational reflection might be thought to create new desires. The paradigm of a rationally created new desire is the desire that results from deliberation as described in *EN* III.iii. Here a desire with a new intentional object arises as a direct result of deliberation, which is a rational process. However, as deliberation is described in that passage it is a way of finding technical means to an end that is already desired (see below chapter 7,

section 4). The desire for the means that is created by deliberation is therefore a 'poietic' one. What we are looking for,
by contrast, are ways in which new 'practical' desires may be
created. For the desiderative state that is presupposed by
phronēsis is a state of 'practical' desire.

One such way might be the following. Suppose a person
believes that one should act nobly and wants to act in that
way. Such a person will have a determinate grasp of *eupraxia*
or *eudaimonia*, but a grasp that is so vague and general that
there will be plenty of room left for deliberation about what
type of act will instantiate acting nobly in the particular case.
Here, then, is a situation in which reason might be thought to
create a new desire, moreover a very important one. For
when, in the next chapter, we come to discuss the cognitive
side of *phronēsis*, we shall see that there is a central role for
phronēsis to play in discovering what a view of *eudaimonia*
that is only indistinct, though true enough as far as it goes,
will in practice imply for the question of how to act in a
given particular situation.

Let us note that the new desire that will be created in the
above way is in fact a 'practical' one. For although the
particular desire that results from the deliberation is related
to a *determinate* view of *eupraxia*, viz. the view that one
constituent of *eupraxia* is acting nobly, it is a desire for
what that determinate constituent of *eupraxia is* in the
particular situation, and the act that is the object of the
desire should therefore be understood as directly related,
though of course via the notion of acting nobly, to the end
of *eupraxia*. The act that is the object of the desire will
therefore remain a *praxis*.

But precisely because the relationship of the object of the
newly created desire and 'acting nobly' is that the former is
what the latter *is* in the particular situation, we cannot say that
a genuinely new desire has been created. And in our search
for a rationally created new desire we are therefore confronted
with the more fundamental question whether rational reflection will be able to make a man want to act nobly.

6.2. Now we saw in chapter 2 that in *EN* IX.viii Aristotle
distinguishes between the morally good man, who sees that

he should act nobly, and the many, who do not, in terms of their relationship to different parts of their souls. Where the former 'gratifies' his reason, the latter gratify their non-rational part of soul. He also says that the former loves what he (and any human being) in a favoured sense (*malista*, 1169a2) *is*, whereas the latter do not. Thus he is making use of the idea of one type of person who is in accordance with what he is (in a favoured sense) and another type of person who is not. What this implies will be clear if we consider Aristotle's remarks in the transitional passage in *EN* X between the analysis of pleasure and the discussion of *eudaimonia*, v.8-11.

Each (type of) animal has its proper pleasure, as it has its characteristic activity (*ergon*), viz. the pleasure which is 'in accordance with', or 'perfects', that activity (v.8, 1176a3-5). Thus there is a proper pleasure of horse, dog, and man (a5-6). But in the case of humans (alone, a8-10) there are differences between the things individuals of the species find pleasure in. Some are attracted by some things, others by others (v.9, a10-15). However, what seems pleasant to the good man (*ho spoudaios*) is what is truly pleasant (v.10, a15-19). But why, then, do not all people find those things pleasant? The reason is that 'men may be ruined and spoilt in many ways' (a21, *pollai gar phthorai kai lymai anthrōpōn ginontai*).

Here we again meet the idea of a person (the good man) who is what man is (by implication — for he is neither ruined nor spoilt) and has pleasures accordingly. If, on the basis of this passage, we ask what reason Aristotle might have given for the fact that, as *EN* IX.viii has it, the many do not gratify what they 'really' are (viz. their reason) and consequently do not find pleasure in acting nobly, the answer must be, so it seems, that they are 'ruined and spoilt in many ways'. But in that case it hardly seems likely that Aristotle could also have meant that simply by going through the argument that shows noble behaviour to be part of *eudaimonia* for man the many might mend their ways: how could rational reflection by itself change what is a destruction (*phthora*) and corruption (*lymē*) of the reflecting person?

Similarly if it were suggested that consideration of the

basic argument in the *Ethics*, viz. the *ergon* argument, might make a person want to act morally well, I believe that the passage just paraphrased shows that view to be distinctly un-Aristotelian. What might follow from consideration of that argument for the person who is not already good will just be the realization that since he has the desires he has, he is not in accordance with human nature, but ruined and spoilt.

There are evidently difficulties in such a monolithic view of human nature as the Aristotelian one, but the point is that if one has that view and if, consequently, one sees types of behaviour that do not conform to that view as expressions of a genuine 'deterioration' of human nature, then it is highly unlikely that one will allow reflection the power to set things right.

6.3. It is most important, however, that we do not press the general view of the relationship of reason and desire that I am ascribing to Aristotle. The point is certainly not that reason has no part at all to play in connection with a 'practical' desire. We have already seen that it has. If a person just wants to act nobly, much will need to be done before he will be able to see what to do in particular situations. My claim is only that if a person decides to perform an act which is morally good, then at the basis of his decision, and independently of any reasoning he may have gone through, there will always be a certain 'practical', including a desiderative, attitude of his. No matter how many arguments he may go through, if that 'practical' attitude is not there, he will not end up by deciding to perform the act. So reasoned argument is not sufficient to make a man want to act nobly, but it may well have a very important role to play in making a man see in particular situations what the type of act in fact is which he 'already' wants to do.

7.1. Both points come out in *EN* X.ix.1–8; the former, however, more clearly than the latter. The passage is worth some attention.

Aristotle has been talking of *eudaimonia* and the virtues, of friendship, and of pleasure; but, so he asks, has he concluded his programme? Hardly, for the end in practical matters is not to analyse (*theōrēsai*) and understand (*gnōnai*), but rather actually to perform the acts (ix.1, 1179a33-b2). Therefore, in the case of moral virtue too it is not sufficient to know what it is, but one must (oneself) try to reach the end of having or rather using it, or if virtue is acquired in some other way (than by one's own efforts), then that way should be brought into play (ix.2, b2-4).

It is clear from these two paragraphs that Aristotle distinguishes sharply between knowing what virtue is and possessing it. It is also clear that he takes the only possible result of the kind of discussion of virtue that he has been engaged in to be knowledge of virtue, and in the last sentence of the two paragraphs he more or less clearly talks of other ways (than that of theoretical inquiry) in which one may come to possess virtue.

And in fact the whole direction of his argument in the paragraphs that follow is towards making the two points that what is required for people to become good is that they get the proper training for virtue from childhood and that this is best brought about if they grow up under good laws (ix.8, 1179b31-32). These two points are made in the middle of ix.8, which partly sums up the earlier paragraphs, on the necessity for the proper training for virtue, partly makes a new point, on the need for good laws. Let us consider how, in ix.3-8, Aristotle gets to his conclusion concerning the role of education.

7.2. The paragraphs fall into two sections: ix.3-5 and 6-8 (1179b31). The content of the two sections is rather similar and it has been suggested that they are alternative versions of the same argument.[3] It is true that the remark about an alternative way of 'becoming good' at the end of ix.2 is taken up fairly directly at the beginning of ix.6, where Aristotle starts by enumerating various ways in which people are thought to 'become good'. But I believe that it can be shown that the content of the two sections is rather more different than has been thought, and in an important way

[3] Cf. Gauthier (p. 9).

which makes it possible to detect a progression of the line of thought from §§ 3-5 to 6-8.

The connection between the beginning of § 3 and the two preceding paragraphs is just as close as the one just mentioned between § 6 and the end of § 2. Aristotle starts off in § 3 by stating that arguments (*logoi*) are not by themselves sufficient to make people good, and this is precisely the idea that we detected in his remarks in the two first paragraphs about knowing and possessing and about the possible result of his discussion of various practical concepts in the *Ethics*. Such discussion may make somebody know, e.g. what virtue is, but it will not make him possess virtue: arguments (*logoi*) are insufficient to make people good. What more, then, is needed?

7.3. I paraphrase ix.3-5 as follows. Arguments cannot by themselves make people good. What they can do is to encourage (*protrepsasthai*) and stimulate (*parhormēsai*) those young people who are generous-minded and have a character that is well born and has a true love of the noble. On the other hand, they cannot encourage the many to noble-and-goodness. By nature the many are not (*ou . . . pephykasin*) such as to obey a sense of shame (*aidōs*) nor to keep from what is morally bad, just because it is base. The many have no idea of the noble and truly pleasant. They can only obey fear (*phobos*) and abstain from what is morally bad because of punishment. So if they do what is good, they will do so for fear of punishment. For they live by passion only (*pathei*) and pursue their own (*oikeiai*) pleasures. And what type of argument (*logos*) could remould (*metarrythmisai*) such people? It is impossible (b16-17), or at least not easy (b17), to change (*metastēsai*) what has formed part of people's characters for a long time.

This passage contains a large number of words that are pregnant with meaning. I shall mention only some of them. First, there is the contrast between the effect of reasoned argument on those fortunate people who are well born, and the effect on the many which argument might have been hoped to have, but in fact has not: reason may encourage and stimulate (*p r o trepsasthai* and *p a r hormēsai*), but it cannot remould or change (*m e t arrythmisai* and *m e t a stēsai*). Secondly, the remark that the many pursue 'their own' pleasures and that they have no idea of the truly pleasant points directly back to Aristotle's remarks in X.v.8-11 about the private (*oikeiai*) pleasures of people who are 'ruined' or 'spoilt' and whose pleasures *are* not, therefore, but only *seem* to be pleasures. Thirdly, the concept of living by passion must be mentioned. What is contrasted with living by passion is living in accordance with reason. Two things hold of the person who lives in accordance with reason. First, he will have a settled state of character; for the reason in accordance with which he lives is universal and unless he has a *hexis*, he will not, therefore, necessarily always follow his reason. Secondly, he will have a *good hexis*, moral virtue; for the reason in accordance with which he lives is not just reason but right reason. If this is what living in accordance with reason means, then, by contrast, living by passion will apply to a person who either has a settled state that goes in the wrong direction or has no settled state, but now has one type of passion and now has another.

But now the main point of the passage is surely that in order for reasoned argument to have any effect with respect to making people good it is necessary that the character of the person to whom the argument is directed is already 'attuned' to virtue in such a way that the argument will reinforce a tendency which is already there (hence *protrepsasthai* and *parhormēsai*) instead of effecting a change (*metarrythmisai* and *metastēsai*) in the passions. We may conclude, therefore, for our question whether rational reflection may create new 'practical' desires, that the passage definitely implies a negative answer: creating a truly new 'practical' desire is identical with changing a person's passions, and reasoned argument does not have the 'power' to do that. (For the notion of power cf. ix.3, b8 *ischyein* and ix.6, b24 *ischyei*, to be mentioned in a moment.)

7.4. But then is it impossible, according to Aristotle, to undergo a change in one's passions, to get new, 'practical' desires, to become good? Of course not. For then moral

virtue and vice would be inborn, and Aristotle denied, in
EN II.i.2-4, that they are. In fact this is precisely the point
where habituation comes in. And I believe that the relation
between the two sections, *EN* X.ix.3-5 and 6-8, the first of
which I have just discussed, is precisely that the second more
or less explicitly makes the point that it does not follow
from what was said in the first section that human beings
cannot at all change their passions: they can, there is some
other way, viz. that of habituation.

In the second section Aristotle starts by mentioning three
ways in which people may become good: by nature (*physei*),
by habituation (*ethei*), by teaching (*didachēi*). But the part
of nature is uninteresting, and as for the role of reason
(*logos*) and teaching (*didachē*) its power is limited (b24, *ouk
en hapasin ischyei*): for it to have any effect the soul of the
listener must have been 'cultivated' in advance in its habits
so as to have the proper passions (b24-26). For the person
who lives in accordance with passion would hardly listen to
an argument that dissuades him, nor would he, if he did
listen to it, 'understand' (*synienai*) it (b26-28). And how
would it be possible to change by rational argument (*meta-
peisai*) such a person (b28)? No, 'it seems a general truth that
passion does not yield to reason but to force' (*bia*, b28-29).
So it is necessary that there is in advance a character 'with a
kinship to' virtue, one that loves what is noble and repudiates
what is base (b29-31).

At first sight what Aristotle is saying here seems identical
with what he said in the earlier paragraphs. But there is an
important difference. In the former section Aristotle made
his point about the impotence of reason by considering what
effect reasoned argument will have on people who have
different types of character *by nature*. Note his reference to
the 'nature' of the many (ix.4, b11 *pephykasin*) and the
predicate 'well born' (ix.3, b8, *eugenes*) that is attached to
the character which must be there for argument to have any
effect. In the later section, by contrast, the possibility that
people may have their characters by nature is immediately
put on one side. Instead Aristotle concentrates exclusively
on the idea that in order for argument to have an effect the
character of the person to whom the argument is directed

must be of a certain kind *as a result of habituation* — compare, e.g., his claim that the soul of the listener must have been 'cultivated' in advance (and *nature* hardly 'cultivates' people's minds) in its habits (this is quite explicit).

So while both sections make the same explicit point, viz. that in order for argument to have an effect it is necessary that there be already a character 'with a kinship to' virtue, it is also the case that there is a progression of thought from the earlier section to the later one: while it might seem on the basis of the former section that there is no way in which people may change their passions (they have them by nature and that is that), in the later section Aristotle introduces the idea, which is important to him in the following paragraphs, that passions may of course be changed, viz. by habituation.

7.5. I conclude that *EN* X.ix.1-8 is quite explicit on the power of reason in relation to 'practical' desire. Still the passage does not seem to exclude an important role for reason. Reasoning is not sufficient — but it may apparently be needed; and what is provided by nature or habituation seems to be described as general dispositions: having a character that is well born and has a true love of the noble, liking and disliking nobly, loving the noble and repudiating the base — 'like earth which is to nourish the seed' (ix.6, 1179b26).

In fact, as we shall become increasingly aware, Aristotle seems to vacillate between two views of the role of reason, one according to which reason has no role at all to play in the actual discovery of what should be done (the view represented in the dilemma of *EN* VI.xii.1, see chapter 8, section 2.1), and another according to which, although the person must independently have a basic 'practical' attitude towards acting in a certain way, there is still some room left for reason to discover exactly what should be done in a given type of situation (which seems to be the position of *EN* VI.xiii.1-2, see chapter 8, section 2.9, and chapter 7, sections 5.1-7.7 on deliberation and *phronēsis*).

There is no real inconsistency between these two positions. Aristotle would presumably accept the second as the one that represents the situation as it normally is. What is important, for my general argument in this chapter and in part II of this book as a whole, is that the does allow the *possibility* of the first position. He does this, I suggest, because of the importance he attaches to the point that at the basis of any view of the good life there lies a 'practical' attitude that is there independently of reason and cannot be changed by it. The position that he allows as possible, which is the position that either a natural or (more probably) a habituated moral virtue is sufficient to make a man perform those acts which are good, represents an extreme case, but precisely one that is a direct extension of that other basic point.

8. Before leaving the question as to the rationale behind Aristotle's idea that moral virtue is acquired in a non-rational way, I wish to discuss one more passage that contains the same message as the one I obtained from X.ix.1-8. The passage is one of the ever-fascinating methodological passages in *EN* I: iii.6-7.

Aristotle starts here from the idea which formed his starting-point in X.ix too. The aim of attending a course in ethics is action (*praxis*), not knowledge (*gnōsis*, iii.6, 1095a 5-6). Therefore it will be pointless and useless to attend such a course if one is such as to 'follow one's passions' (a4-5) or to 'live in accordance with passion' (iii.7, a8): the result will only be that one does not act, as one should, on the knowledge one may acquire. What is required, by contrast, is that the listener desires and acts in accordance with reason; then knowledge about these matters will be extremely useful (a10-11).

I have already made clear how I understand the contrast between living in accordance with passion and desiring and acting in accordance with reason. According to that interpretation the person who does the latter will have a settled state of the *orektikon* and a state of the right kind, moral virtue. But then we may well ask: why should the listener be as described in order for the true end of attending a course in ethics to be achieved? He must already have the correct desires, which will make him *act* correctly (this must be the point of *kai prattousi* in 1095a10), but why must he? The answer will surely be that no matter how

cogent the knowledge will be that he acquires, it cannot by
itself effect a change in his passions, cannot make him stop
living in accordance with passion, and cannot therefore make
him have the desires which he must have if he is to act and
put his knowledge into practice. Such a view, then, of the
relation of reason to desire is implied at the very beginning
of the book, as well as at its very end.

9. It is worth going back to *EN* X.ix in order to consider
a few points that show how it is that habituation may accomplish what reason cannot. Passions, Aristotle said, seem to
yield not to reason, but to force (*bia*); when the many do
what is proper, they do so for fear of punishment.

It will be helpful to dwell for a moment on the notion
of force. In *EN* III.i Aristotle more or less explicitly (cf.
i.10, 1110b1-7) distinguishes between two types of acts
that are enforced (*biaia*). There are 'acts' that are enforced
because the agent contributes nothing at all to the act, as
when somebody directs one's hand while one is asleep.
These 'acts' are truly enforced, and they are unintentional
(*akousia*). But there are also acts where the agent does
contribute something but is subject to psychological pressure,
as when a tyrant has one's parents and children in his power
and orders one to perform some disgraceful act (i.3, 1110a
4-7). Such acts are enforced in a different sense, and they
are not unintentional but intentional (*hekousia*), though in
themselves unwished for (*akousia* in a second sense). For
although they are in themselves unwished for, they are
chosen, viz. as preferable to not performing the acts with
the consequence that this would have.

It will be immediately clear that in this analysis of acts
done under psychological pressure the means-end relation
plays an important role. One performs an act which is not
wanted in itself in order to avoid some larger evil. But this is
precisely the mechanism that lies behind the efficacy of
habituation. The person who is being habituated is 'forced'
to do some particular act in order to avoid evils that he takes
to be greater. This is the point of the remark about passions
yielding to force and the mention of fear of punishment.

But then, it will be asked, how will this mechanism, which

trades on the means-end relationship, result in new *passions*, new 'practical' desires – and that, surely, is the whole point of habituation? Aristotle's answer to this question consists in pointing to something that is taken as an empirical fact, viz. that things which are at first felt to be painful are no longer so 'when they have become customary' (*synēthē genomena*, ix.8, 1179b35-36, cf. also *Rhet.* I.10, 1369b16-18). Thus the mechanism of the process of habituation depends for its effect on a fact about the phenomenon of 'custom' (*synētheia*).

10. In the present chapter I have argued, on the basis of *EN* VI.ii, that *phronēsis* presupposes a certain desiderative state (in a sense of 'presuppose' that I have specified), and I suggested that the point that is made in the passage is only interesting if Aristotle's idea is that the desiderative state must be present *independently* of the rational grasp that is part of *phronēsis*. I have further tried to show that Aristotle's view of the relationship of reason and desire is such that he must hold the latter view. Thus if I have succeeded, I have also explained *why phronēsis* presupposes a desiderative state, and why if a person does not yet possess moral virtue, he must, in order to acquire it, necessarily undergo habituation. My discussion in this part of the chapter was centred on the question whether rational reflection is itself sufficient to make a man want to act nobly. I have also briefly suggested how it is that the non-rational process of habituation may accomplish what reason cannot, viz. changing a man's passions.

Before concluding the chapter, I shall turn briefly to a few passages in the *Nicomachean Ethics* that make slightly different points, but agree in claiming that what makes a man's view of practical principles (*praktikai archai*) right (*orthos*) and what makes it false (*pseudēs*) is his desiderative state. It is worth trying to bring out exactly what points Aristotle is making in those passages. They are the following: III.iv.5-6 (1113a31-b2); VI.v.5-6, 1140b11-20; VI.xii.10, 1144a29-b1; VII.viii.4, 1151a15-19.

11.1. We may start from *EN* VI.xii.10. Aristotle's explicit point here is that the state of seeing that is part of *phronēsis* does not come into being without moral virtue (1144a29-30, 36-b1). A (true) practical principle (*archē*, a32) does not appear (*phainetai*, a34) to a man unless he is good.

This may be understood in three different ways. The point might be (*a*) simply that since, as we know from our discussion of VI.ii, the grasp that is part of *phronēsis* is a fully asserted and a 'practical' grasp, for it to be present a certain 'corresponding' state of desire is required. The point might also be (*b*) that not only is a certain state of desire required for there to be a fully asserted grasp, but the desiderative state must be present *independently* of the grasp. And finally the point might be (*c*) that not only are (*a*) and (*b*) true; it is also the case that the grasp *arises* in some way, e.g. by induction, *from* the desiderative state. In the present chapter I shall leave undiscussed what the implications of point (*c*) may be for the question of the role of reason in full moral virtue. Is the role of reason 'only' that it formulates knowledge which is already there as part of the non-rational moral virtue that is presupposed? Or is there a more important role for reason to play? I shall come back to this basic question in the next two chapters.

To return to the passage under consideration: in a moment we shall see that elsewhere Aristotle does wish to make point (*c*), and there may be a hint of it in the present passage when he states (a34-36), in justification of his point about the condition for a true practical principle to appear to a man, that 'vice perverts (*diastrephei*) a man and *makes him have false beliefs* about practical principles.' Still point (*c*) does not seem to be explicitly made in the passage. Point (*a*), on the other hand, seems ruled out by the sentence I have just quoted, which must imply a stronger view. If vice perverts a man and is responsible for (by making him have) his false beliefs about practical principles, the idea can hardly be just that a certain desiderative state is admittedly required for a grasp to *appear* properly, but that this is no problem since if the grasp is sufficiently backed by argument, the desiderative state will come into being. I take it, then, that Aristotle is at least making point (*b*), in fact the point I took him to be making already in VI.ii.

It should be noted that on this reading, and in fact on the

two other possible readings too, I am implying that when Aristotle talks of 'perverting' or 'changing in a bad direction' (*diastrephein*), he is just dramatizing an essentially abstract, 'static' relationship. His point is not that *first* we have a person who has a fully asserted and true grasp of practical principles, and *then* this grasp may be changed in a bad direction due to the bad desiderative state of his soul, since if he at first does have a fully asserted and true grasp, he will not have a bad desiderative state (hence a longer story must be told in order to show why, in the supposed case, he gave up his former view). Instead, Aristotle is wanting to bring out the exact relationship between a man's view of practical principles and his desiderative state when he *is* good or *is* bad. What he is saying is perhaps (*c*), that if a person has a false grasp of practical principles, this is due to the fact that such principles *arise from* the desiderative state of the person and the person in question does have a bad desiderative state, and certainly (*b*), that if a person has a false grasp of practical principles, this is partly due to the fact that he has a bad desiderative state, and that he has it *independently* of what other things, if any, may account for his having the grasp.

11.2. In *EN* VII.viii.4, 1151a15-19 Aristotle again uses dramatic language. Virtue and vice respectively preserve and destroy the (grasp of the) principle (a15-16). I take it that this too is a way of dramatizing an abstract relationship. In that case, in view of the context (a10-14) the point might be taken to be only (cf. (*a*) above) that a certain ethical state is required for the person to be properly convinced of (*pepeisthai*, a13), i.e. to 'have' in the full sense, a grasp of the end. But Aristotle continues in the following way: 'and in acts that-for-the-sake-of-which is a principle in the way in which in mathematics hypotheses are so; neither in the former case, then, nor in the latter is reason the teacher of principles, but (moral) virtue, whether natural (*physikē*) or habituated (*ethistē*), (is the teacher) of having the right belief (*orthodoxein*) about the principle' (a16-19). The reason, then, why a person is properly convinced of the truth of his grasp of the end is that it has been acquired not by rational argument but directly from the person's moral state. Here, then, Aristotle is in fact making point (*c*) above, and since (*c*) presupposes (*b*), we may conclude that point (*b*) certainly expresses an Aristotelian view.

11.3. In *EN* VI.v.5–6, 1140b11–20 Aristotle again talks dramatically. Temperance (*sophrosynē*) preserves (*sōizein*) the grasp (*hypolēpsis*) that is *phronēsis*, viz. the grasp of the good for man. For pleasure and pain do not destroy (*diaphtheirein*) or pervert (*diastrephein*) *any* type of grasp, e.g. those of geometry, but only practical ones. It turns out later that Aristotle's explicit point is slightly different from what we might expect on the basis of the passages already considered. His point is that when a person is perverted by pleasure or pain, no practical principle *whatever* will appear to him. The point is not that he will admittedly have a grasp of a principle but a false one: he will have no grasp at all.

It seems likely that Aristotle is here thinking of a person who has no settled desideratiave state at all. His desires change from one moment to the other, so that he is incapable of keeping in view some more distant end and of subordinating his acts to the achievement of that end. He is in fact like the people described in *EN* I.iii.6–7, 1095a4–11 as living in accordance with passion. But if we continue to understand Aristotle's dramatic language as we did before, his point will be that if a person's character is such that he lives in accordance with passion in that sense, then he will not be able fully to possess a grasp of practical principles; such principles will not fully appear to him at all. Once more the point may be any of the three I have distinguished, and once more the fact that Aristotle is using his dramatic language suggests that his point cannot just be the one made under (*a*). His aim must at least be to indicate the independent role that is played in the formation of *phronēsis* by the desiderative state that is presupposed when *phronēsis* is present.

11.4. *EN* III.iv.5–6 runs:

For each state has its own beliefs about what is noble and pleasant, and what makes the good man most conspicuous is perhaps that he sees the truth in each matter, which makes him a sort of criterion and measure of them. In the case of the many, by contrast, illusion arises due, as it seems, to (bodily) pleasure. For although it is not a good thing, it appears so. So they choose the pleasant as something good and avoid pain as something bad.

I will not discuss the passage in detail. It seems certain that Aristotle is at least here relying on his general thesis that a certain desiderative state must be there independently of any view of what is noble, good, and pleasant for such a view to be genuinely possessed. He may again even be making the stronger claim (c) that such a view arises from the person's desiderative state, but that claim precisely presupposes the former one.

12. I have explained why *phronēsis* presupposes a certain desiderative state and why such a state will have to be present independently of the grasp that is part of *phronēsis*. In so doing I have brought out the rationale behind Aristotle's claim that if it is not present by birth, moral virtue must be acquired by the non-rational process of habituation. In the last few pages of the chapter I have also approached the question of what the role of reason will be if the view I have just stated is correct. That question is the topic of the following three chapters.

7

MORAL INSIGHT
AND DELIBERATION

1. We have seen, in the preceding chapter, that *phronēsis* presupposes a desiderative state which must be present independently of any cognitive grasp that is part of *phronēsis*. In the present chapter I shall discuss (*i*) what types of grasp do go into *phronēsis*, and I shall try to show (*ii*) that when we concentrate on *phronēsis* as a state of cognition too, we shall have to say that it presupposes a certain *non-rational* state. Thus *phronēsis* presupposes not just a desiderative state but also a non-rational *cognitive* one.

This claim can hardly come as a surprise. For we know that *phronēsis* presupposes a desiderative state which is there independently of the grasp that is *phronēsis*; we also know that if this state is an acquired one, it is the result of the non-rational process of habituation; and finally we know that a desiderative state necessarily implies a cognitive one. The interesting point is not, therefore, the claim that *phronēsis* presupposes a non-rational cognitive state, but (*iii*) the question why it does so. By answering that question I shall *eo ipso* answer the question why, if a person is not already virtuous, he must undergo habituation in order to become so, *even with respect to the cognitive side* of being virtuous.

Aristotle's account of *phronēsis* (in *EN* VI) proceeds on the assumption, for which he argues, that there is an especially close connection between *phronēsis* and deliberation. And since his notion of deliberation is articulated in terms of the distinction between means and ends, his account of *phronēsis* relies on that distinction too. Therefore when I claim that *phronēsis* presupposes a non-rational cognitive grasp, I am claiming that it does so both with respect to its grasp of the end and with respect to its ability to find the means to that end. I shall try to show (*iv*) that that is something Aristotle wants to say.

But then if the non-rational grasp that is presupposed, and with respect to means as well as to ends, is paradigmatically part of non-rational moral virtue as the result of habituation, the following question arises: how does the distinction between means and ends in fact fare, in connection with *phronēsis*, if the grasp of both, on the part of the *phronimos*, presupposes the *same* sort of cognitive state, viz. the one that results from habituation? I shall try (*v*) to answer that question too.

The textual basis for my discussion will be passages in *EN* VI. I intend to discuss in some detail *EN* VI.v.1–4, vii.6–viii.9, ix, xi.4–6, thus bringing us, basically, from VI.ii, which was discussed in the previous chapter, to VI.xii–xiii, which will be discussed in the next chapter.

2. I start by introducing two points about *phronēsis* and the *phronimos* which are not elaborated by Aristotle, but are, I believe, certainly presupposed by him: they are two premisses for what he says about *phronēsis*. The first point is that *phronēsis* is always true. Whatever grasp forms part of *phronēsis* is a true one. The second point is that *phronēsis* is an unerring guide to action. The *phronimos* knows what to do in any practical situation. The two points are, of course, different. *Phronēsis* might always be true even if the *phronimos* did not always know categorically what to do. The correctness of the second, stronger point is the more difficult to prove.

The first point is shown to be true by the following lines (*EN* VI.vi.2, 1141a3–5): 'If, then, the states in accordance with which we possess truth and are never wrong about things that do not allow of being otherwise, and also about things that do allow of being otherwise, are scientific knowledge (*epistēmē*), moral insight (*phronēsis*), wisdom (*sophia*), and insight (*nous*) . . .'.

The second point is proved, I believe, by Aristotle's statement that the person who is without qualification good at deliberation, i.e. the *phronimos*, is the man who is *stochastikos*, in accordance with his reasoning, of the best for man that is achievable by action (*EN* VI.vii.6, 1141b12-14). Is Aristotle here saying that the *phronimos* is 'the man who is capable of *aiming* in accordance with calculation at . . .' (Ross, my emphasis)? It is true that *stochazesthai* means 'aiming at'; *stochastikos*, however, (according to Liddell/Scott/Jones, who cite the present passage) means 'skilful in aiming at, able to hit'. It is better, therefore, to take the *phronimos* to be 'the man who can in his calculation *reach* the best . . .' (Greenwood, my emphasis).

For Liddell/Scott/Jones are right about the sense. The term *stochastikos* is rare in Aristotle. In one passage outside the *Nicomachean Ethics* (*Rhet.* I.1, 1355a7) the word is certainly used to signify successful aiming and is connected with the notion of *tychein* (hitting upon). Another passage (*Probl.* XVIII.4, 916b38) is best taken in the same way.[1] The few occurrences of the word in the *Nicomachean Ethics* are to be found in book II, where Aristotle three times describes moral virtue as being *stochastikē* of the mean: vi.9, 1106b15-16; vi.13, 1106b28; ix.1, 1109a22.

In the last passage it certainly means 'able to hit'. For Aristotle adds that his point about moral virtue connects with the point that it is *difficult* to be good, and in the next few lines talks of *finding* the mean (*to meson labein*, ix.2, a25) and *hitting* it (*tou mesou tychein*, ix.4, a34) as the things that are difficult.[2] It is likely, therefore, that it means the same in the two earlier passages.

Two points support this claim. First, just before concluding (in II.vi.13) that moral virtue is a mean since it is *stochastikē* of it, Aristotle points out that the mean is praised and 'is a form of success' (Ross, *katorthoutai*, vi.12, 1106b26-27), and that 'being praised and being successful are both characteristics of virtue' (hence virtue is of the mean). It is clear that Aristotle's explicit aim (in the passage as a whole, starting at vi.4) is to bring out the general connection between virtue and the idea of the mean, but still the introduction of

---

[1] Note, in context, 917a1-2: ῥήτωρ . . . ἀγαθός ἐστιν ὁ δυνάμενος πλέον ἔχειν.

[2] This point is not invalidated by the fact that at ix.3, 1109a30 Aristotle uses *stochazesthai* in its usual sense of 'aiming at'. For here he is talking of the person who does not yet possess moral virtue, but is trying to *become* virtuous.

the idea of succeeding (*katorthoun*) seems significant. In fact, and this is the second but connected point, in the paragraph (vi.14) that immediately follows on the conclusion in vi.13 Aristotle takes up precisely the idea of succeeding (*katorthoun*, 1106b31) and connects it, in the manner we are already familiar with from II.ix, with the point about the difficulty of 'hitting the mark successfully' (to spell out, pleonastically, the sense of *epitychein*, b33).

I conclude that the morally good man of *EN* II is *able* to hit the mean and that the man who is without qualification good at deliberation is *able* to hit on the best thing a man may attain by action.

3. Let us now turn to a point about the *phronimos* which has already been implied: the *phronimos* is (without quali-fication) good at deliberation. The point is basic, as we shall see, to Aristotle's discussion of *phronēsis* in *EN* VI. I shall first go back to the official discussion of deliberation (*boul-eusis*) in *EN* III.iii, move on to the account of good deliberation (*euboulia*) in VI.ix, and eventually discuss deliberation as an element in *phronēsis* on the basis of VI.v.1-4, vii.6-viii.9, and xi.4-6.

4. The passage on deliberation in *EN* III.iii is well known and I shall only extract from it a few important points.

(*i*) There is no deliberation in connection with types of knowledge that are exact (*akribeis*) and self-sufficient (*autarkeis*). Deliberation presupposes that there is a problem to be solved: how should I act? Compare, for the latter point, the idea of 'being in doubt' (*distazein*) that is mentioned in iii.8-9, 1112b2 and 8, and the idea of 'being engaged in a search for how to act' that is mentioned in iii.17, 1113a5. The same idea is expressed in iii.11-12, 1112b20-23, where deliberation is called a *zētēsis*. Deliberation is a search for a solution to a problem.

(*ii*) Deliberation presupposes that there is an end which is (1) kept fixed, (2) achievable by action, and (3) determinate. That the end is kept fixed and is achievable by action is stated fairly explicitly in the text. For the first point see iii.11, 1112b11-16; for the second compare the same passage with the line of thought in iii.1-7, which leads to the claim that deliberation is about things in our power and achievable by action (iii.7, 1112a31 and 34). That the end is determinate is not part of the official doctrine of the passage, but is clear from Aristotle's examples at iii.11, 1112b13-14.

(*iii*) Deliberation, according to the passage, is concerned with the 'poietic' means to a given end, and this is to be understood in the sense that deliberation concerns how in a particular situation to bring about ('poietically') the end. Here care is required. That deliberation is not concerned directly with the end but with means, in the vaguest sense, is immediately clear. That deliberation is concerned with 'poietic' means is not stated explicitly in the passage, but is, once more, clear from the examples given in iii.11, 1112b 13-14. This point should cause no disquiet. It is of course true that Aristotle provides his account of ('poietic') deliberation in order to elucidate the notion of *prohairesis*, and moreover *prohairesis* in its role in the moral area (compare the way in which he introduces the topic of *prohairesis* at *EN* III.ii.1). The fact remains, however, that in III.iii Aristotle discusses deliberation on the model of the type of reasoning that belongs to the productive arts (*technai*). During the last decades this fact has intrigued commentators, but I believe that we have now reached a stage in the exegesis of the *Ethics* at which we may confidently say that it is a basic device of Aristotle's in that work to make use of the immediately more intelligible model of technical reasoning in order to elucidate moral reasoning, which is not 'poietic'. See further sections 5.4 and 12 below.

The claim, by contrast, that deliberation concerns the concrete realization of the end in a particular situation requires discussion and clarification. It seems clear from what Aristotle says in iii.15-16 that deliberation is, as it were, suspended between two poles: the end, which is presupposed (it is an object of desire), and a particular situation, which is an object of perception. Now the end is present to the deliberator's mind in universal form, it is a 'form' (an *eidos*), according to *Metaph.* Zeta 7, 1032b1, that is present in his mind: health, a house, etc. Similarly deliberation will as a rational process proceed at a universal level; it will constantly be directed towards formulating universal rules: in order to produce health in this type of patient one must do this or that type of act, in order to do that one must do this, etc. Deliberation, then, as a rational process, proceeds at the universal level. Still it starts and ends at the concrete level. As for its start, while the end to be achieved is present to the deliberator as a universal, it remains the case that the aim of the deliberator is that the end should be realized in some particular situation or other. What he attempts to bring about is that health is present in *this* man, that there is a house *here*, etc. As for the end of deliberation, what deliberation results in is a reasoned decision to act, a *prohairesis*. But since any act is a particular event in a particular situation, although a *prohairesis* is a decision to perform some *type* of act, it is a decision to perform that type of act in this or that particular situation. Hence stopping one's deliberation at a *prohairesis* presupposes that one believes oneself either to be now in a certain particular situation, or to be able immediately to get into a certain particular situation, in which one may perform the act (type) decided on. Thus while deliberation itself proceeds at the universal level, it is tied at both ends to a particular situation. At one end it is tied to the situation which sets the problem: I must produce health *here* — how can I do that? And at the other end too it is tied to a particular situation: either the situation one finds oneself in at the moment or a situation one believes oneself able to get into without having to do any more deliberation. And this particular situation is the one in which one will put into practice the result of one's deliberation.

It is important to see, and anyway immediately obvious, that the particular situation, or situations, to which deliberation is tied determines the whole way the process of deliberation proceeds. Deliberation consists in bringing the end 'down' to this situation, something one can immediately do; hence, evidently, if one were in a different situation, one's deliberation would proceed differently.

In this way, then, although deliberation itself proceeds at the universal level, it is nevertheless concerned with the question of how to realize the end, or of what steps to take towards realizing it, in some particular situation.

This point is not, I believe, made in Aristotle's remark about the 'last thing in the analysis' which is 'the first thing in the bringing about' (*EN* III.iii.12, 1112b23–24); for both things will be *types* of act. But the point is, I believe, justified on its own. And it receives support from Aristotle's remark (in iii.13) about how a piece of deliberation may come to a stop: either at something which is impossible (*adynaton*) — then one stops deliberating and moves on to something else; or at something which is possible (*dynaton*) — and then one acts. These impossible and possible things are presumably acts as universally described, a token of which one can or cannot bring into being. But whether what one ends up with it something possible or something impossible is a question that depends on one thing alone, viz. whether the situation in which one finds oneself at present, or a situation that one may immediately bring oneself into, is such that it allows a token of the universally described act to be instantiated in it.

I conclude that deliberation as described in *EN* III.iii is a genuine search for a 'poietic' means that the deliberator believes it possible for him to do immediately (either now or in a future situation that he can immediately bring himself into) to a specific (i.e. fixed and determinate) end that is achievable by action.

5.1. So much for the official passage on deliberation. How many of the points that it makes may be taken over when, in *EN* VI, Aristotle comes to discuss deliberation in connection with *phronēsis*? Consideration of the chapter on *euboulia* or good deliberation (VI.ix) will provide part of the answer.

In the first part of the chapter (ix.1–4, 1142a31–b17) the text is slightly disturbed but may fairly easily be remedied.[3] The line of thought is clear. *Euboulia* is contrasted (*i*) with skill in conjecture (*eustochia*) and quickness of mind (*anchinoia*), and (*ii*) with scientific knowledge (*epistēmē*) and belief (*doxa*). For (*i*) deliberation is a rational activity and (*ii*) a search. And Aristotle concludes that *euboulia* is 'correctness of reasoning' (*orthotēs boulēs*).

It is clear from Aristotle's detailed remarks that *euboulia*

---

[3] Gauther/Jolif well sum up textual work on this section.

is neither an ability (a *dynamis*) nor a state (*hexis*). In fact it is not a property of the mind at all, but a type of event (though of course a mental one), viz. the event which is deliberation and which qualifies as good deliberation.[4] If a person is deliberating and if his deliberation proceeds in such a way that it fulfils the conditions for good deliberation, then there is *euboulia*.

In the second half of the chapter Aristotle attempts to define what the correctness of *euboulia* consists in (ix.4–7, 1142b17–33). The passage divides into two. §§ 4–6 work towards a preliminary definition, and § 7 introduces a distinction that leads to the more restricted, final definition. The preliminary definition runs (end of § 6, b27–28): '(*euboulia* is) correctness concerning the means (*kata to ōphelimon*), and for what is proper (*hou dei*) and as and when (is proper).' So *euboulia* concerns the means, but Aristotle has insisted (in § 4, b17–22) that it concerns the means to a good end only (hence 'what is proper' in the definition).

5.2. Now the final paragraph of the chapter. Aristotle introduces (§ 7, 1142b28) the distinction that will lead him to his final definition. The distinction is the same as one already drawn in VI.v.1–2, 1140a25–31 (on this passage, see section 6 below), between deliberating in some particular respect (*kata meros* or *peri ti*) and deliberating with a view to the general end of living well (*pros to eu zēn holōs*). It is possible, so he now says, to have deliberated well both without qualification (*haplōs*) and with reference to a particular end (*pros ti telos*, b29); *euboulia* without qualification is the type of deliberation which is successful in relation to what is the end without qualification (*pros to telos to haplōs*, b30), 'special' *euboulia* is the one which is successful in relation to some particular end.

This distinction is then made use of in the final definition of *euboulia*, which is in fact a definition of *euboulia* without qualification alone. The definition with its introductory premiss runs (b31–33): 'If, then, it is a characteristic of people

---

[4] I am developing here some remarks on *euboulia* by Greenwood, pp. 65–6.

who are *phronimoi* to have deliberated well, *euboulia* will be correctness concerning the means to the end of which *phronēsis* is a true grasp.' Here, in the concluding lines of the chapter, Aristotle suddenly introduces *phronēsis* — but not accidentally. On the contrary, it is quite clear that the lines constitute the culmination of the whole chapter. For although they seem on the surface concerned to define *euboulia* as such, they in fact define *euboulia* without qualification, and if one does work with a distinction between special and unqualified *euboulia*, no account of the concept can avoid discussing the latter species. So Aristotle discusses *euboulia* because, as he implies in VI.vii.6, 1141b12-14, the man who is without qualification good at deliberation (*ho haplōs euboulos*, b12-13) is the *phronimos*.

In that case we may, on the basis of the chapter on *euboulia*, suggest the following answer to the question of what sort of man the *phronimos* is. He is a person who will be engaged, unsurprisingly, in a *rational* process of discovering what to do; he is not just guessing (successfully), as when a man has quickness of mind and displays skill in conjecture, but, of course, deliberating. He is also a man who is engaged in a rational *search* for an answer to the practical question; for *euboulia* is neither scientific knowledge nor belief, but precisely a search (*zētēsis*). Finally, he is a mean who already has a true grasp of the end, the object of his rational search being the means to that end. These three points are precisely what we should expect on the basis of Aristotle's account of deliberation in *EN* III.iii. I have not argued for the interpretation of ix.7, 1142b31-33 that delivers the third point, but we may consider it as certain that what *phronēsis* is there stated to be a true grasp of is the end, not the means: *hou* in b33 refers back to *to telos* in the same line, not to *to sympheron* in the preceding one. In any case I have already argued for a similar view in my discussion of *EN* VI.ii (chapter 6, sections 2.2, 2.7); and when I come, in the next chapter, to discuss VI.xii.7 ff., I shall try to show that the same view is implied in that passage.

5.3. However, the close connection between the chapter on *euboulia* and the discussion of deliberation in *EN* III.iii raises a problem. There we saw Aristotle to be talking of a rational search for means to an end, where 'means' were understood as 'poietic' means. In *EN* VI.ix, by contrast, since he is talking of deliberation in connection with *phronēsis*, he cannot be thinking of a search for 'poietic' means. For *phronēsis* issues in *praxeis* proper. The problem has often been raised, but I do not find it a serious one. We already know from our discussion in chapter 4, sections 2.2–2.3 of *EN* VI.xii.1–5 that Aristotle is quite prepared to use heavily 'poietic' vocabulary while at the same time reinterpreting it to cover the 'practical' case. He will be doing the same in the chapter on *euboulia*.

The more interesting question is, therefore, how the distinction between means and ends fares when reinterpreted in this way. What will the form be of the grasp (of the end) that the *phronimos* already has when he starts deliberating? And what will the form be of the insight (into 'means') that he will end up having as a result of deliberation? These are the two questions that will concern us when we consider VI.vii.6–viii.9 and xi.4–6. For, as I shall attempt to show, the former passage is concerned with the cognitive relation of the *phronimos* to the means, while the latter passage is concerned with his grasp of the end.

6. First, however, I will consider a few points in the passage that introduces *phronēsis* into *EN* VI: v.1–2. It is fascinating to try to follow Aristotle's argument in detail, but I shall be brief on the passage.

Aristotle's aim is to identify *phronēsis* as the special type of state he has introduced at the beginning of the preceding chapter (iv.2, 1140a3–4): a rational state that is 'practical' (in the strict sense, as opposed to 'poietic'). He reaches his aim by showing (*i*) that the *phronimos* is a man who deliberates, and (*ii*) that his deliberation is of a special type (in fact 'practical'). The point (*i*) that *phronēsis* involves deliberation is extremely important for Aristotle's whole account of *phronēsis* in the book. Thus he uses it already in v.3 to distinguish *phronēsis* from scientific knowledge (*epistēmē*), and it constitutes the basis (cf. vii.6) for his account of *phronēsis* in that very informative passage, vii.6–viii.9.

The point (*ii*) that the deliberation involved in *phronēsis* is of a special type deserves comment. It is a characteristic, says Aristotle (v.1, 1140a25–28), of the *phronimos* 'to be able to deliberate well about what is good and beneficial to himself, not in some special context (*kata meros*), e.g. about what is conductive to health or physical strength, but about what is conducive to living well in general (*pros to eu zēn holōs*)'. In view of Aristotle's examples of 'special' and 'general' deliberation it looks as if he has in mind here the distinction between *poiēsis* and *praxis*. For e.g. health will be an obvious example of a result of an act that is a case of *poiēsis*. In that case his talk of a partial end (*kata meros*) and a general one (*holōs*) brings to mind his specific way of distinguishing between *poiēsis* and *praxis* in VI.ii.5, 1139b1–4. What he is saying in v.1 will then be this. In the final outcome any act will have *eu zēn* (living well) as its end — the general, all-comprising end. Nevertheless it remains possible to talk of a particular end of some acts, e.g. health. Such acts are not directly related to living well in general. They are *poiēseis*. Other acts, however, will be directly related to living well in general. They are *praxeis*.

But then the problem returns. Will it be possible, on this understanding of Aristotle's distinction in v.1, to accommodate his explicit point that the general end of living well is an end *for deliberation*, with all that this implies? For we know that deliberation presupposes at least some determinate grasp of the end, since it includes, according to VI.ix.7, a true *hypolēpsis* (grasp) of the end. We also know that the *phronimos* does not start deliberating from scratch, since some grasp of the end is already implied in the non-rational state of desire that is presupposed by *phronēsis*. So will not this determinate grasp express something which is a 'particular' end, and will not, therefore, the act that the *phronimos* decides to do as being conducive to (*pros*) that end be a case of *poiēsis*?

I have touched on the problem before (chapter 6, section 6.1). My answer is negative. For the particular act that the *phronimos* decides to do remains directly related to living well in general because the relation between the particular act and the initial determinate grasp of living well in general is such that the particular act may be said to *be* what the grasp enjoins in the particular situation. Thus if one had an initial grasp of living well in general as being (possibly *inter alia*) acting nobly and some idea of what acting nobly consists in the particular situation, the act that one might decide to do as a result of deliberation would remain a *praxis*, since it would be seen as what the initially grasped type of act would be in the particular situation. By contrast, if one decided to perform a certain act as conducive to health, the relation between the act and health is not such that the act may be regarded as directly related to living well in general.

7.1. Let us now turn to VI.vii.6–viii.9 (excluding viii.1–4, which is definitely out of place: it rudely breaks the intimate connection of vii.7 and viii.5).

From vii.3, 1141a20 onwards Aristotle has been comparing and contrasting *phronēsis* with scientific knowledge (*epistēmē*), theoretical insight (*nous*), and theoretical wisdom (*sophia*). And his explicit aim in vii.6 ff. remains the same (cf. viii.8). The special importance of the new section lies, therefore, in the fact that it throws new light on the type of knowledge that is *phronēsis*.

Aristotle starts from the point that the *phronimos* is first and foremost a deliberator (vii.6, especially 1141b9–10), but the crucial step is taken when he concludes from this, first, that *phronēsis* concerns action (b12), and then, as a consequence of this, that it includes knowledge *of particulars*. The latter point is made at the beginning of vii.7: 'Nor is *phronēsis* about universal things only: it must also know particulars. For it is practical, and action is about particulars' (1141b14–16). The purpose of the rest of the passage is to spell out in detail, as has not been done before, what follows for the concept of *phronēsis* from the fact that it is concerned with particulars.[5]

---

[5] It will already be clear that I take the Greek terms *ta kath' hekasta* and *to eschaton*, in *EN* VI.vii.7 ff., to stand for genuine particulars (although Aristotle will of course in each case be talking of the particular 'as of some kind': a *tode ti*). J. M. Cooper, in his *Reason and Human Good in Aristotle*, Cambridge, Mass., 1975, pp. 33–44 and Appendix, argues that *to eschaton*, and presumably *to kath' hekaston* too (although he is not so explicit on that), refers to *types* of act that a person decides on as a result of deliberation: 'the final outcome of deliberation,

7.2. Aristotle makes a number of points:

(*a*) That *phronēsis* is also knowledge of particulars goes well with the well-known fact that in other areas too certain people who do not know in the full sense, but are experienced (*empeiroi*, 1141b18), are better able to act than others who do know (vii.7, b16-22). Similarly, says Aristotle in viii.5 (1142a11-16), which takes up vii.7 directly, the implied point that *phronēsis* presupposes experience is shown to be correct by the fact that young people may become mathematicians, but not *phronimoi*: *phronēsis* includes knowledge of particulars; particulars become known from experience (*empeiria*); and young people are not experienced, since experience requires a certain amount of time. The first point, then, is that *phronēsis* presupposes *empeiria*. (I should make it explicit that I do not take Aristotle to be using the term *empeiria* here in the restricted sense I attributed to him in the official passages on the concept. Rather, he is using *empeiria* as equivalent to our 'experience'.)

(*b*) But Aristotle has not forgotten that *phronēsis* involves deliberation. A second point, therefore, which is made in viii.7 (1142a20-23), is that deliberation concerns both universal facts and particular ones. The exact relation of this

---

according to Aristotle, is the selection of a specific action and not of an explicitly individual action to perform' (p. 39). And Cooper uses this suggestion for a special interpretation of the relationship between deliberation and the practical syllogism. It is basic, however, to almost everything I say of *phronēsis* in the present chapter that *phronēsis* is taken by Aristotle to be (also) concerned with genuine particulars. It follows that there will be several quite general arguments that may be deployed against Cooper's suggestion. If, however, one concentrates on the immediately relevant passages, one may argue as follows. In some of its instances in the relevant passages the term *ta kath' hekasta* is undoubtedly used by Aristotle to indicate genuine particulars, e.g. in viii.5, 1142a14 (in spite of the example Aristotle gives of *empeiria* in vii.7, 1141b20) and in xi.4, 1143b4. It follows that since it is *a priori* likely that the sense of the term is the same in the other instances too, and since, in the passages in question, Aristotle uses '*ta kath' hekasta*' interchangeably with '*ta eschata*' (cf. xi.3, 1143a32-33 and compare viii.8 (1142a23-25) with vii.7, 1141b14-16), his use of the former term will fix the sense of the latter. As for Cooper's suggestion that deliberation always terminates in a decision to perform a certain *type* of act, I have already (this chapter, section 4) offered an interpretation of deliberation, as described in the official passage (*EN* III.iii), which accommodates Cooper's point while at the same time insisting that deliberation terminates in the decision to perform a certain type of act *in a particular situation*, either now or at some determinate point in the future.

point to the basic claim that *phronēsis* is (also) concerned with particulars is not immediately clear, and I shall return to it.

(*c*) A third point, which is made in viii.9, 1142a25–30 (see below), is that *phronēsis* is a sort of perception.

We shall clearly have gained in insight into Aristotle's concept of *phronēsis* if we discover the connection between these three points. *Phronēsis* presupposes *empeiria* and is a sort of perception, both of which are non-rational phenomena. It also involves deliberation, which is a rational phenomenon. How do the three phenomena work together in *phronēsis*?

7.3. First, however, there are two preliminary points to be made.

(α) The two facts that Aristotle introduces the whole passage in vii.6 by drawing on the connection between *phronēsis* and deliberation and that he explicitly mentions deliberation again in viii.7 show that he is talking of the type of knowledge the *phronimos* must have if he is to be able to find the *means* to some end, of which he has at least some determinate grasp. As described in the official passage, *EN* III.iii, deliberation is, as we know, concerned with means, and the chapter on *euboulia* shows, as we have also seen, that in *EN* VI Aristotle sticks to the means-end view of deliberation in connection with *phronēsis*.

(β) In the passage under consideration Aristotle talks of particulars as opposed to universals: the second preliminary point, therefore, concerns the sense of this claim. Particulars are particulars. However, it is not clear to me that when Aristotle insists that *phronēsis* must include knowledge of particulars (vii.7, 1141b15), he is in fact talking only of particulars in the strict sense. Rather, what he means by 'knowledge of particulars' is knowledge of the world of particulars, empirical knowledge, including even universally formulable (though not, as we shall see, already formulated) empirical knowledge.

I have three connected reasons for this suggestion.

(*i*) Although Aristotle's point that *phronēsis* is a sort of perception evidently does not require that he is talking of empirical knowledge in general (as opposed to the sheer ability to grasp a particular), his suggestion that *phronēsis* presupposes *empeiria* certainly does. For no matter whether *empeiria* is used in the strict Aristotelian sense or in the laxer sense of the English 'experience', the whole point must be that it contains the implicit universal grasp I introduced in chapter 5, section 7.3.

(*ii*) Aristotle himself contrasts the type of knowledge he is ascribing to the *phronimos* with the knowledge of the geometer or the mathematician. But they are evidently just the people to fix on if one is trying to express the concept of empirical knowledge (whether universal or not) by contrasting it with other types of knowledge.

(*iii*) Finally, my suggestion makes good sense of viii.6, 1142a16-20. Here Aristotle adds, in what looks like an appended note, that one may also wonder why a child may become a skilled mathematician, but not 'wise' (*sophos*) in the sense of[6] a natural scientist (*physikos*). The reason, he suggests, is that whereas the objects of mathematics are 'abstract' (*di' aphaireseōs*), the principles of natural science are acquired from experience (*ex empeirias*).

I conclude that Aristotle is in some way trying to say that since *phronēsis* is concerned with action, which is something particular, the *phronimos* must have empirical knowledge.

7.4. But if this is what he means when he insists that *phronēsis* includes knowledge of particulars, what becomes of the contrast with knowledge of universals, which he makes in vii.7, 1141b14-16? And can 'knowledge of particulars' really be taken to mean empirical knowledge in general?

Here we shall be helped, I believe, if we return to the problem of reconciling Aristotle's claim that *phronēsis* presupposes *empeiria* and is a form of perception, with his claim that the *phronimos* is a deliberator, i.e. a person who is engaged in a rational activity.

Deliberation is a process which is rational inasmuch as the deliberator will fulfil the requirements for rationality I specified in chapter 5 (on the basis of *EE* II.x.18-19,

---

[6] This is how I prefer to understand ἤ ('or, to be more precise'), but it hardly matters greatly whether we take Aristotle to be contrasting the mathematician with the natural scientist only or with the 'philosopher' (the metaphysician) as well as the natural scientist.

1226b21-30). He will have a clear grasp of the end (in some determinate form) and will keep in mind, though not necessarily in any 'active' sense, the means-end relationship. The material, however, for his discovery of the answer to practical questions will not always be present to him in rational form. On the contrary, he will quite often have to rely on non-rational experience and on his perceptual 'appreciation' of the situation. But the point is that the process remains one of deliberation, i.e. a rational one, since when he does rely on his non-rational insight, he *rationalizes* it, because he now uses it *in a rational context*. There is no inconsistency, then, in the fact that Aristotle talks of *empeiria* and perception at the same time as he is talking of *phronēsis* and deliberation. Though the *phronimos* genuinely does use his non-rational insight, he nevertheless turns it into rational knowledge by using it in the deliberative context.

But if this is the way to reconcile Aristotle's point about the need for *empeiria* and perception, on the one hand, with his talk of deliberation on the other, then we may suggest that when he concludes, from the fact that *phronēsis* is concerned with action and hence with particulars, that *phronēsis* presupposes *empeiria* and is a form of perception, what he means to say is that *phronēsis* presupposes empirical knowledge which is univeral *but is as yet unformulated*: it precisely becomes formulated when the *phronimos* starts deliberating.

What I am suggesting, then, is this. When Aristotle states that *phronēsis* (also) involves knowledge of particulars, he means to say that it (also) involves empirical knowledge which is not yet formulated universally (but will become so when the *phronimos* engages in deliberation). There are two points, therefore, in his claim that *phronēsis* is also knowledge of particulars. One is that it involves empirical knowledge in general, as opposed to the kind of knowledge that is had, e.g., by a mathematician. And the other is that the (empirical) knowledge it involves is not yet universally formulated: it is the knowledge of non-rational experience.

If this is correct, we may conclude that Aristotle is talking of the knowledge the *phronimos* must have in order to be able to discover the means; that he is claiming such knowledge to be empirical knowledge; that he is implying that such knowledge includes knowledge of universal connections; but that he is also implying that it is non-rational, unformulated knowledge; and finally, that he is envisaging the relationship of such knowledge to deliberation as being that deliberation rationalizes the as yet non-rational, unformulated knowledge that the *phronimos* is required to have.

7.5. I believe that the view I have argued for of the way in which *empeiria* and perception are part of *phronēsis* is supported by the difficult final paragraph (viii.9) of the section we have been considering.

Aristotle is turning from the comparison of *phronēsis* with *epistēmē* to its relation to *nous*:[7] that relation is one of 'correspondence at the other end' (*antikeisthai*, 1142a25). 'For *nous* has as its objects the terms or propositions (*horoi*) of which there is no rational account (*logos*), whereas *phronēsis* has as its object the particular, of which there is no knowledge based on a rational account (*epistēmē*) but only perception . . .' (a25–27).

These lines already throw some light on the idea of 'corresponding at the other end'; but the point will become clearer if we introduce VI.ix.4, 1143a35–b3, which I shall discuss in more detail later. In the latter passage Aristotle speaks of *nous* as concerned with 'ultimates' (*ta eschata*) in both directions, i.e. both with the primary, theoretical terms or propositions (*horoi*) and with the last things in the practical sphere, particulars. I suggest that in viii.9, 1142a25–27 he is relying on the same idea of a similarity between the grasp of ultimates in both directions, but that he is here dividing the task of grasping those things between *nous*, which is said to be concerned with the primary terms or propositions only, and *phronēsis*, which is given the role of grasping the particular, a role that was in 1143a35–b3 also assigned to *nous*.

But why the difference between the two passages? The reason is that whereas, as I shall argue, in xi.4 the grasp of

---

[7] The 'progressive' sense of μὲν δὴ at the beginning of viii.9, 1142a25 shows that Aristotle is starting on a new point, one that concerns the relation of *phronēsis* to *nous* (and not to *epistēmē*). For this sense of μὲν δὴ cf. J. D. Denniston, *The Greek Particles*, Oxford, 1959², p. 393.

practial particulars is ascribed to *nous* in virtue of the fact that it is there seen as leading to, or having as its end, a *universal* grasp, in viii.9 the end of the grasp is the grasp of something *particular*. More of this later.

So *phronēsis* 'corresponds' to *nous* in that they concern things that lie 'above' and 'below' the area covered by *epistēmē* or 'knowledge in terms of a rational account (*logos*)'.

7.6. But *phronēsis* was also implied to be a sort of perception. The second half of viii.9 provides some hints of what type of perception *phronēsis* is. We may note, before considering these difficult lines, that we should expect them to contain at least some indication of how *phronēsis*, as a sort of perception, may be said to *resemble nous* by 'corresponding' to it (albeit 'at the other end').

So what type of perception is *phronēsis*? I shall propose an interpretaion which has not, to my knowledge, been suggested before. I am relying heavily on other discussions of the passage,[8] and I do not attempt to provide any real argument for the truth of my suggestion.

The relevant lines run (a27–30):

(*Phronēsis* concerns the particular, of which there is no *epistēmē*, but only) perception – not the one of the proper sensible objects, but the one by which we perceive in mathematics that the last thing is a triangle. For there too it will come to an end. But this is perception more clearly than is *phronēsis*,[9] though it is of a different form from the one that was initially mentioned.

The following initial account will, I suppose, command general agreement. Aristotle is contrasting two types of perception: (*a*) perception of proper sensibles, and (*b*) the perception by which we perceive that the last thing in a geometrical context is a triangle. And he states that the latter type, (*b*), is more clearly perception than is *phronēsis*, but that it remains different from (*a*).

The description of geometrical analysis in *EN* III.iii.12 throws some light on 'geometrical perception', (*b*). It is the

[8] J. M. Cooper's discussion is particularly helpful, *Reason and Human Good in Aristotle*, pp. 33–41.
[9] At 1142a30 I accept Burnet's suggestion that we should read ἢ ἡ for the ἢ or ἡ of the MSS. Cf. Gauthier's note ad loc.

result of a search (*zētēsis*) — compare the idea of 'coming to a halt' in the present passage (1142a29). So the geometer will start from some problem that he wants to solve. The problem is presumably that of understanding or giving an account of some complex figure, and what the geometer is looking for when analysing the figure is some simple figure that he already understands and on the basis of which he may construct the complex figure, thereby proving his analysis of it to be correct. In that case when he makes a halt at the triangle, his perception of the triangle will contain two elements: (1) he will see that his analysis has led him to a triangle, he actually sees a triangle in the sand or on the paper (if he has performed the analysis by actually drawing the relevant figures) or at least has a *phantasia* of it (if he has gone through the analysis in his mind, cf. *Mem.* 1, 450a1–7); but (2) he will also 'see' or be aware of the triangle *as* the last step in the analysis (and if he wants to go further, as the first step in the construction).

Of these two elements in 'geometrical perception' the former is evidently a straightforward example of 'common' perception. The latter, on the other hand, is none of Aristotle's three types of perception, and hence it is no case of genuine perception at all. It is, we might say, 'awareness of some particular as having a certain role in a special context', but since it is an awareness of a particular, one can understand why Aristotle should be prepared to call it a type of perception too — although perception of a special sort. What the peculiar property of that type of perception is, is also clear from the geometrical case that serves as an example. It is that the particular is perceived as having a certain role in a *rational* context. For geometrical analysis is a rational activity. The geometer keeps in mind a problem to be solved and is looking for ways to solve it. Thus whether one takes (*a*) perception 'of proper sensibles' to stand for perception of special sensibles alone or to include perception of common qualities (since these too might be said to be genuine or proper objects of perception), 'geometrical perception' (*b*) will differ from it in virtue of the fact that it contains what we may call 'contextual perception'.

How, then, are we to understand the type of perception which is *phronēsis*? It is first stated to be like 'geometrical perception', but is then said to be a less clear example of perception than 'geometrical perception'. The straightforward way to understand this is clearly, if my account of 'geometrical perception' was correct, to say that the perception that is *phronēsis* is 'contextual perception', or a grasp of some particular as having a role in some specific, rational context, and just that. For in that case the perception that is *phronēsis* will not contain the element which made 'geometrical perception' close to being a genuine type of perception, but it will contain an element which makes it *like* 'geometrical perception' and indeed distinguishes it from perception proper.

If this is correct, we can see the precise point of Aristotle's talk of a correspondence of *phronēsis* and *nous*, particularly if we may once more draw on xi.4. There, as I have promised to argue, Aristotle states that *nous* grasps practical particulars because the grasp of them is seen as *leading to* a universal, rational grasp. In the present passage, however, the idea may be the different but precisely 'opposite' one (cf. *antikeisthai*) that the grasp of practical particulars that is part of *phronēsis* is rational too in the sense that the *phronimos* grasps the particular 'in the light of' some universal, rational grasp or, precisely, grasps it *in a rational context*. On this reading there is a genuine point to the suggestion of a correspondence of *nous* and *phronēsis*, which there is not if we just take the claim to be that *nous* and *phronēsis* are similar, since they are both a grasp that lies 'beyond' (viz. at either end of) the type of grasp that is *epistēmē*.

7.7. If this interpretation of viii.9 is correct, the passage states exactly what we should expect. Since *phronēsis* is (also) concerned with the particular, it requires perception (and *empeiria*), but this fact does not diminish the rational character of *phronēsis*, since by grasping the particular in a rational context the *phronimos* will rationalize the non-rational insight that accounts for his grasp of the particular. *Phronēsis*, then, corresponds to *nous*, not by being a state that accounts for some special type of rational, 'intuitive' grasp of particulars, but in the way that it makes use of a person's non-rational, empirical knowledge of the world of particulars in the rational, deliberative context of trying to discover what should be done in order to live a life of *eupraxia*. I conclude that there is more or less explicit textual support for the answer I have suggested to the question of how to tie together the concepts of deliberation, *empeiria*, and perception, all of which are mentioned in the section we have been considering (vii.6–viii.9).

8.1. But then comes a crucial question. I have argued that the point of the whole passage we have been considering is that *phronēsis* presupposes non-rational empirical knowledge. We know already that *phronēsis* will presuppose such knowledge. For *phronēsis* presupposes a certain desiderative state, and such a state will necessarily include a certain (non-rational) cognitive state. But why is it that *phronēsis* presupposes *non-rational* empirical knowledge?

This question raises more problems than I shall be able to solve. The connection between VI.viii.5 and 6 shows that the question will include the question of the difference between *phronēsis* and natural science (*hē physikē*, cf. viii.6, 1142a18), on the one hand, and mathematics on the other. This difference, i.e. the one between what I have called empirical and non-empirical knowledge, is described elsewhere by Aristotle (e.g. in *EN* VI.iii.2 and iv.4) as a difference between types of grasp that have as their objects things which may be otherwise and types of grasp which have as their objects things that are 'of necessity'. Aristotle is quite clear throughout his ethical treatises that practical knowledge belongs on the former side, and he repeats the point (see, e.g., *EN* I.iii.4) that such knowledge will as a consequence be knowledge that is only true 'for the most part' (*hōs epi to poly*). But the notions of being capable of being otherwise, as applied to a certain thing, and of being true for the most part only, as applied to a certain type of knowledge, are unclear to me. The following remarks will not, therefore, probe very deeply. Nevertheless, since I believe they do answer part of the general question of the status of 'the area of practice' in Aristotle, they should be made.

8.2. Why, then, is the non-rational insight of experience needed for a man to possess knowledge of matters of practice, viz. either *technē* or *phronēsis*, or knowledge of the matters of nature, viz. natural science (*physikē epistēmē*)? The answer to my question will presumably mention two facts, one about what is known and one about rationality, which when taken together have the consequence that what is known when a man has experience is such that it cannot be learned by rational means.

It is natural to suppose, from my discussion of rationality in Aristotle, that the relevant fact about rationality has something to do with what I took to be a sign of rationality, according to Aristotle, viz. that for a grasp of some universal to be rational it must be immediately formulable in a sentence by the person who has it. But then it may be guessed that the relevant fact about rationality is that any rational grasp may only contain a very limited amount of information. Sentences may not exceed a certain very short length before 'falling apart', and similarly it seems a fact about human beings that they can only 'keep in one view' at any time a relatively small amount of information.

But if this is indeed the relevant fact about rationality, then, conversely, the relevant fact about what is known when a man has experience will be that it is a highly complex set of knowledge and that this complexity reflects a complexity of the practical area itself.

If these are the two relevant facts about what is known and about rationality, then it will follow that what is known when a man has experience cannot be learned by rational means.

But are they the two relevant facts? Here we should remember that when we ask why experience is required for a man to have knowledge in the area of practice, we are at the same time asking for an explanation of Aristotle's claim, as made in *EN* II.i, that knowledge in that area is acquired by habituation. We know that Aristotle is in fact making that claim in that passage. For the moral state that results from habituation is (also) a cognitive state. What, then, is the point of habituation?

Two elements are central in this process: that of repetition, and that of being oneself confronted with particular situations. The point of repetition seems to be that of making the person who is being habituated aware of what elements in a situation are relevant to the question of how to bring about some end. By being repeatedly told in different situations to do the same thing with a view to some end the person will come to classify those different situations as tokens of the same type, and by comparing the various tokens he has been presented with he will become able to see what elements in those situations are the bearers of that classification.

But it is the second element which is important in the present context. For the reason why somebody needs to be actually confronted with particular situations must surely be that only thus will he have any chance of coming to know all those elements in a given situation which play a role in the classification of the situation. It is simply not possible to tell somebody in advance exactly what the relevant features of a situation are for it to require a certain response relative to some end; this is something the person must come to see for himself in and through practice. If this is indeed the point of actually being confronted with particular situations, then knowledge that results from habituation will be particularly rich. But such knowledge is perceptual or non-rational. In that case it is reasonable to suppose that the reason why experience is required for a man to have knowledge in the area of practice is that man's non-rational capacities are better able to do justice to the complexity of the practical area.

8.3. I believe that this interpretation of the role of experience is important for the proper understanding of certain passages in which Aristotle claims a certain priority for perception over reason with respect to coming to a decision about what to do in particular situations. Take *EN* II.ix.8, 1109b20–23, which runs: 'But up to what point and to what extent a man must deviate [sc. from the mean] before he becomes blameworthy, it is not easy to determine in principle (*tōi logōi*). For neither is anything else among perceptible things. Such things belong under particulars, and the decision rests with perception (*en tēi aisthēsei hē krisis*).'

What will explain this failure of rationality (*logos*), and what will explain the corresponding success of perception? In my discussion of Aristotle's concept of rationality I introduced the notion of a perceptual implicit grasp of a universal, and I have just suggested that such a grasp, which is the one that will result from habituation, is better able to do justice to the complexity of the practical area than a rational, explicit grasp of universals will be. It seems to me that precisely this suggestion will make satisfactory sense of the claim that in particular cases the decision rests with perception. If this is correct, it will follow that when Aristotle refers us to perception for a decision about particulars, he is not referring us to some mysterious capacity for intuition. On the contrary, in *EN* II.i he is at pains to emphasize the role of habituation precisely in order to introduce it as one part of a general and systematic theory of how people come to decide about what to do in particular situations. Similarly when he talks of perception in connection with *phronēsis*, he is not performing some desperate move that is intended to introduce perception as an unexplained stop-word for the question of how the *phronimos* may be able to find the proper answer to the practical question. On the contrary, he is incorporating into his account of the deliberation engaged in by the *phronimos* a point about perception and rationality that has been well prepared in advance.

9.1. I have discussed Aristotle's claim that *phronēsis* presupposes non-rational experience in connection with his claim that *phronēsis* involves deliberation, i.e. in connection with the ability of the *phronimos* to discover the means. We shall now concentrate on the grasp of the end which must be there for a man to start deliberation at all. Here too, as we shall see, Aristotle insists on the need for experience. We must consider why, and we shall, as a consequence of that discussion, work towards greater clarity concerning the role of the means-end scheme in connection with the *phronimos* and the type of deliberation he engages in.

9.2. How, then, will a person come to have the more or less determinate grasp of the good which in any particular case is presupposed by deliberation? One answer might be: by reasoning. This answer might seem false on two counts, but I believe neither presents a genuine problem. First, it might be thought that the grasp that is presupposed by deliberation, which is a type of reasoning, cannot itself be acquired by reasoning. This is false. The grasp that is presupposed by deliberation is only kept fixed in the particular context; in another situation it may itself be the object and result of reasoning. Secondly, we know that a fully asserted grasp of the end cannot be acquired by reasoning alone, since a certain desiderative state is presupposed. But this does not, of course, exclude that if that state is present in some general form, e.g. by birth (so-called natural virtue), the cognitive grasp of the end of deliberation might be acquired by reasoning. An example of such reasoning might be the argument that shows acting nobly to be part of one's *eudaimonia*, or in general the type of reasoning that is instantiated in the *Ethics* as a whole.

However, Aristotle does not say that the grasp of the end is acquired by reasoning. I have already discussed (chapter 6, sections 11.1–11.4) certain passages in *EN* VI and VII that imply, and even state, that the true grasp of the end arises from natural or habituated virtue. And I shall now consider a passage in *EN* VI that makes the same point: VI.xi.4–6. This passage makes it explicit that the grasp of the end is acquired by induction (*epagōgē*). Now *epagōgē* is a process that presupposes the faculty of *nous* (in the very mundane sense that possession of *nous* is a necessary condition for a man to have a universal grasp of anything, and if a man has been engaged in *epagōgē*, he will have such a grasp); hence *epagōgē* is to that extent a rational process. But *epagōgē* does not imply genuine reasoning in the sense intended above. So the point stands that the grasp of the end is not acquired, according to Aristotle, by reasoning (in that sense).

But then the question arises whether Aristotle altogether excludes the possibility that reason may have something of its own to contribute to the formulation of the grasp of the end — in addition, that is, to being responsible for the sheer inductive formulation of that grasp. I shall return to this question in the next chapter, where I shall claim that Aristotle does grant an independent role to reason. In the present chapter I shall concentrate on his apparent claim that the grasp of the end is not acquired by reasoning but inductively, based on non-rational, natural or habituated virtue. So VI.xi.4–6.

10.1. The explicit aim of VI.xi.4-5, 1143b5 is to show that *nous* is concerned with particulars. For in that case, as Aristotle argues in xi.2-3, it will join with judgement (*gnōmē*), understanding (*synesis*), and *phronēsis*, which are also concerned with particulars, in 'converging to the same point'. I suggest that we should take this to mean that *nous*, judgement, and understanding distinguish parts of the wider mental state that is *phronēsis*. That at least would fit what Aristotle says, immediately before, of understanding (VI.x) and of judgement (VI.xi.1).

It is not quite clear what is in fact meant by *nous* in the whole of xi.2-6. In § 2 it is coupled with judgement, understanding, and *phronēsis* (1143a26), and Aristotle talks (a27-28) of having *nous* as co-ordinate with having judgement and being *phronimos* and a man of understanding. Judgement, understanding, and *phronēsis* are states of mind and one expects *nous* to be the same. Then, in §§ 2-3, a29-35, Aristotle discusses together the convergence of judgement, understanding, and *phronēsis* and only in § 4, a35 turns to *nous*. Here, moreover, *nous* does not seem to be a state of mind, but a faculty. For it is difficult to understand in any other way the suggestion (see below) that the 'perception' of particulars that one must have if one is to arrive at a universal grasp of the end *is nous*. It seems that *nous* is here the faculty that enables a man to go from a grasp of particulars to a grasp of the end. But then Aristotle later (§ 5, b6 ff.) returns to talking of *having nous* as something co-ordinate with having judgement (b7 and 9) and having understanding (b7), as if *nous* were, once more, a state of mind.

I believe this lack of clarity is revealing. (*a*) 'Having *nous*' (*noun echein*) seems to be an everyday expression for a state of mind which is not necessarily rational. It is 'to have sense, be sensible' (Liddell/Scott/Jones, s.v. *noos* 2.a), i.e. a state of mind which in Aristotle's psychological theory should be placed on the non-rational side. A comparable case is Aristotle's concession that we may even call animals *phronima*, viz. when they seem to have the capacity for foresight concerning their own lives (*EN* VI.vii.4, 1141a26-28), although animals are non-rational. And in fact, as b6 ff.

makes clear (see below), one may 'have *nous*' based on (non-rational) *experience*. (*b*) When, however, in xi.4, a35 Aristotle comes to argue that *nous*, as something one may 'have', is co-ordinate with judgement, understanding, and *phronēsis*, he does so by introducing *nous* in the role of the *faculty* that explains how human beings may acquire a universal grasp of the end, a somewhat different role from the one it plays in 'having *nous*'. For *nous* (the faculty) is certainly a rational phenomenon: it is the faculty that enables a rational grasp to be formed.

Nevertheless, the connection between the two roles of *nous* seems sufficiently close. For *nous* (the faculty) is introduced, not just as the faculty that accounts for a rational grasp, but as the one that allows a man to acquire a universal grasp, in the area of practice, on the basis of the non-rational insight into particulars that he will have if he 'has *nous*'.

This is somewhat to anticipate later conclusions. Let us go back to §§ 4–5 and 5–6 and consider whether the points I have just made concerning *nous* in the former passage and 'having *nous*' in the latter are borne out by the text.

10.2. We already know the beginning of xi.4–5. *Nous* is concerned with ultimates at both ends: primary terms or propositions in connection with (theoretical) demonstrations, and 'in connection with practical "demonstrations" the particular, that which admits of being otherwise, and the minor premiss.[10] For these[11] are starting-points for the that-for-the-sake-of-which. For universals arise from particulars. Of those things, then, one must have perception (*aisthesis*) and that perception is *nous*'. So *nous* is in fact concerned with particulars.

How does Aristotle's argument go? *Nous* in practical

---

[10] I take it that when Aristotle says that *nous* in the practical area grasps 'the minor premiss', he means that it grasps what in a practical syllogism *goes into* or *is mentioned in* the minor premiss, viz. some particular case. He is not yet talking of a practical syllogism, but of what when such a syllogism will be formed will be mentioned in the minor premiss: the particular case. We should understand him, then, as if he were saying that *nous* in connection with practical 'demonstrations' is of τοῦ ἐσχάτου καὶ ἐνδεχομένου καὶ // τοῦ // τῆς ἑτέρας προτάσεως.

[11] αὗται refers back to τὸ ἔσχατον καὶ ἐνδεχόμενον καὶ // τὸ // τῆς ἑτέρας προτάσεως in the preceding line. The gender is due to attraction by the grammatical predicate ἀρχαί.

matters is concerned with particulars — for it is from them that the that-for-the-sake-of-which comes into being. Till now I have taken it without argument that the 'ultimate thing', what admits of being otherwise, and what belongs to the minor premiss all represent particulars. The relation of xi.4 to xi.2–3 warrants this interpretation, and so does the fact that Aristotle inserts his remark that universals arise from particulars. The latter sentence also shows that the context in which practical *nous* is introduced as grasping particulars is the one of the question of how the grasp of the end (the that-for-the-sake-of-which) comes into being. Thus the sense in which *nous* grasps particulars and may therefore be said to join with *phronēsis* and the other states in converging to the same point is that *nous* grasps the end, which is a universal, but *from* a grasp of particulars. I have already said that this indicates that *nous* is here taken to be the faculty that enables a man to arrive at universal grasps from particulars, in fact the faculty that is required for *epagōgē*. And I have also suggested that understanding *nous* in that way does not lead us too far from the way it is apparently understood in the paragraphs that precede and follow § 4, viz. in the phrase 'having *nous*'. But the point that needs emphasis is that *nous*, as one part of *phronēsis*, is said in the passage to be perception and to grasp particulars because Aristotle is asking how the grasp *of the end* that is part of *phronēsis* comes into being. He is not, in this passage, talking generally of a rational grasp of practical particulars, but assigning to *nous* in connection with practice a specific role in *epagōgē* leading to a rational grasp of the end.

10.3. On this reading of ix.4–5 one can see the precise point of the lines xi.6, 1143b9–11, which are normally, and quite rightly, taken by commentators to belong immediately after b5: 'That is why *nous* is both a starting-point and an end. For demonstrations are *from* these (viz. particulars) and *about* them.'

Nous is a starting-point, because practical 'demonstrations' are from particulars: *nous* is required at the start in order to elicit from particulars that universal grasp that expresses what in practical 'demonstrations' is mentioned as the end, such a 'demonstration' being the setting out of a chain of reasons as a result of deliberation. This is the point Aristotle has just been making in xi.4–5, 1143b5.

And *nous* is an end, because practical 'demonstrations' are about particulars: *nous* is at work at the end of the process, when deliberation results in a reasoned grasp of the particular situation that calls for action and in a rational decision (a *prohairesis*) to perform a particular act in that situation. This point, I suggest, is the one Aristotle was making in viii.9.

If this reading of 1143b9–11 is correct, these lines may be seen as summing up very neatly Aristotle's remarks in vii.6–viii.9, where he was talking of the rational grasp of particulars that is involved in deliberation as far as the grasp of the mean goes, and his remarks in both xi.4–5 and, as we shall see, 5–6, where is talking of the rational grasp of particulars that leads to the grasp of the end that is also involved in deliberation.

10.4. Let us consider the remainder of the passage, xi.5–6, 1143b6–9 and 11–14.[12]

That is why those things seem to be natural (*physika*) and why nobody seems to be *sophos* by nature (*physei*) but (people do seem) to have judgement, understanding, and *nous* (by nature). Here is a sign: we believe they follow with age and that a particular age brings with it *nous* and judgement; and we ascribe the cause to nature. . . . Therefore one should attend to the unargued sayings and beliefs of people who are experienced (*empeiroi*) and elderly or *phronimoi* no less than to demonstrations. For since such people have an eye (*omma*) as a result of experience (*ex empeirias*), they see aright.

Aristotle is stating a corollary of the whole of xi.2–5. The types of insight that he has discussed there are 'natural', present 'by nature', 'caused by nature' — and this is presumably connected with the fact that they grasp particulars. But what does he mean? In view of the fact that he starts talking, in the latter half of the quoted passage, of *empeiria*, it is likely that he has in mind a point that is closely connected with his emphasis, as expressed in viii.5–6, on the need for *empeiria* in connection with *phronēsis* and natural science as

---

[12] The division into paragraphs is silly here. § 5 ought to start with διὸ καὶ φυσικὰ . . . , i.e. after (b5) τούτων οὖν ἔχειν δεῖ αἴσθησιν, αὕτη δ᾽ ἐστὶ νοῦς, instead of before it, or even better after (b9–11) διὸ καὶ ἀρχὴ . . . περὶ τούτων, when these lines have been inserted in their proper place between b5 and b6.

against, e.g., mathematics. In that case the sense of saying that the states he has been discussing are natural will be that they 'grow up in us naturally . . . , as we gain experience in life' (Stewart ad loc.). The sense cannot be that the states are 'natural endowments' or states that are either present at birth, like the faculty of perception, or automatically become fully present at some later stage in life, like the capacity for reasoning. Rather, the point must be that if a person leads a certain sort of life and is confronted, as he goes through life, with particular situations and cases of certain types, then due to the capacity he has by nature for experience, for learning by himself from particular cases, he will gradually acquire the states in question without having been taught or having been engaged in a rational search for the insight that they represent. The insight into particulars that is part of understanding, judgement, *phronēsis*, and *nous* (as something one 'has') comes about by itself. The person just sees for himself and 'naturally' learns.

By contrast nobody becomes *sophos* 'by nature'. It is difficult to decide exactly how to translate *sophos* here. Most modern translations talk of being a philosopher or philosophically wise. This seem either too restricted or, if it is intended in a wide sense, entirely unhelpful. But no matter what translation we opt for, the idea must be that insight that is rational in the sense that it is the result of rational analysis (philosophical knowledge, mathematical knowledge or, for that matter, the truly justificatory and explanatory elements in *phronēsis* and natural science, see below) does not arise in a man by itself: it is either taught or acquired by rational analysis engaged in by the person himself.

10.5. In *EN* VI.xi.4-6, then, we have a view of how the end is grasped that is closely similar to the one we saw to be contained in the passages that claim that the true grasp of the end arises from moral virtue. It is true that Aristotle does not in xi.4-6 refer the grasp of the end back to moral virtue, but to experience. But this hardly matters. For although in these contexts Aristotle normally talks of both natural and habituated moral virtue as what gives rise to the true grasp of the end, it is clear, e.g. from *EN* II.i, that the central form of non-rational moral virtue is the habituated one — and this type of virtue includes experience. In fact undergoing habituation is precisely an enforced way of acquiring *empeiria* (at the same time as one is having one's desiderative state adapted). So the grasp of the end arises from (non-rational) moral virtue in the way that moral virtue *qua* a (non-rational) cognitive state of experience of what it would be pleasant to do in different situations delivers material (in the form of *phantasiai aisthētikai*) for the formulation of the inductive universal grasp. This picture will hold for moral virtue as habituated, but not, I suppose, for the other species of non-rational moral virtue, viz. natural moral virtue. Here empirical insight will be at first lacking. The naturally virtuous man has the proper 'bent of character', but he does not always see what act will best express or reach his real aim. In his case there is no need for habituation, since his desiderative state has no need to be adapted. What he needs is precisely experience.

11. But now saying that the insight into particulars that is part of understanding, judgement, 'having *nous*', and *phronēsis* is experience is evidently not saying that such non-rational insight is all that goes into those states. I am only concerned here with *phronēsis*. As far as that state goes, we may say, first, that since, as I have been implying all through, the grasp of the end for which *nous* is responsible is identical with the 'true grasp of the end' which in VI.ix.7, 1142b33 is stated to be (part of) *phronēsis*, *phronēsis* will at least also contain the rational element which is a conceptualization of the non-rational insight, viz. a universal grasp of the end, based on *epagōgē*. And secondly, as we shall see in the next chapter, *phronēsis* contains a whole body of theory that will provide genuine justification of the empirical knowledge as conceptualized.

Nevertheless, it is evident that in connection with the grasp of ends too Aristotle is particularly keen on emphasizing what we may call the empirical content of *phronēsis*. The reason is not difficult to find. The distinctive capacity of the *phronimos* is the one of being able to find in a given particular situation what should be done as part of the good life. This, of course, is a highly empirical job. It requires a grasp of the world of particulars that will make a man see in the particular situation that the act that will possess certain moral properties (of being, e.g., noble or just or courageous) is this or that. Now one could have a view of *phronēsis* according to which the grasp of the end would consist solely, e.g., in the grasp that one should act nobly. In that case the job of finding what acting nobly in fact is, in the particular situation, would be left to deliberation as a process that looks for means. But this picture is unsatisfactory for a number of reasons. First, Aristotle is surely right to stress that human beings in fact come to see what should (unconditionally) be done as they grow up, and hence before being able to formulate and see the truth of such a general idea as that one should act nobly. As they grow up human beings do acquire *some* determinate grasp of the end. And secondly, just because of its generality it is difficult to see how one could attach any sense to the general idea that one should act nobly, unless one were able to 'cash' it in more specific beliefs about what should (unconditionally) be done. It is reasonable, therefore, to say of the end what is said of the means, viz. that the grasp of it requires experience. For the normal case will be that the end, which in any given situation is fixed and to which a means is sought, is not itself just the very vague and general one of acting nobly, but is already more specifically described. We can see, therefore, why Aristotle stresses the importance of practical experience in connection with ends too, and it has become clear that with his introduction of the notion of habituation at the beginning of *EN* II he has been preparing his claim about the role of moral virtue for the grasp of ends too.

There remains the question of the role of reason in connection with the grasp of the end: whether reason has anything to contribute in addition to being responsible for the sheer formulation of the universal grasp that results from *epagōgē*. This question will be discussed in the next chapter.

12. Before concluding the present chapter we should take special notice of a point that concerns Aristotle's use of the terms 'means' and 'end' in connection with the reasoning

engaged in by the *phronimos*. I have at various points in the present chapter claimed that there is no problem about describing that reasoning in terms of the means-end scheme implied in the concept of deliberation and at the same time claiming that what results from such reasoning is a decision to perform an act which is a genuine *praxis*. We have also seen that Aristotle makes the same claim about the necessity for non-rational experience in connection with the grasp of the end that the *phronimos* has and in connection with his ability to discover the means. What both facts point to is the conclusion that in connection with *phronēsis* the sharp distinction between means and ends in deliberation is weakened.

When the *phronimos* deliberates, he will start from some rational grasp of the end, which is based on his moral virtue, his previous experience, and in addition whatever arguments for acting in certain ways he has gone through. (*i*) He believes e.g. that one should act nobly and that to act nobly in this situation will be to act in this or that way, where the description of the act is still a fairly vague one — for if the recommended way of acting is described in wholly specific terms, there will be nothing for him to deliberate about. (*ii*) And he wants to act in accordance with his belief. Starting from there his deliberation will then consist in discovering (by activating his non-rational experience) the means to acting in the ways described, but of course 'means' in the sense that allows the act he eventually decides on to remain a *praxis*. But if his deliberation will in this way consist in narrowing down his initial fairly general grasp of the end to a more specific grasp of it which will fit exactly the situation that he is confronted with, and if, furthermore, this narrowing down will partly include the formulation of more specific, but still universally formulated ways of acting, then the result of his deliberation will be that he has a clearer, because more specific, grasp of the end itself, viz. a clear grasp of what the end consists in in that particular type of situation.

So reason has an important role to play for the discovery of what to do,[13] and Aristotle is well advised to discuss the

[13] My account here is greatly indebted to the paper by D. Wiggins, 'Deliberation and Practical Reason', *PAS* 76 (1975–6), 29–51. The problem of the role of

role of reason on the basis of the conceptual scheme that is implied in the concept of deliberation — although he hardly stresses sufficiently the existence of the whole body of theory that the *phronimos* may bring in in justification of his empirical grasp of the end. (See next chapter.) Nevertheless in connection with *phronēsis* the means-end scheme does not in the end remain so rigid as it is in the technical case.

13. In the present chapter I have been discussing material from *EN* VI that throws light on deliberation as a process engaged in by the *phronimos*. Following Aristotle I have concentrated on the connection between deliberation and the non-rational grasp of particulars, i.e. experience, which is apparently had by the *phronimos* in connection with his grasp of means as well as his grasp of the end. What has been left on one side is an element in *phronēsis* which is not actually mentioned in *EN* VI, but which must nevertheless be taken to belong as part of that state, viz. the element of rational justification of the grasp of the end that arises

---

reason in the discovery of what to do is also the subject of T. H. Irwin's paper, 'First Principles In Aristotle's Ethics', *Midwest Studies in Philosophy, vol. III: Studies in Ethical Theory*, University of Minnesota, Morris, 1978, 252-72, in which he develops the interpretation of the relationship of reason and desire in Aristotelian ethics that he sketched in 'Aristotle on Reason, Desire, and Virtue', *JP* 72 (1975), 567-78. While agreeing with almost everything said by Wiggins and Irwin about the importance and function of practical reason, I believe that they both attach too little importance to the role of non-rational habituated virtue in delivering material for the rational grasp of practical ends. Irwin is unhappy about the parts of the *Ethics* in which Aristotle emphasizes, in connection with the determination of the end, the need for experience, which a man will possess if he has non-rational habituated virtue, and believes these parts inconsistent with the parts in which he implies, in the same connection, the need for deliberation. But they are not — unless one takes the effect of deliberation to be that of providing a genuine change in a man's desires. I have argued that this is not Aristotle's view, but also that it does not follow from this that reason is just 'the slave of the passions'. Wiggins, too, combats the view that it is moral virtue that fixes what the end will consist in in particular situations. I agree that there is plenty of room for deliberation, but insist that there is no actual inconsistency between the two views. When Wiggins ends up by finding at the root of deliberation 'situational appreciation' (Aristotle's *aisthēsis*), he is himself in fact reconciling the two views. For situational appreciation is precisely due to the form of experience which is part of a habituated moral virtue. If, however, Wiggins and Irwin mean to suggest that rational reflection may result in what I have called a genuine change in a man's desires and views of what is good, I believe they are taking an un-Aristotelian view of the matter.

from the person's moral state.

In the next chapter I shall turn to that element and try to show how it should be thought to combine with the inductive grasp of the end. I shall then try to show that although that element must in fact, for a special reason, be thought to be part of *phronēsis*, Aristotle nevertheless toys with the idea that the only rational element in *phronēsis* (as far as the grasp of ends goes) is the one of conceptualization of the person's implicit grasp of the end. I shall discuss what, in that hypothetical case, the point will be, according to Aristotle, of being *phronimos* as opposed to being just non-rationally good.

8
THE POINT OF
MORAL INSIGHT

1.1. We have seen in the previous two chapters that a certain desiderative state and a certain non-rationally cognitive state are required for a man to be, and become, *phronimos*. We have also seen why Aristotle makes that claim. But we also know, of course, that *phronēsis* is a rational state, and we have till now been concerned with two respects in which this is so: the *phronimos* is able to find the *means* to the end by the rational process of deliberation, and he has a rational grasp of that *end* as a result of *epagōgē*. I also suggested, at the end of the preceding chapter, that these two points should not be sharply contrasted. When the *phronimos* deliberates, i.e. seeks for means, he is *eo ipso*, since the area is a strictly 'practical' one, articulating and developing his conception of the end. And with respect to means as well as to ends he will need the kind of non-rational experience that is part of his non-rational virtue.

But the *phronimos* will know more. For he is a man who acts for the sake of the noble. In chapter 2 I developed what follows from this. The *phronimos* will have grasped the two principles of nobility and of utility. He will see that 'the moral question' is the one of how to share natural goods, and he will apply as the criterion for good action insights that are formulated in the two principles. The *phronimos*, therefore, will have a profound insight into the whole human condition, an insight which goes far beyond the mere capacity to see in a particular situation what should be done. Moreover, the insight is of such a nature as to *justify* the grasp that the *phronimos* has of what should be done. The *phronimos* sees that a particular type of act should be done as one thing that constitutes *eudaimonia* (this, of course, follows from the fact that he performs *praxeis*), but the reason why acting in that way is in fact part of the person's happiness is precisely that the act is noble (with all that is implied in this), and reason tells him that acting nobly *is* part of his happiness. So if the idea of acting for the sake of the noble has the sense I have attached to it, and if it has the importance I claim for it, and if, furthermore, the *phronimos* will in fact act for the sake of the noble, we may conclude that *phronēsis* includes insight of the type I indicated.

1.2. But now we know already that this fact is not mentioned in *EN* VI at all. There, at least in the passages we have been considering till now, the rational element in *phronēsis* is stated to consist in (*i*) the ability to deliberate and (*ii*) the simple possession in explicit form of the grasp of the end that is presupposed by deliberation (with all that is implied in the concept of an end, including the reference to *eudaimonia* and *eupraxia*). As we shall see in a moment, Aristotle sticks to this picture in the remaining chapters of *EN* VI, viz. xii–xiii; but here, at least, it is clearer why he does so.

In general, then, we must work with three conceptions or levels of moral goodness. First, there is the state of mind of the person who is morally good by nature or habituation, i.e. non-rationally so. Next, there is the state of mind of the person who in addition to possessing non-rational moral virtue is able to deliberate and has a rational grasp of the end, i.e. the person who conceptualizes his non-rational insight and refers it to *eudaimonia* and *eupraxia*. And thirdly, there is the state of mind of the person who is also able to justify his insight by reference to the notion of the noble, with all that this implies.

I claim, then, that as the *phronimos* is described in *EN* VI he belongs at the second level, and that the purpose of *EN* VI.xii–xiii is to distinguish that level from the first one and to explain why the second level is so important. But if I am right in insisting that there is a third level, viz. that of the *phronimos* as noble-and-good, we must consider why that level is neglected by Aristotle in *EN* VI. Consideration of his reason, as given in VI.xii–xiii, for taking the second level to be important will lead us to an answer to this question.

The ultimate aim will be to define, by making use of the concepts of *praxis* (second level) and the noble (third level), the basic elements in moral goodness according to Aristotle.

2.1. I have already discussed parts of *EN* VI.xii–xiii. For remarks about the structure of the two chapters as a whole see chapter 4, section 2.1. The passage I am concerned with at present is xii.7–xiii.6. Here Aristotle takes up one part of the whole question of the utility of *sophia* and *phronēsis* that he raised in xii.1–2 (1143b18–33). The part is the one that concerns the utility of *phronēsis* for a man who is already good.

xii.1, 1143b21–28 runs:

> For what purpose should one have *phronēsis*? If *phronēsis* is concerned with things just, noble, and good for man, and these are the things that the good man will do, we shall not be better able to act by knowing about them, if, that is, the virtues are states. Similarly (we shall) not (be better able to do) healthy or vigorous things — where 'healthy' and 'vigorous' are to be understood as 'manifesting health or vigour' rather than 'creating them'; for we shall not be better able to act (if we are already healthy or vigorous) by possessing the art of medicine or of gymnastics.

It is most important to see the significance of the fact that Aristotle raises the question of the utility of *phronēsis* in this way. It seems clear that he is in fact drawing on the distinction between the two first levels of moral goodness that I introduced. He is saying, 'Being morally good is (primarily, at least) a question of *acting* well; but this is something that men may do who just have the right moral state, a moral virtue, without *knowing* about acting well. Why, then, should one become better able to act by acquiring *phronēsis*, since *phronesis* is concerned with knowing?'

The distinction is clearly the one between having a non-rational moral state and having a state that involves knowledge. Now we are well prepared for the suggestion that a man may be able to act well without having the relevant knowledge — in the rational sense: he may 'know' how to act without knowing it in that sense. For the moral state that is the result of habituation precisely is a state that will issue in particular (true) judgements (*phantasiai aisthētikai*) of what should be done and a corresponding desire to act in accordance with that judgement. Moreover, we have seen Aristotle stressing, in the earlier parts of *EN* VI, the need for non-rational experience even when a man is fully *phronimos*. So it is eminently natural that he should feel the need to discuss the question he is embarking upon. Indeed, the fact that he raises the question of the utility of *phronēsis* in this particular way supports the view I have developed in the previous two chapters of the importance for *phronēsis* of non-rational moral virtue.

2.2. What, then, is Aristotle's solution to the problem he has raised?

First we should note that there are indications that xii.7–xiii.6, which contains his answer, forms a single connected piece. Just before that passage (in xii.4–6) Aristotle presents three arguments, which I have already discussed in detail, for the claim that both *sophia* and *phronēsis* are useful in certain respects. And immediately after the passage (in xiii.7) he recapitulates two of those arguments, but only in so far as they are concerned with the utility of *phronēsis*, not of *sophia*. The two facts that in xiii.7 he returns to xii.4–6 and that he now concentrates on *phronēsis* alone (for the reason that that is what he has been concerned with in the intervening passage) suggest, though they do not of course prove, that the intervening passage does constitute a single piece.

This is important. For in the passage itself it is rather difficult to see exactly how Aristotle's thought develops from section to section; if, then, we may take it from the very start that the passage forms a connected whole, we may use that suggestion as a guiding principle for its interpretation. Let us suppose, then, that in the passage as a whole Aristotle's basic aim is to show exactly how *phronēsis* is required for a man to be fully morally good, even though he may not by acquiring *phronēsis* become better able to act.

Various points within the passage itself support the view that it constitutes a single piece. Aristotle starts off (beginning of xii.7) in a way that clearly marks off what follows from the preceding arguments: 'Concerning the point that we shall be no better able, because of *phronēsis*, to perform noble and just acts, let us start a little further back and take the follow-ing as our starting-point' (1144a11-13). Now the point from which Aristotle intends to start (introduced, idiomatically, by *gar* in a13) cannot take up less than the following eight lines (a13-20), since they constitute a single sentence. I shall come back to them in a moment. But then if these lines provide what is only a starting-point, unless the text is badly damaged the line of thought that is started in 1144a11(a13) must be continued in a20. This is important since, in the whole of xii.7-xiii.6, the transition in 1144a20 is the most difficult to understand. From xii.8, 1144a20-22 the thought becomes easier to follow. In a20-22 Aristotle introduces two more things, moral virtue (*aretē*) and 'a different capacity' (*hetera dynamis*). He then announces (in a22-23) that both of these need more careful consideration. Accordingly, in xii.9-10, a23-29 he discusses the capacity mentioned, and this discussion, as I shall try to show, leads naturally on to the one contained in xii.10, a29-b1. In xiii.1-2 (1144b1-17) he returns to the other thing mentioned, moral virtue, and his discussion culminates in xiii.3-6, b17-32. Thus the remark about procedure contained in 1144a22-23 may be seen to articulate the whole of the following discussion — a point which is supported by the similarity between the concluding parts of the two sections, i.e. xii.10, 1144a36-b1 and xiii.2, 1144b16-17, and the way they are summarized together in xiii.6, 1144b30-32.

2.3. Let us start the interpretation of xii.7-xiii.6 as a whole. Having stated the problem which is to be solved Aristotle first (xii.7, 1144a13-20) makes the following point. Certain people who perform just acts are not yet called just, e.g. if they only do what the laws bid, or act unwillingly or from ignorance, or for some other purpose, i.e. not for the acts themselves — and this in spite of the fact that they do act as they should and as a man must act if he is to be good. Similarly if one is to be good, one must apparently be in a certain state when performing one's acts: one must perform them '"prohairetically" (*dia prohairesin*) and for the sake of the acts themselves' (a19-20).

Now if the whole passage is to make sense (and I am

supposing it does), it will be natural to conclude, after
1144a20, that in some way the utility of having *phronēsis*
is connected with a man's acting 'prohairetically' and for
the sake of the acts themselves.

However, Aristotle continues as follows: 'Now the *prohairesis* is made right by virtue, but the question of finding
what must be done for the sake of the *prohairesis* belongs,
not to virtue, but to a different capacity' (1144a20-22).
Here Aristotle is probably taking up (compare *oun* at a20)
the third of the arguments that precede our passage, viz. the
one that claims (xii.6) that man's proper job (*ergon*) is
achieved if he has *phronēsis* and moral virtue, inasmuch as
virtue makes the aim (*skopos*) right while *phronēsis* makes a
man able to find the means. But then it is natural to ask the
following two questions. (*i*) Is the 'other capacity' identical
with *phronēsis*? (*ii*) And if this is what Aristotle means, how
is it that the fact that *phronēsis* is identical with that 'other
capacity', which is concerned with means, *explains* why
people who possess *phronēsis* will act 'prohairetically' and for
the sake of the acts themselves? That is, while Aristotle could
mean, by 1144a20-22, that the possession of *phronēsis* is a
necessary condition for a man to be able to act well inasmuch
as *phronēsis* is responsible for finding out what must be done
for the sake of the *prohairesis*, we would, if that were the
case, be entitled to ask him how this function of *phronēsis*
will also make it the case that the possession of *phronēsis* is a
necessary condition for a man's being good in the sense
indicated in 1144a13-20, viz. such that he acts 'prohairetically' and for the sake of the acts themselves.

2.4. However, let us proceed. Having announced that the
two things mentioned, viz. moral virtue and the other
capacity, must be more carefully considered, Aristotle first
discusses the capacity. This turns out to be the one that
people normally call cleverness (*deinotēs*) — for that is
precisely an ability to find the means to a given end. Now
cleverness is peculiar by being morally neutral. It is the
ability to find the means to some end whether that end be
good or bad. Hence it is only when the end is good that
cleverness is laudable, otherwise it is 'villainy' (*panourgia*).

But then if we return to the question whether *phronēsis*, as we were half led to believe from 1144a20-22, is identical with the ability to find means, i.e. with cleverness, it will be immediately clear that the only kind of cleverness that could be identical with *phronēsis* is the one that is laudable. However, I do not think that this is what Aristotle intends to convey. For if we equate *phronēsis* with laudable cleverness, it will still be extremely difficult to see how the possession of *phronēsis* (in that sense) is a necessary condition for a man's acting 'prohairetically' and for the sake of the acts themselves. I suggest, therefore, that we understand 1144a 28-29, where Aristotle states that *phronēsis* is not identical with the capacity he has been considering but presupposes it, as making the point that although the presence of cleverness may well be (and Aristotle states that it is) a necessary condition for a man's being *phronimos*, *phronēsis* is different from cleverness *even in its laudable version*.

2.5. But then, of course, we must ask what more must be part of *phronēsis* for it to be the case that it is the possession of *phronēsis* that makes a man act 'prohairetically' and for the sake of the acts themselves. An answer to this question is contained, I believe, in xii.10, 1144a29-b1.

I have discussed the passage before (chapter 6, section 11.1).

The state of that psychic eye does not come into being without moral virtue. This has been said before and is evident. For reasoning about practical matters has as its starting-point this: 'since the end and the best is x', and this does not appear to a man unless he is good. For vice perverts and makes a man have false beliefs about practical principles. Hence, clearly, a man cannot be *phronimos* without being good.

I take it that the state of the 'psychic eye' that Aristotle is here talking of is a grasp of practical principles and that both the state and the grasp form part of *phronēsis*. Otherwise the concluding words will not make sense. Aristotle's explicit point in the passage will then ᴜᵉ that for a man to have that grasp, or rather, as the talk of false beliefs makes clear, for a man to have a true grasp of practical principles, moral virtue is required.

I have discussed earlier what the exact sense of this may be. The important point in the present context is that the passage clearly implies that the grasp of practical principles is part of *phronēsis*. This is important in several respects. First, it is welcome confirmation of a point I made in chapter 7 (section 5.2), and which should not anyway be doubted (though it has been), viz. the point that *phronēsis* includes a grasp of the end. But secondly, it is precisely the point that will answer the question I raised a little while ago, viz. what more than laudable cleverness will make up *phronēsis*? The answer is that it is the grasp of practical principles.

Moreover, if I am right in insisting on the essential connectedness of whatever Aristotle says from vii.7 onwards, we should see the section I have just discussed as *correcting* an inference one might make on the basis of xii.6, a6-9, and xii.8, a20-22, viz. that the role of *phronēsis* lies exclusively in finding the means. This, apparently, is not true. There is more to *phronēsis* than that.

2.6. If this is a justifiable way of reading a29-b1 together with what precedes, we may now turn back to a20-22. When considering those lines (against the background of a11-20) we asked how we should relate *phronēsis* to the two things that are mentioned there, moral virtue and 'the other capacity' (i.e. cleverness). We have now seen that *phronēsis* is not identified with the other capacity (even when this is laudable), but that *phronēsis* in addition includes a grasp of the principles. That is, *phronēsis* is also involved in connection with the *prohairesis* of a20 which is made right by moral virtue, this *prohairesis* being what is expressed in a practical principle. But it is this fact which shows why, if he has *phronēsis*, a man will act 'prohairetically' and for the sake of the acts themselves.

In order to see how this is so, we must consider, first, what *type* of grasp of practical principles is part of *phronēsis*, according to xii.10, and secondly, why in that same passage Aristotle introduces moral virtue at all. The two questions may be considered together. Suppose I have been right in connecting the point that is made in xii.10 with the one made in a20-22 and a6-9. In that case it will follow from the way in which a6-9, in particular, reminds one of VII.viii.4, 1151a15-19, where, as we saw in chapter 6 (section 11.2),

Aristotle claims that the true belief about the end arises inductively from moral virtue, that he is in fact making the same point in VI.xii.10. I have already discussed in chapter 6 (section 11.1) the problem of the exact sense of the point made in xii.10. I suggested that there is at least a hint in the passage that Aristotle is saying that *phronēsis* requires moral virtue because the grasp of the end that is part of *phronēsis* arises from moral virtue − point (*c*) in that discussion. Now that we have seen the connection of xii.10 with xii.6 (via xii.8, a20-22) and (via xii.6) with VII.viii.4, we can see that there is a stronger justification for taking Aristotle in xii.10 to be making that point.

In that case we shall also know what kind of grasp of practical principles Aristotle is talking of in xii.10. It is that rational grasp of what should be done in certain types of situation which is acquired by induction. It follows that when Aristotle argues, in xii.7 ff., for the need for *phronēsis*, he is arguing that moral goodness of the kind that belongs at the *first* of the three levels I distinguished at the start of this chapter is insufficient: goodness of the kind that belongs at the *second* level is required − in order that a man may act 'prohairetically' and for the sake of the acts themselves.

Now the grasp of practical principles that is apparently part of *phronēsis* will not only be a grasp of universal propositions stating what should be done in certain types of situation. For in xii.10, 1144a32-33 Aristotle gives the following as the form of the starting-point of practical reasoning (deliberation): 'since the end and the best is x'. I take this to imply that the *phronimos* has a grasp that in this type of situation this type of act should be done because that is what *eudaimonia*, which is identical with 'the end and the best', consists in.

Why, then, does Aristotle suddenly make the point, in xii.10, that moral virtue is required for a man to be *phronimos* in the sense of having a grasp of the stated type?

Here, at last, comes the answer to our basic question of how *phronēsis* will secure that a man acts 'prohairetically' and for the sake of the acts themselves. Aristotle is aiming at making the point that if a man is to be good (this was the premiss in 1144a18-19), *he must perform praxeis*. The

requirement that for a man to be good he must act 'prohairetically' and for the sake of the acts themselves is nothing
but the requirement that he must perform *praxeis*. The
praxeis must of course be good, but that is not Aristotle's
point. His point is that for a man to be *truly* good (the
second level), not just non-rationally so (the first level), he
must perform *praxeis* — *and this requires two things*. First,
the man must have a grasp of the *end* of such a kind (*i*) that
it contains a reference to *eudaimonia* (or, we may now say,
eupraxia) — for performing a *praxis* implies bringing the act
under the concept of *eudaimonia* (or *eupraxia*); and (*ii*) that
it contains a specification of *eudaimonia* which is such that
the particular act that is performed may be related directly
to *eudaimonia* even when it is related to it via that specification. And the second requirement is that the man must
want to do the particular act he decides to do irrespective
of any additional reason he may have for doing it. These are
the two things that must hold for a man to perform a *praxis*,
as we saw at the end of chapter 1. And these are the two
things that will hold when a man is *phronimos, if phronēsis
is what xii.10 states it to be*. So *phronēsis*, as described in
xii.10, is in fact required for a man to act 'prohairetically'
and for the sake of the acts themselves. Hence by possessing
phronēsis we do become, not better able to act (as this
turn of phrase was used in xii.1), but able, and now for the
first time, to act in the full and proper sense, to perform
praxeis.

So since *phronēsis* is not just cleverness, even in its laudable form; since it also contains a grasp of the end; since that
grasp is a grasp of what type of activity in a certain type of
situation is *eudaimonia* or *eupraxia*; since that grasp arises
from moral virtue; and since, therefore, the person who has
the grasp will want *anyway* to do the particular acts that are
enjoined by his grasp: therefore possession of *phronēsis* is
what makes a man capable of acting 'prohaireticaly' and for
the sake of the acts themselves.

And we now know why *phronēsis* is required, what the point
of it is: for a man to be truly good, he must perform *praxeis*.

2.7. Let us take up Aristotle's discussion from xiii.1,

1144b1. He now turns to the other thing mentioned in
a20-22, viz. moral virtue. Renewed analysis of that is called
for, he says. 'For in the case of virtue too there is a relationship: as *phronēsis* is related to cleverness — not identical,
but similar to it — so natural virtue is related to genuine
virtue (*kyria aretē*)' (b1-4). Stating that relationship to be
one of 'similarity' is not very revealing. We know of course
from xii.10, 1144a28-29, that *phronēsis* is 'similar' to
cleverness in the sense that it presupposes it, and I have tried
to establish what more is required for cleverness to turn into
phronēsis. Will the same relationship hold between natural
and genuine virtue?

Before commenting on the details of the distinction
between natural and genuine virtue (xiii.1), we may supply
the answer as given in xiii.2. The answer is positive. Genuine
virtue presupposes natural virtue, or at least, in order to
include habituated virtue, non-rational moral virtue. Moreover, just as *phronēsis* and cleverness were said to be not
identical but similar, so the state that results when something
has been added to natural virtue, and which will then be
genuine virtue, is stated to be similar to the state of natural
virtue that was there from the beginning (xiii.2, b13-14).
Now what must be added to natural virtue to make genuine
virtue is *phronēsis*. Aristotle concludes xiii.1-2 as follows:
'So that just as there are two species in the believing part
(*to doxastikon*), viz. cleverness and *phronēsis*, so in the
moral part too (*to ēthikon*) there are two species: natural
virtue and genuine virtue; and of these genuine virtue presupposes *phronēsis*' (b14-17).

2.8. The latter point is the one Aristotle is wanting to
make in xiii.1-2. We must ask, therefore, what the relation
is between that point and the preceding passage, which we
have already discussed (xii.7-10). In particular, does xiii.1-2
throw light on the question of how possession of *phronēsis*
is necessary for a man to act 'prohairetically' and for the
sake of the acts themselves?

The answer to the second question should, I believe, be
negative. For I have argued that that question is already
answered at the end of xii.10. If this is correct, one might

expect the point of xiii.1–2 to be the following. We started from a view according to which it is moral virtue that makes the aim right and *phronēsis* that is responsible for finding the means. Here, as VII.viii.4 makes clear, by 'moral virtue' Aristotle may well mean just non-rational, i.e. natural or habituated, virtue. We then saw that additions had to be made to this picture: *phronēsis* also contains a grasp of the end, and moreover a grasp that arises from the (non-rational) moral virtue. But then if we recall the basic psychological theory I argued in chapter 5 lies behind everything Aristotle says of wanting, viz. that it involves a cognitive component as well as a 'purely' desiderative one, it will be natural to conclude that moral virtue proper is not after all just the desiderative state with its non-rational cognitive component, but the desiderative state which has as its cognitive component the *rational* cognitive state that *phronēsis* was seen to be. And if one wants, sensibly enough, to retain the idea that the type of desiderative state that *gives rise* to *phronēsis*, viz. non-rational moral virtue, is in fact moral virtue, one might wish to distinguish that state as a *form* of moral virtue from the moral virtue that includes *phronēsis* and, since it is apparently required that a man acts 'prohairetically' and for the sake of the acts themselves if he is to be *truly* good, call the latter type of moral virtue *genuine* moral virtue (*kyria aretē*): I take it that this is precisely the point Aristotle wishes to make in xiii.1–2. And I believe this claim is supported by the way he proceeds in xiii.3 ff.

2.9. However, the fact remains that in xiii.1 he argues in a slightly unexpected way.

What he says is, first (b4–8), that although moral properties (being just, 'fitted for moderation', brave, etc.) may in some way be present in people already from birth, we nevertheless consider what is genuinely good to be something that is present in a different way. And then (b8–13) he *explains* this by remarking that natural (moral) states 'are clearly hurtful without *nous*', as the case of children and animals shows. Just as a strong body may stumble badly if it moves around without sight, so in the case of beings who have only natural moral states. But if a man acquires *nous*, he will excel in acting.

Here Aristotle seems to be arguing that *phronēsis*, which is what *nous* must stand for here, is required, not, as I argued, in order to make a man who does the proper acts do them *from the right motive or from the right state of mind* (1144a 18-20), but, at a lower level, in order that he may do the proper acts in the first place, no matter what his state of mind is. *Nous*, and *phronēsis*, is required to make a man *see* what is to be done. I believe that this is an unfortunate move on Aristotle's part. It will, it is true, make it abundantly clear that *phronēsis* is useful — and showing that, as we know, is one basic aim of VI.xii–xiii as a whole. But the suggestion completely neglects the point that is so imporant in the passage in which Aristotle introduces the whole problem of the utility of *phronēsis*, viz. the point that a man may act just as well without *phronēsis* as with it.

I believe, however, that one can see a reason for Aristotle's procedure in xiii.1. The point is that although, if the interpretation I have given above of the aim of xiii.1-2 is correct, Aristotle is intending to make a terminological distinction between genuine virtue and non-rational moral virtue in general, including both natural and habituated virtue, he nevertheless talks of natural virtue alone. But we have already seen (in chapter 7, section 10.5) that there is the difference between natural and habituated virtue that the former may lack what the latter possesses, viz. the amount of experience that is required to make one see exactly how to bring about what one wants to do. It seems to be this fact about natural moral virtue that Aristotle is making use of in xiii.1. But if I am right about the difference between natural and habituated virtue on this point, then he just cannot generalize this argument in xiii.1 to cover habituated virtue too. Hence had he wished to remain entirely faithful to the way in which he introduces the whole problem of the utility of *phronēsis* in xii.1, he would have had to cancel his suggestion that possession of *nous*, and *phronēsis*, affects the very way in which a man acts.

2.10. So at the end of xiii.2 Aristotle has distinguished between natural and genuine virtue and he has stated that genuine virtue presupposes *phronēsis*. At the end of xii.10

he concluded that *phronēsis* presupposes moral virtue. There is no problem here, since the type of moral virtue that is presupposed by *phronēsis* is *non-rational* moral virtue, as I have argued. Everything is ready, then, for the summary: 'It is clear, then, from what has been said that it is not possible to be genuinely good without *phronēsis*, nor is it possible to be *phronimos* without moral virtue.' This summary comes in xiii.6, 1144b30-32. We must consider the intervening passage, xiii.3-5.

2.11. The aim of the passage is twofold. Aristotle first (§§ 3-4) wishes to show that his claim that (genuine) virtue presupposes *phronēsis* has general support. He is not interested in the exact kind of presupposition that is involved, but only wishes to show that others too have believed that virtue 'involves' (in whatever way) *phronēsis*. Socrates, for example, did. He even claimed the virtues to *be* types of *phronēsis*. This was false, but he was right in taking virtue to presuppose *phronēsis*, i.e. in *connecting* it with *phronēsis* (xiii.3, b17-21). And there is another indication (a sign, *sēmeion*) that people take virtue to involve *phronēsis*: everybody will define virtue as a state in accordance with right reason — but right reason is reason in accordance with *phronēsis*. Once more the exact way in which people connect virtue and *phronēsis* is un-important. (They talk of the relationship as the one of being 'in accordance with', *kata*.) The point is that they do connect virtue with *phronēsis* (xiii.4, b21-25).

Aristotle next (xiii.5, b25 ff.) turns to his second aim, which is to clarify the relationship of (genuine) virtue to *phronēsis*. Exactly how does genuine virtue 'involve' *phronēsis*? Now we started from the view that *phronēsis* is a *sine qua non* of genuine virtue. We were then introduced to the Socratic view (call it *A*) that *phronēsis* and virtue are identical, but this view went too far. Socrates was only right in so far as *A* implies the initial, *sine qua non* view. Next we were introduced to a more generally accepted view (call it *C*) that virtue is 'in accordance with' *phronēsis*. 'But we must change the position slightly. For not only the state that is in accor-dance with (*C*) right reason is virtue, but the one that is "with" right reason (*meta*, call this view *B*). But right reason about these matters is *phronēsis*. (So virtue is a state "with" *phronēsis* (B).) Now *Socrates*, to go back to him,[1] believed that the virtues *are* forms of reason (A) — for he took them all to be types of *epistēmē* — but *we* believe that they are "with" reason (B)' (xiii.4, b25–30). So the relation of *sine qua non* is the one of 'with'.

But what is meant? My discussion of xii.7 ff. provides the answer. Genuine virtue presupposes *phronēsis* in the sense that *phronēsis* as a grasp of the end, of what *eudaimonia* or *eupraxia* consists in, is *the cognitive element* (in rational form) *in a state of desire*, the other element being the 'purely' desiderative one that according to *EN* VI.ii 'corresponds to' and 'asserts' the cognitive grasp.

3. Thus at the end of *EN* VI Aristotle at last brings into the open a number of crucial points concerning *phronēsis*. (*i*) *Phronēsis* is not only concerned with the means: it also includes a grasp of the end. (*ii*) This grasp is a grasp of the end as something that is part of *eudaimonia*; and it presupposes and arises from non-rational moral virtue. (*iii*) As a grasp of the end it is the cognitive element in a state that deserves a special name: *kyria aretē*. All of these points have been hinted at or implied earlier in the book, but not stated so clearly as here. The doctrinal connections with VI.ii are particularly close. But then that passage, though well integrated into the whole, does look like an elaboration, at first sight barely intelligible, of earlier material, a sort of brief for the rest of the book. *EN* VI.xii–xiii, by contrast, represents Aristotle's crowning effect.

But the two chapters are also of special interest since, as I have argued, they contain Aristotle's answer to the basic question of the whole point of *phronēsis*. That point is that genuine moral acts are *praxeis*, and that it is the possession of *phronēsis*, as a grasp of the end which brings it under the concept of *eudaimonia* and presupposes non-rational moral virtue (points *i* and *ii* above), which makes a man perform (good) *praxeis*.

---

[1] Cf. 1144b28–29 Σωκράτης μὲν οὖν with my remark on 1139a31 πράξεως μὲν οὖν in chapter 6, section 2.5 (with n. 2).

4. But then the problem I sketched at the beginning of this chapter (sections 1.1–1.2) will be felt even more acutely. If the *phronimos* is not just a man who performs (good) *praxeis*, but also one who has the rational grasp that is implied in acting for the sake of the noble; if, that is, true moral goodness belongs at the third level rather than at the second one, then why is Aristotle content to place the good man at the second level only and to contrast him only with the man who belongs at the first level?

I believe that there are two reasons for this. But I shall reserve the second one for the next chapter.

5. The first reason is that when he comes to develop in *EN* VI the concept of rational moral insight, Aristotle wishes to concentrate on a type of insight which is necessarily motivational.

This point does not require much discussion. *Phronēsis*, as the concept is developed in *EN* VI, is a state of mind that rationalizes the desiderative attitude of the agent and his non-rational beliefs about what should be done by bringing them under the concept of *eudaimonia*. This is true of *phronēsis* both as a state of mind that contains a universal grasp of the good already formulated and as a state of mind that makes a person able to *discover* (by deliberation) what should be done, in situations in which this is not yet clear to him. Therefore since *phronēsis* presupposes a certain desiderative state, it is necessarily motivational. A person who has *phronēsis*, as the concept is described at the second level of moral goodness, is *praktikos* not just in the sense that he is able to act correctly, or that his acts are *praxeis* proper, but in the sense that he *will* act (and in the right way).

The insight, on the other hand, that is brought in when we move from the second to the third level of moral goodness, i.e. when we move to genuine noble-and-goodness, is not by itself motivational. A person may see and believe that human happiness consists, in part, in noble behaviour, and he may see and believe that acts are noble if they possess the features I brought out in chapter 2. But he may still decide that such insight, though of course relevant to his own case, is not binding for his own behaviour. For nothing prevents him from choosing to be 'less than human', and hence from opting for a type of happiness that is 'less than human'. By contrast, the insight that goes into *phronēsis*, as the concept is developed in *EN* VI, cannot at all be properly had unless one has the corresponding desiderative state. That type of insight, then, but not the one that is added at the third level, is by itself, necessarily motivational. And if it is asked why Aristotle wishes to pay special attention to the element in full *phronēsis* that makes it motivational, the answer seems simple. The type of insight he is discussing is after all *moral* insight, and the whole point of insight in that area lies in action — just as, as Aristotle stresses over and over again, the point of engaging in the study of ethical theory lies in action as opposed to mere knowledge.

I conclude that there is at least one good reason why Aristotle should concentrate on the second level of moral goodness. In the next chapter I shall discuss a second reason, which resides in his view of human responsibility for moral acts.

9

MORAL INSIGHT
AND RESPONSIBILITY

1. At the end of the preceding chapter I offered one reason why Aristotle emphasizes the second level of moral goodness that I distinguished, as against the third one. I shall now offer one more reason for his emphasis on moral acts as *praxeis*, but this time a reason that stresses the importance of that second level as compared with the first one. My suggestion will be that the second level introduces an element that creates a type of responsibility for moral acts that is peculiar to human beings.

The Aristotelian concept of responsibility is extremely difficult, and so is the chapter in the *Nicomachean Ethics* that we shall have to discuss in detail, *EN* III.v (on the volunariness of virtues and vices). It is not even quite clear what Aristotelian concept one is trying to understand when one asks about his concept of responsibility. Aristotle talks of man as being an originator (*archē*) of acts and as being 'the master' (*kyrios*) of them. He talks of acts as being up to us (*eph' hēmin*). He talks of them as being voluntary (*hekousia*) and of agents as acting voluntarily (*hekontes*). And he talks of men as 'causing' acts (as being *aitioi* of them). As is shown e.g. by *EE* II.vi.8–11, these various locutions should, initially at least, be kept distinct. I shall be concerned with the conditions for stating moral acts and states to be 'voluntary', and with the sense in which human beings are said to be *aitioi* ('causing') of moral states. And I shall translate *aitios* as 'responsible'.

2.1. In *EN* III, before chapter v, Aristotle has been discussing the concepts of voluntariness, *prohairesis*, and wish (*boulēsis*). The conditions for an act to be voluntary are (III.i.20, 1111a22–24) that the origin (*archē*) of the act is in

the agent and that he is not ignorant of one or more of the
particular elements that constitute the act (from some point
of view). Aristotle expressly denies that ignorance of the
proper moral *end* of acts (*hē en tēi prohairesei agnoia*) is
ignorance of the type that renders an act involuntary (III.i.15,
1110b31-33). His reason is that people are blamed for this
kind of 'universal' ignorance, whereas they are pitied for
ignorance of the particulars of the action. As a piece of justification this observation is clearly worthless. For Aristotle's
project in III.i is to find conditions for voluntariness that
will explain why people may justifiably be praised and
blamed for their voluntary acts. Thus at the end of III.i
there remains the task of explaining why universal ignorance
of the end does not excuse. Why is it that if, as seems reasonable, ignorance excuses, universal ignorance does not? The
answer is given in chapter v.

2.2. Aristotle's aim in that chapter is to show that virtues
and vices are voluntary. A subsidiary aim is to show, against
Socrates (cf. v.4), that vices *no less than* virtues are voluntary.
The latter aim determines the train of argument in v.2-3. In
v.1 Aristotle has argued, in effect, that virtues, which are
states (*hexeis*), are voluntary since the particular acts that
spring from them are so. In v.2-3 he argues that what holds
for virtuous acts holds for vicious acts too, and concludes
from this that both virtue and vice are voluntary. Here he
once more makes use of the argument that concludes from
properties of the particular acts that are the exercise of a
certain moral state to properties of the state itself.

Now this argument is clearly unsatisfactory if III.v is
intended to explain why particular acts that are done in a
special type of ignorance, viz. universal ignorance of the true
end, are nevertheless voluntary. For, as will become clear,
what accounts for the ignorance in question is a man's
moral state. Hence what we expect in III.v is an argument
to show that moral states are voluntary, *independently* of
the claim that acts that spring from them are so. We expect
to be informed why moral states are voluntary and why for
that very reason particular acts that spring from them are in
fact voluntary in spite of the fact that they are done in a

certain type of ignorance, as they were claimed to be.

I believe that Aristotle himself felt his argument to be unsatisfactory. The proof is that in the rest of the chapter he precisely does attempt to show that moral states are voluntary independently of the claim that acts that spring from them are so.

2.3. The way in which he approaches this topic is intriguing. He has concluded (end of v.3) that particular moral acts, both good and bad, are up to us (hence voluntary) and that moral states, both good and bad, are so too. In § 4 he drives home his criticism of Socrates: vice too is voluntary. The relation to this of § § 5-6, however, is difficult to see. If anyone disagrees, says Aristotle, with what precedes, he must also deny something that was said earlier (presumably in iii.15, 1112b31-32), viz. that man is an originator and creator of his acts as he is of his children. But he clearly is, since we cannot refer acts back to any other origin than those in ourselves. So if the origins are in us, the acts themselves will be up to us and voluntary. Here Aristotle is apparently just arguing that particular moral acts are voluntary, which is less than he claimed in § § 3 and 4. Perhaps his idea is the old one that if he can show the exercise of moral states to be voluntary, he has by the same token shown that moral states are so too. In fact he continues, in § 7, to talk as if he were only concerned with the voluntariness of moral acts. It is a sign, he says, of the truth of the point he has just made, viz. that particular moral acts are voluntary, that people who act morally badly are punished while those who act nobly are honoured; people are punished, that is, or honoured for their good or bad moral acts.

But gradually Aristotle introduces a new point. People who act morally badly are punished, he says, unless they act under compulsion or as a result of ignorance — but ignorance for which they are not themselves responsible (v.7, 1113b24-25). Here we meet for the first time the basic idea of the chapter. The ignorance that Aristotle is talking of is a cognitive state that is connected with the moral *state* of the person, and Aristotle's basic aim in the chapter is to show that virtue and vice are voluntary because we are ourselves responsible for our moral *states*. The immediate, important point, however, is this. We saw that in § § 5-6 Aristotle was apparently *arguing* that particular moral acts are voluntary — he did not take it for granted but presented a brief argument for that claim. He is now moving towards showing that moral *states* are voluntary because we are ourselves responsible for them. But in v.7, 1113b24-25 he connects the two points. It is as if he were saying: 'In my earlier account of what makes an act voluntary I stated that acts are voluntary if they are not done under compulsion or from ignorance. But now morally bad acts *are* done from ignorance. So are they involuntary? No, for they are done as a result of ignorance for which the man is himself responsible. Now, as will become clearer, his ignorance is due to his moral state. So he must himself be responsible for his moral state. We must say, therefore, that when we consider particular *moral* acts the earlier account of voluntariness should be supplemented. A particular moral act may be voluntary in spite of the fact that it is done as a result of ignorance, viz. if it is done in an ignorance of the true end of acts which is due to the moral *state* of the person, and if he is himself responsible for that state. We must distinguish, therefore, between types of ignorance — I hinted at this in III.i.15.'

2.4. This movement from talking of particular acts to talking of states is continued in § § 8-9, in which Aristotle takes up the point about ignorance. A man is punished for his very ignorance if he (himself) seems responsible (*aitios*) for it. Thus in the case of a man who has acted badly from drunkenness. For the starting-point is in himself, since he is (himself) 'the master' (*kyrios*) of not getting drunk — and his getting drunk was the cause of his ignorance. Similarly if people are ignorant of something in the laws which one ought to know and which is not difficult (v.8). And similarly in other areas where the ignorance seems due to carelessness. For since people are (themselves) 'the masters' (*kyrioi*) of taking care, it is up to themselves not to be ignorant (v.9).

In these two paragraphs Aristotle is quite clearly concerned to show why particular acts that are done as a result of ignorance may still be in some way considered voluntary and hence liable to punishment. In addition we should note that he is considering different types of ignorance, one of which, viz. that of the drunken man, clearly includes ignorance of the particular circumstances of the act, and that he is considering cases that are not, at least directly, moral ones. But these two facts are unimportant. In § 10 Aristotle reverts to the moral case, via the case of (unspecified) carelessness. And no matter what type of ignorance will be involved in the various types of case he is considering, the general point he wishes to make will be the same for all: acts may be voluntary even though they are done in ignorance of some vital element or other — if the agent is himself responsible for the state that causes his ignorance.

It is clear, then, when we come to v.10 ff., that the reason why Aristotle engages in showing that virtues and vices are voluntary is that only if that can be shown, and independently of the claim that the particular moral acts that spring from the virtue and vice are voluntary, is the latter claim justified. At the same time it will be clear that moral acts that are performed by beings who are themselves responsible for the states from which the acts spring are voluntary in a fuller sense than the same acts when performed by a being who is not himself responsible for his state. Thus, to anticipate somewhat, a child may perform a bad moral act and do so voluntarily, i.e. as a result of his own desire and with knowledge of the particulars of the act and situation. And an adult human being may perform the same act, and voluntarily too. But in the latter case the voluntariness of the act is a deeper one. For it includes the state of ignorance, viz. of the end of the act, which, in a sense, is common to both but for which only the adult is himself responsible. Since he is himself responsible for the state that causes his ignorance of the true end of acts, his act is voluntary not just in the sense that he wants it and knows the particulars of the case, but also that his ignorance of the end, an ignorance which is a vital element in the full description of the act, is voluntary. His *acts*, then, are voluntary in a fuller sense that those of the child.

3.1. But then what is meant by the claim that we are ourselves responsible for our moral states? § § 10–14 contain the answer. § 10 starts from an objection that relates to the case of carelessness that was mentioned in § 9. Perhaps the man who acts carelessly is not, after all, 'the master' of taking care: perhaps he just is the kind of man not to take care. Aristotle's reply follows immediately. Such people will themselves (*autoi*) be responsible (*aitioi*), by their dissolute lives, for being men of that kind. In the next sentence he makes the same point for people who are unjust and immoderate, i.e. morally bad, and then turns to explaining (v.10–14) in what sense these people are themselves responsible for being the kind of men they are.

People become the kind of men they are from doing the corresponding (types of) acts. Now (1) 'not to know that states come into being as a result of acting (in a certain way) in particular cases reveals an extreme lack of sense. . . . But if while knowing this one performs acts as a result of which one will become unjust one will be voluntarily unjust' (v.12, 1114a9–10 and v.13, a12–13). (2) 'Furthermore, it is irrational to think that a man who acts unjustly does not *want* to be unjust or that a man who acts immoderately does not want to be immoderate' (v.13, 1114a11–12). These are difficult reasons, as we shall see in a moment.

Let us first consider the paragraph that follows (14).

A man who acts unjustly must want to be unjust (according to § 13) — but it does not follow that if he is unjust already, he may become just simply by wanting to. The case is like that of (self-induced) illness. A man may be ill voluntarily if his illness is due to his living incontinently and disobeying his doctors. Once the illness has started, he has thrown away his chance. But before he fell ill, it was up to him not to fall ill, since the starting-point was in himself. 'Similarly at the start (*ex archēs*) it was up to the unjust and to the immoderate man not to become that kind of person (that is why they are so voluntarily), but when they have become so it is no longer possible for them not to be so' (v.14, 1114a19–21).

The obvious interpretation of this is that we are ourselves responsible for our moral states since at some particular point during our lives (*a*) we did not have those states, and (*b*) it was up to us to take, as it were, the first step that was to lead to our having them.

This solution raises a number of difficulties, as commentators have been quick to see.[1] In what sense was it 'up to us' at the fictitious starting-point not to take that fatal first step? Since the point that is made in § 12 (point (1) above) can only apply to adults, the starting-point will itself, in many cases at least, be a state, viz. a habituated one that has been acquired as the person grew up; and if that state is already there, how will it be possible to maintain that it is *at that point* 'up to' the person not to become, say, unjust — for he may already be so? So Aristotle seems to have forgotten what he himself has stressed so much, viz. that moral states are already being formed during childhood. The difficulty has two parts. First, there is the logical absurdity of saying that at some point it is up to a man not to become what he already is. Secondly, there is the difficulty of supposing it to be up to a man whether to develop in a certain way or not if at the fictitious starting-point he already has a settled desiderative state: how, if I am an ingrained thief, will it be psychologically possible for me not to perform those acts of stealing by the performance of which I become personally responsible for my moral state?

A further difficulty in the obvious interpretation is that on that interpretation the point made in v.13, 1114a11–12 (point (2) above) directly contradicts a point Aristotle makes elsewhere (*EN* III.xii.4, 1119a31–33): that whereas the particular acts of the immoderate man are voluntary, his whole state is not; 'for nobody wants to be immoderate.'

3.2. I believe that the fact that Aristotle seems, on the obvious interpretation of the passage, to be both forgetful of parts of his own doctrine and contradicting himself indicates that that interpretation is false. Let us first consider in what sense it was 'up to' the agent at the fictitious starting-point not to take the fatal step. This will relate to the second part of the first difficulty stated.

Take the case of illness: in what sense is the illness voluntary? Aristotle's point must be that at some moment the factor that determines whether a man is to be ill or not

---

[1] Cf., e.g., Gauthier p. 215; W. F. R. Hardie, *Aristotle's Ethical Theory*, Oxford, 1968, p. 175.

changes. Before that moment the factor is (partly) the man himself, after that moment it is nature (alone). The illness is voluntary, therefore, in the sense that at the start it is (to some degree) dependent on the man, as opposed to nature, whether the illness is to occur or not. Now I do not believe that the point is that given what kind of man the person is it was still possible for him at the start of the process not to fall ill. Rather, the illness is dependent on him in the sense that it is precisely a matter of what kind of person he is, e.g. one who lives incontinently and disobeys his doctors, whether he is to fall ill or not. Since the contrast is between the period when it is all nature's business and the antecedent period when something depends on the man, it is most likely that the sense in which the illness 'depends on the man' is the minimal one according to which whether the illness is to occur or not is simply a question of what sort of man the given person is.

Let me spell out this point. For purposes of illustration we may draw a rough distinction between three views of the causes of, e.g., illness. One view might be that illness is natural in the sense in which death is so. No matter which human beings we are considering, it is certain that they will die. Similarly, one might think, though on the relevant interpretation of 'natural' the view is just false, it is natural that whatever illness in fact occurs should occur. This view, of course, is not Aristotle's. For in the passage we are considering he clearly speaks of self-induced illness. A second view one might hold, then, is that it is not all nature's business. Something depends on us in the sense that different people may react differently as far as illness goes if placed in relevantly identical situations: one man will do what will cause him to fall ill, another will not. And a third view will be that not only is it not all nature's business; the illness is not determined in advance even in the sense that given what kind of man the person is he will, or will not, fall ill. On the contrary, no matter how settled a state a man has, it is still 'up to' him, in some sense, not to do what he is bent on doing. These three views may be placed on a scale with the first one at the one end and the third one at the other. My point is that since it is the first view that Aristotle brings in as the one to be contrasted with the view that something is 'up to us', it is most likely that the latter view is the second one.[2]

If we apply this to the moral case, what we shall get is a suggestion that the moral state for which a person is responsible is acquired by a process the start of which was dependent on the man in the sense that it was simply due to the fact that he was as he was that the process took the course it took. It follows that if it turns out that we can make sense of the idea that there is a starting-point of a state in the adult period, even when the person may already possess some state, the claim that at the starting-point it is up to us whether the process that leads to the possession of the final state gets started or not is not incompatible with the possibility that at the starting-point we already possess a certain state, i.e. have a settled desiderative attitude. For whether it will be impossible or not *for the individual* to decide on a different course of action than the one that will turn out to have been the fatal first step, it will remain the case that the process that was to lead to the final moral state was dependent on *him*, on what kind of person *he* was. This point, then, will remove the second part of the first difficulty I raised.

3.3. What, then, about the first part of that difficulty: will it be possible to make sense of the idea of a starting-point for the process that leads to the possession of a moral state in the adult period, i.e. in a period in which a man may already possess a certain moral state, viz. a habituated one?

This is where I shall make my crucial suggestion. If the person is an adult human being, then the kind of virtue or vice of which he is capable is not just the non-rational state of mind that results from habituation or from nature plus experience; it is the state of mind that is later in the *Ethics* called genuine virtue. This state of mind includes, as we know, *phronēsis*, i.e. a universal grasp of what should be done and the belief that acting in that way is what *eudaimonia* or *eupraxia* consists in. Now this type of state is one for which the given person may be said to be himself responsible in the following way. Since he is an adult, he must know

---

[2] This point ultimately goes back to R. Loening, *Die Zurechnungslehre des Aristoteles*, Jena, 1903, pp. 262-5.

that if he performs some particular act, he will accomplish one of two things. If he does not already possess a settled desiderative state, he will move one further step in the direction of having it. If, on the other hand, he already does possess a settled desiderative state, he will confirm his possession of it. But now since he is an adult, he will also know that in an adult human being having a certain desiderative state *means or turns into having a certain view of eudaimonia.* Our man will know that by having a certain (non-rational) desiderative state one comes to have a certain genuine moral state, whether good or bad, one comes to be a certain type of person in the full sense of a man who has a certain view of *eudaimonia.* But if while knowing this (and Aristotle states that not to know this shows lack of sense, v.12, 1114a 10) he performs the given act, then he will be making the non-rational desiderative state that he either already has or is about to create *his own.* He will 'create' himself as a certain type of person in the full sense. For although he may have no choice not to act as he eventually does, he now knows that by so acting he will become a man with a certain view (true or false) of *eudaimonia.* Thus he himself becomes responsible, not (necessarily) for his non-rational state (if he already has one), but for the genuine moral state that consists of the non-rational desiderative state plus the corresponding view of *eudaimonia.*

3.4. If this is correct, we may try to solve the second difficulty we encountered, i.e. the difficulty that in v.13, 1114a11–12 Aristotle seems flatly to contradict his later remark in III.xii.4. For if he is envisaging a situation in which a man performs a certain act while knowing that by performing the act he will become a certain type of person (in the sense suggested), then it is in fact irrational (1114a11) to deny that the man wants to become that type of person. It is not, of course, that he wants 'to be unjust' or 'to be immoderate' — and the point of III.xii.4 may be precisely that nobody wants *that.* But he does seem to want to be 'the kind of person who performs that (type of) act', viz. the type of act he in fact decides to perform; in that sense he does want to be an unjust or immoderate man.

3.5. So adult human beings are responsible for their moral states because they seem to fulfil both conditions for voluntariness that were introduced in III.i. They must, on pain of showing lack of sense, *know* that they will become a certain type of person (in the full sense) by behaving as they do. Therefore, if they persevere, they must *want* to become that type of person. Adult human beings, therefore, become fully good or bad by their own making.

According to this analysis Aristotle is not saying that at some point each individual has himself had any genuine choice between doing or not doing what led to his being a certain type of man — that I have already argued. In fact, as commentators agree,[3] he is not concerned with freedom at all, but with responsibility. A man is responsible for (*aitios* of) a certain phenomenon if he knew that it would come about and still wanted to do the act that brought it about. Therefore an adult is himself responsible for his (genuine) moral state, whereas a child is not — in his case the praise and blame must go to those responsible for his education (cf. *EE* II.vi.10, 1223a10–13). And therefore acts of an adult are voluntary even if they are done in ignorance of the true end, i.e. even if they are bad moral acts. For the man is himself responsible for the state of ignorance from which they spring. Moreover, such acts are fully voluntary as opposed to similar acts when performed by children in full knowledge of the relevant particulars of the case but (necessarily) in ignorance of the true end. The latter acts *are* voluntary, as Aristotle insists in III.i, but they are not fully so, since they are done in ignorance of a certain vital element, viz. what the true end of acts is. By contrast, the same acts when performed by the adult, fully vicious person are fully voluntary. For although they too are done in ignorance of that vital element, the vicious person is himself responsible for that ignorance.

4.1. It is necessary to try out this interpretation of what accounts for the voluntariness of moral virtues and vices by considering § § 17–20 in our chapter. The passage will show,

---

[3] Cf., e.g., D. J. Furley, in *Two Studies in the Greek Atomists*, Princeton, 1967, pp. 223 and 225 n. 17.

first, that Aristotle does in fact take it that the genuine
alternative to his own view of the way in which moral states
are voluntary is that they result *from nature*. Hence it is less
likely that the voluntariness of moral states that he is arguing
for is one that depends on a claim that each *individual* has
at some point had a genuine choice: it is enough that it was
not just nature's business whether a given person was to
develop in a certain way, but was also to some degree dependent on what kind of man he was — and he might have been
different, as is revealed by the fact that other people are
different. Secondly, the passage will show that the kind of
moral state for which we are ourselves responsible is in fact
the full, genuine moral state that contains a grasp of *eudaimonia* — and that, of course, was a crucial point in the
interpretation I proposed. Finally, I shall suggest that although
the passage does not clearly indicate exactly in what way we
are ourselves responsible for our moral states, nevertheless,
if we press it, we come very close to the answer that was
suggested by § § 10-14.

4.2. Aristotle starts (v.17, 1114a31-b1) by introducing an
objection that might be made to his claim that vice is voluntary. Somebody might argue that everybody desires the
apparent good: what is desired, even by the vicious man,
is something that appears good — to him. And furthermore,
the objector claims, people are not 'the masters' of their
phantasia: as each man is (in terms of his character), so the
end appears to him. So, as we may complete the objection,
since vice contains a (false) view of the good and since, as
the objector has claimed, a person is not responsible for his
views of the good, a vicious person cannot be held responsible
for his vice, which cannot, therefore, be voluntary.

If this completion of the objection is correct, then it
already seems implied that the type of vice that is being
discussed is full or genuine vice, i.e. a state of mind that
includes a grasp (in this case a false one) of the good. For
the point that vice is voluntary turns on the idea that human
beings are not responsible for the view of the good that is
part of vice. It might be objected here that the *phantasia* of
the good that Aristotle is talking of need not be the *rational*

grasp that goes into full vice, but just the grasp of the end that is implied, and precisely just *implied*, in the particular *perceptual phantasiai* that e.g. children may have. The objection can hardly be maintained. For when Aristotle talks of 'the apparent good' and states that the end will appear in a certain way, his language seems to reflect the vocabulary of III.iv on wish (*boulēsis*), and in that chapter he is certainly talking of a grasp of the end which is rational.

Aristotle continues by introducing two possible views. One view (v.17, b1–3) is that each person is himself in some way responsible for his state. In that case he will himself also be in some way responsible for his *phantasia*, and hence, as we may complete the line of thought, a crucial premiss in the objection, viz. that we are not 'the masters' of our *phantasiai*, is false.

This view is in fact Aristotle's, as commentators have seen.[4] It turns on the point that a certain state implies a certain *phantasia*, but this point, as we know, is common to Aristotle and the objector. There is no explicit indication in Aristotle's reply that he is talking of a *rational* grasp — nor, of course, need there be. But if I was right about the type of grasp he was operating with when stating the objection, the *phantasia* for which, on Aristotle's own view, the man is himself responsible *will* be the rational grasp of what the good, the end, *eudaimonia*, is.

The second view that is presented begins with the words *ei de mē*, 'otherwise . . .' (b3). The sense is: if it is not the case, as Aristotle's own view has it, that each individual is himself in some way responsible for his state and consequently for his grasp of the good, then . . . There follows an account of the only possible alternative, as Aristotle sees it, to his own view, and moreover the only view that will imply the premiss on which the initial objection relied, viz. that people are not themselves 'the masters' of their *phantasia* of the good.

The view is (b3–12) that nobody is himself responsible for 'doing badly' (b3–4).[5] A man who 'does badly' will act as he does in ignorance of the true end, though believing (falsely) that by his acts he will be happy (b4–5). But he has not

---

[4] e.g. Gauthier ad loc.

[5] The term is *kakopoiein*, which means both acting badly and the contrary of *eudaimonein*.

himself chosen to aim at that specific end (b5–6). On the contrary, this view of the end is something he has from birth: one must be born with an eye, as it were, by which to judge rightly and choose what is truly good (b6–8). The person in whom this right aim and eye is present by nature is the one who is well endowed by nature (b8). The aim and eye is something one cannot acquire or learn from anybody else: as one was born, so one's state is (b9–10).

So Aristotle is constructing a certain view of how people obtain the states and grasps of the end that they have, and fathering that view on the objector as the only one he may possibly turn to in support of his objection. Two things should not noted. First, here at last it is quite clearly implied that the grasp of the end that Aristotle is talking of (and saying one has by nature) is a rational one in my usual sense. For it is explicitly stated that the person who is being described believes that by reaching the end *he will be happy* (b5). The second point to notice is that Aristotle has constructed the view he is fathering on the objector in terms of the distinction between ends and means. As we shall see his refutation of the view turns on precisely that point.

4.3. His refutation, as given in v.17–20, b12–25, consists in an argument *ad hominem*, as commentators have pointed out.[6] And it is a refutation that does not attempt to prove that virtue is voluntary, but only that in spite of the elaborate view that Aristotle has allowed the objector to construct of how people obtain their aims and their 'eyes', it will remain the case that if, as the objector does, one takes virtue to be voluntary, vice will be so too.

If the elaborate view constructed by the objector is true, 'why should virtue be voluntary more than vice? For it must hold equally of both the good man and the bad man that the end appears and is fixed, by nature or in whatever other way, and that the rest is done, in whatever way it is done, by being referred to the end' (v.17–18, b12–16). That is, the account we shall give of the relation to means and ends of the good man and the bad man will be the same. If the bad man is

---

[6] Gauthier ad loc. and Furley, *Two Studies in the Greek Atomists*, pp. 193–4.

related in some particular way to means and ends, so will the good man be. 'If, therefore, the end does *not* appear to each man in whatever way it may be *by nature*, but there is also something that depends on himself (virtue and vice will be equally voluntary)' (v.19, b16–17 with 19–20). This is Aristotle's own view, which he brings in as a reminder. 'If, on the other hand, the *end* is natural, but virtue is voluntary due to the fact that the good man does the *rest* voluntarily, then (too) virtue and vice will be equally voluntary' (b17–20).

This is how the objection is dismissed. The objector agrees that virtue is voluntary, and the way in which he will be able to account for that belief, in terms of the elaborate view he has constructed, is by saying that although the end is present by nature, the good man will do the means to the end voluntarily. But then, Aristotle objects, the same picture will hold for the bad man. 'For "what depends on himself" belongs in the same way to the bad man too — in his acts if not in his end' (b20–21).

Aristotle may conclude, then, that if, as everybody agrees, the virtues are voluntary, the vices will be so too; for the same is true of both (v.20, b21–22 and 24–25). In his formulation of this conclusion Aristotle adds, parenthetically, the following as an explanation of why virtues are voluntary: 'For we are ourselves in some way co-responsible for our states, and it is by being of a certain character that we posit a certain end' (b22–24). This is clearly the view of 1114b1–3 and 16–17 that I have stated to be Aristotle's own view. The fact that he refers to it here, where for argumentative purposes it would be better to refer to the view of the voluntariness of virtue that he has developed against the objector (in 1114b 12–16 and 17–20), makes it clear that the view is his own: when he comes to state, at the end of the chapter, why virtues are voluntary Aristotle decides to provide what according to him is the correct explanation.

4.4. So three times in §§ 17–20 we get a reference to Aristotle's own view (1114b1–3, 16–17, 22–24) that we are ourselves in some way responsible or co-responsible for our states and that therefore virtues and vices are voluntary. But there are no clear indications of how exactly we are to understand that view. I have already suggested that we must rely on §§ 10-14.

However, consideration of the difference between the two views that are contrasted in §§ 17-20 of how we get the proper aim and 'eye' will show that if we press what Aristotle is saying in that passage, we shall obtain exactly the answer to the question of how we are ourselves responsible for our states that I extracted from §§ 10-14. There are two points. First, the only alternative to the Aristotelian view that is allowed in §§ 17-20 is that we have the proper aim and 'eye' *by nature*, in the sense of something inborn that cannot be changed, or as we e.g. have the capacity for perception. But now we know from *EN* II.i that Aristotle is particularly keen on emphasizing that moral states are not natural in that sense but may be changed — by habituation. Taken out of context, therefore (and this is the first point), we should expect the view with which the objector's view is contrasted to be the Aristotelian view from *EN* II.i that moral states arise as a result of habituation. In fact, as we know, it is not. For (and this is the second point) the view with which the objector's view is contrasted in §§ 17-20 is the one that each individual is *himself* responsible for his moral state. It is not surprising, of course, that this is the view that Aristotle advances in the present passage. For his aim is to show that virtues and vices are voluntary, and as he has defined voluntariness earlier in the book, for something to be voluntary it must, in the ways he specifies, be dependent on the particular individual with reference to whom the thing is stated to be voluntary. But then suppose we take these two points as established, (*i*) that the objector's view *brings to mind* Aristotle's own distinction in II.i between acquired, viz. habituated, capacities or states and natural ones, and (*ii*) that it is also made clear that the claim that we are ourselves responsible for our states is after all not just the claim that moral states are not unchangeably present by nature but may be acquired by habituation. In that case we seem forced to look for some 'moment' during our lives at which it will make sense to say that we become *ourselves* responsible for our states *even though* they may also be the result of habituation. Once we have got so far, the only possible solution seems to lie in fixing on the 'moment' when the habituated moral state, if a person has that kind of state, turns into the kind of state that Aristotle is clearly talking of in § § 17-20, viz. a rational moral state that includes the grasp of the good according to which behaviour of a certain type is (part of) what makes up one's *eudaimonia*. And then, of course, we are very close to the suggestion about how we become responsible for our moral states that I extracted from § § 10-14.

5.1. I have little doubt that this reading of *EN* III.v as a whole will seem strained. But it has at least the merit of ascribing to Aristotle an account of how we are ourselves responsible for our moral states that will not immediately appear unsatisfactory. On the obvious interpretation of what he is saying he appears just to push the problem of responsibility for particular acts one step back. If we are responsible for acts because we are responsible for the states from which they spring, in what sense are we then responsible for the states — particularly if the states are, at least often, the result of habituation? On the interpretation I have offered Aristotle's point is not so immediately un-satisfactory. Adult human beings are responsible for their (full) moral states because at some point during their lives there arises in them the capacity that is required for them to be *fully* morally good or bad, viz. the ability to see that by acting in a certain way they will become people of a certain (moral) type. When this ability is present, they become, in a sense, themselves, by adopting the view of the good that is implicitly present in their immediate responses, by making that view their own.

5.2. Suppose, then, that my interpretation is correct. Suppose that virtues and vices are taken by Aristotle to be voluntary in the sense I have given. Suppose that the reason why people are blamed for their states (as they evidently are, cf. III.i.15) is that they have in a sense consciously adopted them, although they may not have had any chance not to do so. And suppose, furthermore, that the reason why particular bad acts are not involuntary in spite of the fact that they spring from a state of ignorance of a certain type, viz. ignorance of the true end, is that the vicious state has been adopted by the person in question in the sense I have explained. In that case we may say that in the moral case Aristotle has not after all been satisfied with the account of voluntariness that he gave in III.i: what he is doing in III.v is to introduce further conditions for moral acts to be *fully* voluntary and consequently for a man to be *fully* responsible for a moral act. The further condition is that the state from which the act springs has been consciously adopted by the agent as expressing his view of what *eudaimonia* consists in.

6.1. It would clearly be welcome if one were able to find confirmation somewhere in the Aristotelian *corpus* that such a view of human responsibility is in fact Aristotle's. Two pieces of Aristotelian doctrine might seem relevant. First, in certain passages he insists that human beings are alone able to *act*. He is presumably using 'acting' in a wide sense, to cover both *poiēsis* and *praxis*. But the question is why humans alone may be said to act. Is there some connection with my suggestion that only adult human beings are fully responsible for their acts? Secondly, in a few passages Aristotle connects praise and blame particularly closely with moral states rather than particular acts. Once more the question is why he does so, and whether his point connects with my suggestion. I shall not pursue these questions very far, but only indicate that three passages in which either of the two points is made and which might seem particularly promising for my purpose do not in fact yield anything that I can build on.

6.2. One passage in which Aristotle makes the first point mentioned is *EE* II.vi.(2, 1222b19-20): '. . . but man is the only animal who is also the originator of certain acts; for we would not say that any other animal acts.' The context (chapter vi as a whole) looks promising inasmuch as the conclusion of the chapter is that virtues and vices are voluntary. Nevertheless, in spite of the very careful argument that is contained in the chapter, the argument for the voluntariness of virtues and vices is just the not very satisfactory one from the fact that virtues and vices are objects of praise and blame (vi.10–11), and it seems impossible to discover any revealing connection between the point about acting and the one about the voluntariness of virtues and vices.

Another passage that makes the point about acting is *EN* VI.ii.2, 1139a18–20. In this passage there is no connection with the idea of the voluntariness of virtues and vices. Rather, Aristotle's point is that only humans may act 'prohairetically' in the sense he develops in ii.2–5 (cf. ii.5, 1139b4–5). Now this sense is the same as the one he strives to bring out in VI.xii–xiii when he attempts to show that the point of *phronēsis* lies in the fact that possession of *phronēsis* makes a person perform *praxeis*. And of course, if one contrasts that type of act with the one that is characteristic of animals and children, one can see why Aristotle should be tempted to claim that only action that is 'prohairetic' is genuine action. It is just a more satisfactory type of action, since it is action that involves a clear grasp of the end of the act, no matter whether the act is a case of *poiēsis* or one of strict *praxis*. Still one would like to hear more about why 'prohairetic' acts alone are genuine acts. And we do not get any more in the passage referred to.

So while there may be some important connection between Aristotle's claim that humans alone may act and the idea I am ascribing to him of when there is full responsibility, the point is not actually made in the two passages I have referred to. What they do, in particular the latter one, is just to make the need for additional explanation be felt more acutely: why is it that only 'prohairetic' action, only action that is fully conscious of its aim, is genuine action?

6.3. The second area that seemed relevant was that of the special connection of praise and blame with moral states. If Aristotle connects praise and blame particularly closely with moral *states*, perhaps his reason is that the voluntariness of moral states, which is a necessary condition for them to be appropriate objects of praise and blame, is a particularly important one.

EE II.xi.9–13 is a relevant passage. Detailed analysis of xi.11–13, 1228a11–18 will, I believe, show that Aristotle in this passage does connect praise and blame particularly closely with moral states rather than particular acts.[7] And in xi.10 he concludes that vice and virtue are voluntary. Once more, however, it seems impossible to establish any clear connection between the two points. Moreover, the argument for the contention concerning vice and virtue, though not entirely clear, seems to be a version of the unsatisfactory argument that concludes from properties of the exercise of moral states to properties of the states themselves.

6.4. So, little has been gained from the two pieces of doctrine that seemed promising. In the two passages from the *Eudemian Ethics* the two points that are made, viz. that only humans may act and that moral states are particularly fit objects of praise and blame, are not clearly connected with the point that is also made in both passages to the effect that virtue and vice and voluntary. Moreover, the two passages give unsatisfactory reasons for the latter claim. What these two passages leave us with, at least when we come from *EN* III.v, is therefore the desire for a more profound explanation of the voluntariness of virtues and vices than those given in the two passages. Similarly the passage from *EN* VI did not yield anything of direct relevance to the notion of human responsibility, but only left us with the desire for further explication of the point that only 'prohairetic' action is genuine action. But the two questions to which these passages give rise are, of course, respectively the one that is only raised in *EN* III.v itself and the one that led us from *EN* VI.xii–xiii (as discussed in chapter 8) to *EN* III.v. The latter text, then, is central.

7. Suppose, then, that the interpretation I gave of III.v is correct. In that case one can understand why at the end of *EN* VI Aristotle places such emphasis on the second level of moral goodness that I have distinguished. For it is precisely at that level that one may start ascribing to a man a genuine responsibility for his moral acts. Acts that spring from a

---

[7] I take it that the lines referred to contain two additional arguments for the conclusion stated in xi.8, 1228a1–2 that virtue is responsible for making right the *end*, as opposed to the means.

non-rational moral state (level one) may well be voluntary in the basic sense that is brought out in III.i. But they are not voluntary in the full sense, since they do not spring from a rational moral state. Such a state is the only type of virtue and vice for which a man is truly himself responsible. Possession of such a state is therefore a necessary condition for a man to be himself truly responsible for his moral acts.

10

CONCLUSION: PROBLEMS
AND RESULTS

Let me try to gather up the threads of my account. I have said something about a certain number of topics in Aristotle's ethics, but I have had very little to say directly about a few issues that are central to a proper evaluation of Aristotle's achievement in ethics.

One such issue is that of the virtues and vices of Aristotle's type of naturalistic approach to ethics. The importance of this issue is clear. For the naturalistic approach is fundamental to Aristotle's moral philosophy. It is so both in connection with his explication, in the *ergon* argument, of the very notion of the good for man, and in connection with his use of the notion of man's identity at a number of crucial turning-points in his system. And of course it connects closely with his general approach in biology and in metaphysics as centring on the notion of essence.[1] But the question of the merits or otherwise of Aristotle's naturalistic approach to ethics is also important because of the continuing controversy over naturalistic and non-naturalistic theories of ethics. In this connection there are good grounds for discussing precisely Aristotle's theory, since it certainly constitutes one of the more powerful versions of naturalism.

So there is ample material for discussion. I have at various points had occasion to show the importance for Aristotle's ethical theory of his anthropology, e.g. in my account in chapter 2 of the sense of acting nobly, and in my discussion in chapter 4 of the 'recipe' for the good life. But I have not tried to evaluate properly the *ergon* argument. Nor shall I try to do so here.[2]

[1] For the general issue see esp. S. R. L. Clark, *Aristotle's Man, Speculations upon Aristotelian Anthropology*, Oxford, 1975.

[2] For recent attempts at this I refer to S. Hampshire, 'Ethics: A Defense of

There is a second important issue, of which I have said more, but which again I have not confronted directly. Since the beginning of modern Aristotelian studies in the nineteenth century all philosophical discussion of his ethics has been consciously or unconsciously influenced by the question of the relationship in ethics between Aristotle and Kant.[3] This topic is of the greatest importance and complexity. Kant himself is responsible, through his attack on eudaimonism and his insistence on the 'categorical' character of the moral imperative, for creating the impression of a fundamental opposition between his own ethics and that of Aristotle. But he never confronts Aristotle's views directly. The task of analysing Aristotle in terms of Kant's theory was then taken up by the ninteenth-century commentators on Aristotle. It was always combined with a genuine interest on the part of the commentators in the underlying, more general, problems in ethics, one result being that Aristotle would either be censured (or praised) for neglecting points emphasized by Kant, or else he would be praised for having adumbrated points brought into sharper focus by Kant. This enterprise of comparing Aristotle directly with Kant is a valuable one. But it is perhaps even more fruitful to compare his theory with a slightly more general type of Kantian theory, which ignores some idiosyncrasies of Kant's own treatment. Such a task has been undertaken for Platonic ethics by T. H. Irwin in chapter VIII of his brilliant study, *Plato's Moral Theory*.[4] There is much in Irwin's discussion that is highly

Aristotle', *University of Colorado Studies*, Series in Philosophy 3, 1969, 23–38, also in Hampshire's *Freedom of Mind and other Essays*, Princeton, 1971; T. Nagel, 'Aristotle on *Eudaimonia*', *Phr.* 17 (1972), 252–9; Clark, *Aristotle's Man*, ch. II.1; K. V. Wilkes, 'The Good Man and the Good for Man in Aristotle's Ethics', *M* 87 (1978), 553–71.

    [3] See, e.g., for Germany in the 19th century, F. A. Trendelenburg, *Historische Beiträge zur Philosophie iii*, Berlin, 1867; for France at the turn of the century, V. Brochard, 'La Morale ancienne et la morale moderne', *Revue philosophique*, 26 (1901), 1–12, also in his *Études de philosophie ancienne et de philosophie moderne*, Paris, 1926; and for modern Anglo-American philosophy, R. G. Sullivan, 'The Kantian Critique of Aristotle's Moral Philosophy: An Appraisal', *RM* 28 (1974), 24–53, and R. Kraut, 'Aristotle on Choosing Virtue for Itself', *AGP* 58 (1976), 223–39. In its own independent way the following paper is also a case in point: G. E. M. Anscombe, 'Modern Moral Philosophy', *Phil.* 33 (1958), 1–19.
    [4] Oxford, 1977.

relevant to Aristotle too, in particular in connection with his attempt to relate Plato to the distinction between teleological and deontological moral theories, and to the connected problem of egoism and altruism. I shall make no attempt to do for Aristotle what Irwin has done for Plato. But I will try to indicate the relevance of some of my results for such an enterprise.

One central topic in this connection concerns the sense of Aristotle's type of eudaimonism and its status in relation to teleological and deontological moral theories. In chapter 1 of this book I have argued that Aristotle defines the concept of *eudaimonia* as the entirely formal concept of the state which is the end-point of all a man's choices, and that properly understood choosing something for its own sake *means* choosing it for the sake of *eudaimonia* in that sense. But if this interpretation is correct, it will follow that Aristotle's theory offers no basis for at least the cruder forms of the Kantian criticism of eudaimonism. For by saying of moral acts that they are done for the sake of *eudaimonia* Aristotle will certainly not assign a hypothetical value to moral acts. On the contrary he will be insisting that they are choice-worthy for their own sake. Thus Aristotle's use of the concept of *eudaimonia* does leave room in his eudaimonism for deontological considerations. Now Aristotle is in fact no firm deontologist, if a deontological moral theory is defined as implying that the value of moral behaviour is not to be explained in terms of any non-moral values. But this fact has nothing to do with his use of the concept of *eudaimonia*. His eudaimonism is evidently some kind of teleological theory, but his use of the concept of *eudaimonia* does not automatically lay it open to deontological criticism.

In this connection it is worth noticing that the interpretation of *eudaimonia* that I have offered in chapter 1 places Aristotle squarely in the line of development from Plato's early to his middle dialogues that has recently been traced by Irwin. According to Irwin 'Socratic' ethics in the early Platonic dialogues is modelled on technical reasoning in that *eudaimonia*, which is understood by Socrates as some determinate non-moral state, is seen as the end to be attained and moral behaviour as a genuine, technical means to that end.

In the 'Platonic' ethics of the middle dialogues, by contrast, *eudaimonia* is no longer considered a determinate end, nor is moral behaviour said to have technical value in relation to an end that is specified in non-moral terms. On the interpretation I have proposed of Aristotle's use of *eudaimonia* Aristotle should be seen as continuing this development. For I argued in chapter 1 that his conception of *eudaimonia*, as an entirely formal state that implies absolutely nothing for the question of the number and connectedness (or the opposite) of the things that fall under it, represents an advance on Plato's account in the middle dialogues (at least as interpreted by Irwin).

But Aristotle is in fact no deontologist. For, as I have argued in chapter 2, he will account for the value of moral behaviour in non-moral terms, viz. when he implies, in what I have called the principle of utility, that the criterion for noble behaviour is the greatest possible satisfaction of needs for natural goods in a given community. Similarly I accepted in chapter 4 that Aristotle in some way does want to say that the goodness for the agent of moral behaviour lies in the fact that such behaviour somehow enhances his chances of engaging in *theōria*. But then, of course, there were two crucial qualifications. For the defining property of moral behaviour, as I argued in chapters 2 and 3, is that it is an expression of the agent's grasp of the principle of *nobility*, and as for *theōria*, I argued in chapter 4 that it is only incidentally the criterion for the goodness of moral acts; moreover I argued that as an (incidental) aim of moral behaviour it will be overridden by the agent's consideration for the noble in those situations in which the material identity of moral behaviour and of acts that as takings of natural goods have *theōria* as their end is disrupted. When these qualifications have been entered, we are once more far from a teleological theory that is immediately open to the cruder versions of deontological criticism. The concept of moral obligation (if no actual word for it) certainly forms an important part of Aristotle's ethical theory.

The conception of nobility which I have ascribed to Aristotle on the basis of the chapter in the *Nicomachean Ethics* on self-love is developed from certain remarks of his in that chapter about the kind of being that man is, viz. that he is a rational being. The line of thought here is basically identical, I believe, with Kant's development of the idea of 'people as ends'. The similarity is perhaps not fortuitous. For the Aristotelian argument, based on man's rationality, for moral and noble behaviour, conceived basically as justice, is taken up, and in a sharper form, in Stoic ethics in the argument of the Stoics for justice and in their connected argument for the claim that moral virtue is the only thing that is genuinely good;[5] and it is known that Kant was studying Cicero's account of Stoic ethics during the period when he was preparing the *Grundlegung zur Metaphysik der Sitten*.

I submit, therefore, that a thorough examination of the relationship to the distinction between teleological and deontological theories of ethics of Aristotle's type of eudaimonism and of his account of the value of moral behaviour would show that relationship to be a rather subtle one. And the same will hold, I believe, for the relationship of Aristotle's ethical theory to that other pair of concepts, egoism and altruism. Thus it must surely be false to say, with D. J. Allan, that Aristotle's 'explanation of human conduct . . . (is) a *self-centred* one . . . Even the attempt . . . to find room in the scheme for apparently altruistic action proves that for Aristotle the fundamental motive is self-assertion in one form or another.'[6] While it is certainly true that Aristotelian explanation of action is self-*referential* (I do what *I* want to do and what I take to be my own good), this fact does not, of course, rule out the possibility of altruism, as has been stressed e.g. by T. Nagel in his book of the same name.[7] Aristotle's eudaimonism does not rule out concern for others, and his account of acting for the sake of the noble positively includes the idea of such concern.

To conclude these remarks on the first part of the book let me comment briefly on two general objections that will

---

[5] I am referring to the Stoic use of their concept of 'adaptation' (*oikeiōsis*), cf., e.g., Cicero, *De Finibus* III. 16, 20-21, and 62-64.

[6] Allan, 'Individual and State in the *Ethics* and *Politics*', in *La 'Politique' d'Aristote*, Entretiens Hardt 11, Geneva, 1964, 55-85, p. 60 (Allan's emphasis).

[7] Oxford, 1970.

probably be made to the interpretation of moral behaviour I have offered.

The first objection relates to the distinction between two different views of morality, one of which is connected with Kant, and according to which morality is seen as *Moralität*, while the other is connected with Hegel, who sees morality as *Sittlichkeit*. This is another distinction the exact sense and legitimacy of which may only be settled after a substantial amount of analysis. But the objection would be that by arguing for an Aristotelian conception of morality as nobility, which lays emphasis on the agent's own grasp of a rational argument for moral behaviour, I am connecting Aristotle too closely with Kant. Rather, one should praise Aristotle for providing material for a view of morality of the Hegelian type, which plays down the importance of the individual's own justification of moral behaviour and concentrates instead on morality as a set of practices that find expression in the customs and institutions of a given society.[8] I will readily admit that there is not much of Hegel in my interpretation of Aristotle. But the question arises whether the two views of morality are in fact irreconcilably different. And while I have certainly stressed points that belong on the Kantian side of the dichotomy, I have also been at pains to emphasize the importance for Aristotle's ethical theory of the idea of morality as a set of accepted practices that we grow into from childhood. So perhaps in this connection too Aristotle should not be placed unequivocally on either side of the supposed fence.

The second objection relates to a distinction that has re-emerged in some recent discussions of ethics, between act-centred ethical theories and agent-centred ones. Once more the target of the objection will be my account of the noble, but this time it is my development of the principle of utility rather than that of nobility that will be deplored. For do I not precisely miss what seems a virtue in Aristotle's theory, viz. that it focuses on agents instead of acts and on the

---

[8] This is the implied point in J. Ritter's valuable paper 'Das bürgerliche Leben, Zur aristotelischen Theorie des Glücks', *Vierteljahresschrift für wissenschaftliche Pädagogik*, 32 (1956), 60–94. Also in Ritter's *Metaphysik and Politik, Studien zu Aristoteles und Hegel*, Frankfurt am Main, 1977.

question of what sort of person the good man is instead of what makes an act morally right? In this connection too a proper clarification of the issue would require a certain amount of analysis. But it seems *a priori* likely that the distinction between the two types of theory is not an exclusive one. Surely no satisfactory type of ethical theory will be so agent-centred as altogether to exclude from consideration the question of the very 'object' of morality. Aristotle's, I contend, certainly did not.

In the second part of the book I turn to an issue which is also connected with Kant, viz. the question of the roles played by reason and desire in the formulation and adoption of moral ends. At one extreme there is Kant's view that reason may be practical, i.e. that it has motivational power on its own. At the other extreme there is Hume's view of the impotence and non-motivity of reason.

In Aristotelian scholarship discussion of this issue has centred on the question whether the end, according to Aristotle, is fixed by moral virtue, whereas *phronēsis* is concerned with means only, or whether *phronēsis* is concerned with ends in addition to means (the implication being that the end will not, then, be fixed by moral virtue).[9] I have argued in chapters 6 and 7 for an intermediate view. While it is no doubt true (and important) that *phronēsis* concerns ends as well as means, it is also true that the moral end is 'fixed' by moral virtue. The basic point here is a Humean one, of the importance of desire for the adoption of ends, but one that saves Hume's view from triviality.[10] *Phronēsis*, which is the cognitive element in a full state of desire and is therefore necessarily motivational, presupposes a state of desire that must be present *independently* of the cognitive grasp that is *phronēsis* (chapter 6, sections 4 and 11.1-11.4); and as a rational cognitive state it also presupposes, and results from, the progressive, deliberative clarification of

---

[9] Important participants in this controversy are F. A. Trendelenburg, in his *Historische Beiträge zur Philosophie ii*, Berlin, 1855, pp. 373-84, J. Walter, G. Teichmüller, R. Loening, M. Wittmann, D. J. Allan, in 'Aristotle's Account of the Origin of Moral Principles', R.-A. Gauthier, in his commentary pp. 563-8, 576-8, and P. Aubenque. (For bibliographical details see the bibliography under *G* and *M*.)

[10] See, for the risk of triviality, T. H. Irwin, 'Aristotle on Reason, Desire, and Virtue', *JP* 72 (1975), 567-78, pp. 571-6, and ch. 6, sect. 4, above.

non-rational knowledge which is itself the cognitive element in a (natural or habituated) state of desire (chapter 7). Thus it is non-rational moral virtue, as a full state of desire that includes both a non-rationally cognitive state and a 'pure' desiderative one, which makes a man *see* what should be done in the particular situation and makes him *want* to do that thing.

This account does nothing to invalidate the point about the importance of *phronēsis* for the grasp of ends as well as of means. Thus I have embraced almost all the claims made by such more or less professed anti-Humeans as Irwin and D. Wiggins concerning the role of reason and *phronēsis* in the clarification of one's moral ends, and I have even added that reason has a further important role to play in that it provides genuine justification of a man's views of the good by introducing the principles of nobility and utility. So reason has many important functions. But what it cannot do is to effect a genuine change in a man's passions or to make him see in the particular situation exactly what reaction will make him realize his end.

I conclude that as regards the scholarly controversy concerning the scope of *phronēsis* the frontiers in the debate have been too sharply drawn. *Phronēsis* is concerned with ends (and importantly so) as well as with means, but it remains true to say, in the precise sense I have attempted to specify, that it is moral virtue that 'fixes' the end.[11] As regards the opposition of Hume and Kant, by contrast, I have for once settled firmly for locating Aristotle on one side of the fence, the Humean one, though his version of the Humean view is, I would contend, an enlightened one.

But now though these results may be important in themselves, I have only discussed the question of the roles played by reason and desire in the formulation and adoption of moral ends in order to be able to isolate one element in moral goodness that it is the special task of *phronēsis* to introduce.

[11] I believe that G. Teichmüller saw this, *Die praktische Vernunft bei Aristoteles*, Neue Studien zur Geschichte der Begriffe iii, Gotha, 1879, e.g. pp. 206-38; but he was precisely chided for adopting this intermediate view, by R. Loening in his in other respects masterly book, *Die Zurechnungslehre des Aristoteles*, Jena, 1903, p. 28.

One might think that the importance of *phronēsis* would be settled once *phronēsis* was seen as contributing to the clarification of moral ends that are only indistinctly adopted; but then Aristotle toys with the idea that non-rational moral virtue will be sufficient to make a man do the proper moral acts (chapter 8, section 2.1). One might also think that the importance of *phronēsis* would be settled once *phronēsis* was seen as providing genuine justification of a man's views of the good; but Aristotle does not make this point at all in the official account of *phronēsis* in *EN* VI. So the real importance of *phronēsis* will ultimately lie elsewhere, viz. in the fact that it is the possession of *phronēsis* which makes a man perform moral acts from the proper *motive, as praxeis*. I have argued that it does this in two ways, first by including a grasp of ends that refers these directly to the concept of *eudaimonia* or of *eupraxia*, and secondly by being the cognitive element in a state of desire, where the desiderative element is present independently of the cognitive grasp and in the form of a non-rational (natural or habituated) moral state. For what makes an act a *praxis* is, as I argued at the end of chapter 1, that it is referred directly by the agent to the concepts of *eudaimonia* and *eupraxia* and that it is wanted by the agent irrespectively of any reasons he may have for the goodness of the act (with its act-result, where there is one). As described at the end of *EN* VI — so I argued in chapter 8 — *phronēsis* is precisely that state the possession of which will make the agent perform his acts as *praxeis*. That, then, is the very point of Aristotle's concept of moral insight. And in chapter 9, I connect this interpretation with his account of human responsibility for moral states and the acts that spring from them.

I believe that this requirement of Aristotle's, that acts to be moral must be *praxeis* in the specified sense, is an interesting one, and that it should be taken to be so not least by philosophers with an interest in agent-centred theories of ethics. Consideration of a few objections one may make to this claim will confirm the interest of Aristotle's requirement. First it might be objected that the element of rationality that is involved when an act is a *praxis* is only a very limited one, since it consists only in bringing the act under the concept of *eudaimonia*. More will be needed to render an act fully accountable, and I have of course also been talking of a proper justification of acts that the *phronimos* may provide. And secondly it might be asked, as Aristotle himself in a way does in *EN* VI.xii–xiii, why it should in fact be any better to be able to refer an act to the concept of *eudaimonia* than just to be able to see what should be done in the particular situation.

However, in answer to the latter objection one may wish to point out that it is in fact a necessary condition for the very possibility of rational talk of values and for the connected possibility of working with one's own more or less coherent moral views that one has an articulate grasp of those views. And this is precisely what one has when one refers those views to the concept of *eudaimonia*. Furthermore, and with regard to the former objection, the sheer ability to articulate one's moral views does seem to have a special importance, which may be seen if it is compared at the one end with the cognitive state of the child, who is not yet articulate in that specific way, and at the other end with the state of an adult who would not only bring his acts under the concept of *eudaimonia* but whom we might also imagine as for ever deliberating in order to refine his grasp of the good. As for the child there certainly is a sense in which we do not yet quite know what *kind* of person he is, no matter how reliable he may otherwise be in his reactions. And as for the imagined perpetual deliberator the very unreality of such a person contains a lesson. All deliberation must at some point come to an end. This, of course, is the point at which the agent 'chooses'. But it is at this point that we may start seeing him as some particular type of person. The point, then, when a man decides on an act as one thing that falls under *eudaimonia* is crucial. It is the point when we may start seeing him as a being with *his* peculiar view of the good, in fact as a person.

SELECT BIBLIOGRAPHY

The bibliography lists the most important works known to me on the topics treated in the book. It also mentions a few classics or valuable recent work on topics that have not been discussed directly. The distribution under the various headings has sometimes caused difficulty. In particular, there is a considerable overlap between sections (H) and (M).

In addition to the bibliographical help provided by *L'Année philologique*, *The Philosopher's Index*, *Bulletin signalétique*, etc., extensive bibliographies are to be found in the Susemihl/Apelt edition of the *Nichomachean Ethics*, Leipzig, 1912³ pp. XIII-XXIX (for the older literature), and in the commentary by Gauthier and Jolif (see below under (E)), vol. ii.2, pp. 917-40 (for the period 1912-58) and vol. i.1, pp. 315-34 (for 1958-68). And there is a very helpful descriptive bibliography in J. Barnes, M. Schofield, R. Sorabji (edd.), *Articles on Aristotle*, vol. ii, London, 1977, pp. 221-33.

(A) *Greek ethics in general*

Adkins, A. W. H., *Merit and Responsibility, A Study in Greek Value*, Oxford, 1960.

—— *From the Many to the One, A Study of Personality and Views of Human Nature in the Context of Ancient Greek Society, Values and Beliefs*, London, 1970.

Dodds, E. R., *The Greeks and the Irrational*, Sather Classical Lectures 25, Berkeley/Los Angeles, 1951.

Irwin, T. H., *Plato's Moral Theory, The Early and Middle Dialogues*, Oxford, 1977.

Lloyd-Jones, H., *The Justice of Zeus*, Sather Classical Lectures 41, Berkeley/Los Angeles, 1971.

Robin, L., *La Morale antique*, Paris, 1938.

Schwarz, E., *Ethik der Griechen*, Stuttgart, 1951.

Snell, B., *Die Entdeckung des Geistes, Studien zur Entstehung des europäischen Denkens bei den Griechen*, Göttingen, 1975⁴.

Vlastos, G. (ed.), *The Philosphy of Socrates*, New York, 1971.

—— (ed.), *Plato*, vol. ii (Ethics, Politics, and Philosophy of Art and Religion), New York, 1971.

—— *Platonic Studies*, Princeton, 1973.

272 SELECT BIBLIOGRAPHY

(B) *Indices verborum*
Bonitz, H., *Index aristotelicus*, Berlin, 1870.
For the *Nicomachean Ethics* there is a complete, but far from faultless
index verborum in Grant's edition (see under (E) below).
For the *Eudemian Ethics* there is a good index in Susemihl's edition
(below under (E)).

(C) *Aristotle in general*
Allan, D. J., *The Philosophy of Aristotle*, Oxford, 1970².
Brandis, C. A., *Handbuch der Geschichte der Griechisch-Römischen
Philosophie*, ii.2.1-2, Berlin, 1853-7.
Düring, I., *Aristoteles, Darstellung und Interpretation seines Denkens*,
Heidelberg, 1966.
Gomperz, T., *Griechische Denker, Eine Geschichte der antiken Philo-
sophie III*, Leipzig, 1909.
Jaeger, W., *Aristoteles, Grundlegung einer Geschichte seiner Entwick-
lung*, Berlin, 1923.
Lloyd, G. E. R., *Aristotle: The Growth and Structure of his Thought*,
Cambridge, 1968.
Mansion, S., 'Les positions maîtresses de la philosophie d'Aristote', in
Aristote et Saint Thomas d'Aquin, ed. L. De Raeymaeker, Louvain,
1957, 43-91.
Moreau, J., *Aristote et son école*, Paris, 1962.
Robin, L., *Aristote*, Paris, 1944.
Ross, W. D., *Aristote*, London, 1923.
Stigen, A., *The Structure of Aristotle's Thought, An Introduction to
the Study of Aristotle's Writings*, Oslo, 1966.
Stocks, J. L., *Aristotelianism*, London, 1925.
Zeller, E., *Die Philosophie der Griechen in ihrer geschichtlichen Ent-
wicklung*, ii.2, Leipzig, 1879³.

(D) *Philosophical Method*
le Blond, J. M., *Logique et méthode chez Aristote, Étude sur la recherche
des principes dans la physique aristotélicienne*, Paris, 1939.
Eucken, R., *Ueber die Methode und die Grundlagen der Aristotelischen
Ethik*, Frankfurt am Main, 1870.
Owen, G. E. L., 'Tithenai ta Phainomena', in *Aristote et les problèmes
de méthode*, ed. S. Mansion, Louvain, 1961, 83-103. Also in *Aristote*,
ed. J. M. E. Moravcsik, New York, 1967; and in *Articles on Aristotle*,
vol. i, edd. J. Barnes, M. Schofield, R. Sorabji, London, 1975.
Wieland, W., *Die aristotelische Physik*, Göttingen, 1970².

(E) *Texts, translations, annotated translations, commentaries, editions*
Aristotle, *De Anima*, ed. W. D. Ross, Oxford Classical Texts.
—— *Ethica Eudemia*, ed. F. Susemihl, Teubner edition.
—— *Ethica Nicomachea*, ed. I. Bywater, Oxford Classical Texts.
Ackrill, J. L., (tr. with notes), *Aristotle's Ethics*, Selections from
Philosophers, ed. M. Warnock, London, 1973.

Apostle, H. G. (tr. with notes), *Aristotle, The Nichomachean Ethics*, Dordrecht/Boston, 1975.

Burnet, J. (ed.), *The Ethics of Aristotle*, London, 1900.

Dirlmeier, F. (comm.), *Aristoteles, Nikomachische Ethik*, Aristoteles, Werke in deutscher Übersetzung, ed. E. Grumach, vol. vi, Berlin, 1959.

—— (comm.), *Aristoteles, Eudemische Ethik*, Aristoteles, Werke in deutscher Übersetzung, ed. E. Grumach, vol. vii, Berlin, 1962.

Eriksen, T. B. (comm.), *Notes on Aristotle's Ethica Nicomachea X, 6-9*, Oslo, 1974.

Festugière, A. J. (comm.), *Aristote, le plaisir (Eth. Nic. VII 11-14, X 1-5)*, Paris, 1936.

von Fragstein, A. (comm. on the *EE*), *Studien zur Ethik des Aristoteles*, Amsterdam, 1974.

Gauthier, R.-A. and Jolif, J. Y. (comm.), *Aristote, L'Éthique à Nicomaque*, Paris/Louvain, 1970².

Grant, A. (ed.), *The Ethics of Aristotle*, London, 1885².

Greenwood, L. H. G. (ed.), *Aristotle, Nicomachean Ethics Book Six*, Cambridge, 1909.

Hamlyn, D. W. (tr. with notes), *Aristotle's De Anima, Books II and III*, Oxford, 1968.

Joachim, H. H. (comm.), *Aristotle, The Nichomachean Ethics*, Oxford, 1951.

Nussbaum, M. C. (ed.), *Aristotle's De Motu Animalium*, Princeton, 1978.

Rackham, H. (tr.), *Aristotle, The Athenian Constitution, The Eudemian Ethics, On Virtues and Vices*, Loeb edition, 1952².

—— (tr.), *Aristotle, The Nicomachean Ethics*, Loeb edition, 1934².

Ramsauer, G. (ed.), *Aristotelis Ethica Nicomachea*, Leipzig, 1878.

Rodier, G. (ed.), *Aristote, Éthique à Nicomaque, Livre X*, Paris, 1897.

—— (ed.), *Aristote, traité de l'âme*, Paris, 1900.

Rolfes, E. and Bien, G. (tr. with notes), *Aristoteles, Nikomachische Ethik*, Hamburg, 1972².

Ross, W. D. (tr.), *Ethica Nicomachea*, The Works of Aristotle Translated Into English, ed. Ross, vol. ix, Oxford, 1925.

Stewart, J. A. (comm.), *Notes on the Nicomachean Ethics of Aristotle*, Oxford, 1892.

(F) *Authenticity and chronology*

For the *Magna Moralia* see the bibliography in

Dirlmeier, F. (comm.), *Aristoteles, Magna Moralia*, Aristoteles, Werke in deutscher Übersetzung, ed. E. Grumach, vol. viii, Darmstadt, 1973³.

For the *Eudemian* and *Nicomachean Ethics* see the bibliography in

Kenny, A. J. P., *The Aristotelian Ethics*, Oxford, 1978.

There is an excellent survey by A. Mansion of the older literature on these questions in his paper

'Autour des Éthiques attribuées à Aristote', *Revue néoscolastique de philosophie*, 33 (1931), 80-107, 216-36, 360-80.

(G) *Aristotle's ethics, books and general articles*

Ando, T., *Aristotle's Theory of Practical Cognition*, The Hague, 1971³.

Aubenque, P., *La Prudence chez Aristote*, Paris, 1963.

Barnes, J., Schofield, M., and Sorabji, R. (edd.), *Articles on Aristotle, 2. Ethics and Politics*, London, 1977.

Brochard, V., 'La Morale ancienne et la morale moderne', *Revue philosophique*, 26 (1901), 1-12. Also in his *Études de philosophie ancienne et de philosophie moderne*, Paris, 1926.

Clark, S. R. L., *Aristotle's Man, Speculations upon Aristotelian Anthropology*, Oxford, 1975.

Cooper, J. M., *Reason and Human Good in Aristotle*, Cambridge, Mass., 1975.

Fortenbaugh, W. W., *Aristotle on Emotion*, London, 1975.

Gauthier, R.-A., *La Morale d'Aristote*, Paris, 1973³.

Gigon, O., 'Theorie und Praxis bei Platon und Aristoteles', *Museum Helveticum*, 30 (1973), 65-87, 144-65.

Hager, F.-P. (ed.), *Ethik und Politik des Aristoteles*, Wege der Forschung 208, Darmstadt, 1972.

Hamelin, O., 'La morale d'Aristote', *Revue de métaphysique et de morale*, 30 (1923), 497-507.

Hampshire, S., *Two Theories of Morality*, Oxford, 1977.

Hardie, W. F. R., *Aristotle's Ethical Theory*, Oxford, 1968.

Kenny, A. J. P., *The Aristotelian Ethics*, Oxford, 1978.

—— *Aristotle's Theory of the Will*, London, 1979.

Loening, R., *Die Zurechnungslehre des Aristoteles*, Jena, 1903.

Monan, J. D., *Moral Knowledge and its Methodology in Aristotle*, Oxford, 1968.

Ollé-Laprune, L., *Essai sur la morale d'Aristote*, Paris, 1881.

Ritter, J., 'Das bürgerliche Leben, Zur aristotelischen Theorie des Glücks', *Vierteljahresschrift für wissenschaftliche Pädagogik*, 32 (1956), 60-94. Also in Ritter's *Metaphysik und Politik, Studien zu Aristoteles und Hegel*, Frankfurt am Main, 1977.

Rowe, C. J., *The Eudemian and Nicomachean Ethics: A Study in the Development of Aristotle's Thought*, Proceedings of the Cambridge Philological Society, suppl. vol. iii, 1971.

Schilling, H., *Das Ethos der Mesotes*, Heidelberger Abhandlungen zur Philosophie und ihrer Geschichte 22, Tübingen, 1930.

Sullivan, R. J., 'The Kantian Critique of Aristotle's Moral Philosophy: An Appraisal', *RM* 28 (1974), 24-53.

Teichmüller, G., *Die praktische Vernunft bei Aristoteles*, Neue Studien zur Geschichte der Begriffe iii, Gotha, 1879.

Trendelenburg, F. A., *Historische Beiträge zur Philosophie iii*, Berlin, 1867.

Verbeke, G. 'Thèmes de la morale aristotélicienne', *Revue philosophique de Louvain*, 61 (1963), 183-214.

Walsh, J. J., *Aristotle's Conception of Moral Weakness*, New York, 1963.

Walsh, J. J. and Shapiro, H. L. (edd.), *Aristotle's Ethics, Issues and Interpretations*, Belmont, 1967.

SELECT BIBLIOGRAPHY 275

Walter, J., *Die Lehre von der praktischen Vernunft in der griechischen Philosophie*, Jena, 1874.
Weiss, H., *Der Zufall in der Philosophie des Aristoteles*, London, 1942, ch. III.
Wittmann, M., *Die Ethik des Aristoteles*, Regensburg, 1920.

(H) *Goodness and happiness* (*EN* I and X.vi ff.)
Ackrill, J. L., 'Aristotle on *Eudaimonia*', *PBA* 60 (1974), 339-59.
Adkins, A. W. H., '*Theoria* versus *Praxis* in the *Nicomachean Ethics* and the *Republic*', *CP* 73 (1978), 297-313.
Anscombe, G. E. M., *Intention*, Oxford, 1963².
Armstrong, A. MacC., 'Aristotle's Conception of Human Good', *PQ* 8 (1958), 259-60.
Aubenque, P., 'Die Kohärenz der aristotelischen Eudaimonia-Lehre', in *Die Frage nach dem Glück*, ed. G. Bien, Problemata 74, Stuttgart, 1978, 45-57.
Austin, J. L., '*Agathon* and *Eudaimonia* in the *Ethics* of Aristotle', in *Aristotle*, ed. J. M. E. Moravcsik, New York, 1967, 261-96.
Defourny, P., 'L'activité de contemplation dans les Morales d'Aristotle', *Bulletin de l'Institut Historique belge de Rome*, 18 (1937), 89-101. Published in English, with the title 'Contemplation in Aristotle's Ethics', in *Articles on Aristotle*, vol. ii, edd. J. Barnes, M. Schofield, R. Sorabji, London, 1977.
Geach, P. T., 'Good and Evil', *Analysis*, 17 (1956-7), 33-42. Also in *Theories of Ethics*, ed. P. Foot, Oxford, 1967.
Glassen, P., 'A Fallacy in Aristotle's Argument about the Good', *PQ* 7 (1957), 319-22.
Hampshire, S., 'Ethics: A Defense of Aristotle', *University of Colorado Studies*, Series in Philosophy, 3 (1967), 23-38. Also in Hampshire's *Freedom of Mind and other Essays*, Princeton, 1971.
Hardie, W. F. R., 'The Final Good in Aristotle's Ethics', *Phil.* 40 (1965), 277-95. Also in *Aristotle*, ed. J. M. E. Moravcsik, New York, 1967.
—— 'Aristotle on the Best Life for a Man', *Phil.* 54 (1979), 35-50.
Hare, R. M., 'Geach: Good and Evil', *Analysis*, 17 (1956-7), 103-11. Also in *Theories of Ethics*, ed. P. Foot, Oxford, 1967.
Jacobi, K., 'Aristoteles' Einführung des Begriffs "eudaimonia" im I. Buch der "Nikomachischen Ethik", Eine Antwort auf einige neuere Inkonsistenzkritiken', *Phil. Jahr.* 86 (1979), 300-25.
Kearney, J. K., 'Happiness and the Unity of the Nicomachean Ethics Reconsidered', *Proceedings of the American Catholic Philosophical Association*, 40 (1966), 135-43.
Kenny, A. J. P., 'Happiness', *PAS* 66 (1965-6), 93-102. Also, with the title 'Aristotle on Happiness', in Kenny, *The Anatomy of Soul*, Oxford, 1973; and in *Articles on Aristotle*, vol. ii, edd. J. Barnes, M. Schofield, R. Sorabji, London, 1977.
Kirwan, C. A., 'Logic and the Good in Aristotle', *PQ* 17 (1967), 97-114.
Kraut, R., 'Aristotle on Choosing Virtue for Itself', *AGP* 58 (1976), 223-39.

—— 'Two Conceptions of Happiness', *PR* 88 (1979), 167–97.

Léonard, J., *Le Bonheur chez Aristote*, Mémoires de l'Académie Royale de Belgique, classe des lettres et des sciences morales et politiques 44, Brussels, 1948.

Margueritte, H., 'Une lacune dans le Ier livre de l'Éthique à Nicomaque', *Revue d'histoire de la philosophie*, 4 (1930), 176–88.

—— 'La composition du livre A de l'Éthique à Nicomaque', *Revue d'histoire de la philosophie*, 4 (1930), 250–73.

Nagel, T., 'Aristotle on *Eudaimonia*', *Phr*. 17 (1972), 252–59.

Prichard, H. A., 'The Meaning of *agathon* in the *Ethics* of Aristotle', *Phil.* 10 (1935), 27–39. Also in Prichard's *Moral Obligation*, Oxford, 1949; and in Aristotle, ed. J. M. E. Moravcsik, New York, 1967.

Ringbom, M., 'Aristotle's notion of virtue', *Ajatus*, 29 (1967), 51–61.

Ritter, J., 'Die Lehre vom Ursprung und Sinn der Theorie bei Aristoteles', *Veröffentlichungen der Arbeitsgemeinschaft für Forschung des Landes Nordrhein-Westfalen, Geisteswissenschaften 1*, Köln/Opladen, 1953, 32–54. Also in Ritter's *Metaphysik und Politik, Studien zu Aristoteles und Hegel*, Frankfurt am Main, 1977.

Rorty, A. O., 'The Place of Contemplation in Aristotle's Nicomachean Ethics', *M* 87 (1978), 343–58.

Seidl, H., 'Das sittlich Gute (als Glückseligkeit) nach Aristoteles, Formale Bestimmung und metaphysische Voraussetzung', *Phil. Jahr.* 82 (1975), 31–53.

Siegler, F. A., 'Reason, Happiness, and Goodness', in *Aristotle's Ethics, Issues and Interpretations*, edd. J. J. Walsh and H. L. Shapiro, Belmont, 1967, 30–46.

Verbeke, G., 'L'idéal de la perfection humaine chez Aristote et l'évolution de sa noétique', *Miscellanea Giovanni Galbiati 1*, Fontes Ambrosiani 25, Milan, 1951, 79–95.

Verdenius, W. J., 'Human Reason and God in the Eudemian Ethics', in *Untersuchungen zur Eudemischen Ethik*, edd. P. Moraux and D. Harlfinger, Peripatoi i, Berlin, 1971, 285–97.

de Vogel, C. J., 'Quelques remarques à propos du premier chapitre de l'Éthique de Nicomaque', in *Autour d'Aristote*, Recueil de'études . . . offert a Mgr. A. Mansion, Louvain, 1955, 307–23.

—— 'On the character of Aristotle's Ethics', in *Philomathes, Studies and Essays in the Humanities in Memory of Philip Merlan*, edd. R. B. Palmer and R. Hamerton-Kelly, The Hague, 1971, 116–24.

Wilkes, K. V., 'The Good Man and the Good for Man in Aristotle's Ethics', *M* 87 (1978), 553–71.

Williams, B. A. O., 'Aristotle on the Good: a Formal Sketch', *PQ* 12 (1962), 289–96.

von Wright, G. H., *The Varieties of Goodness*, London, 1963, ch. V.

(I) *Plato and the good* (*EN* I.vi)

Ackrill, J. L., 'Aristotle on "Good" and the Categories', in *Islamic Philosophy and the Classical Tradition, Essays Presented to Richard*

Walzer, edd. S. M. Stern, A. Hourani, and V. Brown, Oxford, 1972, 17-25. Also in *Articles on Aristotle*, vol. ii, edd. J. Barnes, M. Schofield, R. Sorabji, London, 1977.

Allan, D. J., 'Aristotle's Criticism of Platonic Doctrine Concerning Goodness and the Good', *PAS* 64 (1963-4), 273-86.

Berti, E., 'Multiplicité et unité du bien selon EE I 8', in *Untersuchungen zur Eudemischen Ethik*, edd. P. Moraux and D. Harlfinger, Peripatoi i, Berlin, 1971, 156-84.

Flashar, H., 'Die Kritik der platonischen Ideenlehre in der Ethik des Aristoteles', in *Synusia, Festgabe für Wolfgang Schadewaldt*, edd. H. Flashar and K. Gaiser, Pfullingen, 1965, 223-46. Published in English, entitled 'The Critique of Plato's Theory of Ideas in Aristotle's Ethics', in *Articles on Aristotle*, vol. ii, edd. J. Barnes, M. Schofield, R. Sorabji, London, 1977.

Kosman, L. A., 'Predicating the Good', *Phr.* 13 (1968), 171-4.

(J) *Moral Virtue in general (EN* II)

Hardie, W. F. R., 'Aristotle's Doctrine that Virtue is a "Mean"', *PAS* 65 (1964-5), 183-204. Also, with new appendix, in *Articles on Aristotle*, vol. ii, edd. J. Barnes, M. Schofield, R. Sorabji, London, 1977.

Joseph, H. W. B., 'Aristotle's Definition of Moral Virtue, and Plato's Account of Justice of the Soul', in his *Essays in Ancient and Modern Philosophy*, Oxford, 1935, 156-77.

Olmsted, E. H., 'The "Moral Sense" Aspect of Aristotle's Ethical Theory', *AJP* 69 (1948), 42-61.

Urmson, J. O., 'Aristotle's Doctrine of the Mean', *APQ* 10 (1973), 223-30.

(K) *Voluntariness and free will (EN* III.i-v)

Austin, J. L., 'A Plea for Excuses', *PAS* 57 (1956-7), 1-30. Also in his *Philosophical Papers*, Oxford, 1961, and in *The Philosophy of Action*, ed. A. R. White, Oxford, 1968.

Bondeson, W., 'Aristotle on Responsibility for One's Character and the Possibility of Character Change', *Phr.* 19 (1974), 59-65.

Furley, D. J., *Two Studies in the Greek Atomists*, Princeton, 1967.

Glover, J., *Responsibility*, London, 1970, ch. I.

Haksar, V., 'Aristotle and the Punishment of Psychopaths', *Phil.* 39 (1964), 323-40. Also in *Aristotle's Ethics, Issues and Interpretations*, edd. J. J. Walsh and H. L. Shapiro, Belmont, 1967.

Hardie, W. F. R., 'Aristotle and the Freewill Problem', *Phil.* 43 (1968), 274-78.

Huby, P., 'The First Discovery of the Freewill Problem', *Phil.* 42 (1967), 353-62.

Seif, K. P., 'Das Problem der Willensfreiheit in der Nikomachischen Ethik des Aristoteles', *Theologie und Philosophie*, 54 (1979), 542-81.

Siegler, F. A., 'Voluntary and Involuntary', *Monist*, 52 (1968), 268-87.

Wittmann, M., 'Aristoteles und die Willensfreiheit, Eine historisch-kritische Untersuchung', *Phil. Jahr.* 34 (1921), 5-30, 131-53.

(L) *Individual virtues* (*EN* III.vi–V)

Allan, D. J., 'Individual and State in the *Ethics* and *Politics*', in *La 'Politique' d'Aristote*, Entretiens Hardt 11, Geneva, 1964, 55–85.

Fortenbaugh, W. W., 'Aristotle and the Questionable Mean-Dispositions', *TAPA* 99 (1968), 203–31.

Gauthier, R.-A., *Magnanimité, l'idéal de la grandeur dans la philosophie païenne et dans la théologie chrétienne*, Paris, 1951.

Hardie, W. F. R., '"Magnanimity" in Aristotle's Ethics', *Phr.* 23 (1978), 63–79.

Hunt, L. H., 'Generosity', *APQ* 12 (1975), 235–44.

Pears, D. F., 'Aristotle's Analysis of Courage', *Midwest Studies in Philosophy 3: Studies in Ethical Theory*, University of Minnesota, Morris, 1978, 273–85.

Schmidt, E. A., 'Ehre und Tugend, Zur Megalopsychia der aristotelischen Ethik', *AGP* 49 (1967), 149–68.

Wilpert, P., 'Die Wahrhaftigkeit in der aristotelischen Ethik', *Phil. Jahr.* 53 (1940), 323–38. Also in *Ethik und Politik des Aristoteles*, ed. F.-P. Hager, Wege der Forschung 208, Darmstadt, 1972.

(M) *Deliberation, prohairesis, praxis/poiēsis, phronēsis* (*EN* VI)

Ackrill, J. L., 'Aristotle's Distinction between *Energeia* and *Kinesis*', in *New Essays in Plato and Aristotle*, ed. R. Bambrough, London, 1965, 121–41.

— — 'Aristotle on Action', *M* 87 (1978), 595–601.

Allan, D. J., 'Aristotle's Account of the Origin of Moral Principles', in *Actes du XIème congrès international de philosophie* 12, Brussels, 1953, 120–27. Also in *Articles on Aristotle*, vol. ii, edd. J. Barnes, M. Schofield, R. Sorabji, London, 1977.

— — 'The practical syllogism', in *Autour d'Aristote*, Recueil d'études ... offert à Mgr. A. Mansion, Louvain, 1955, 325–40.

Anscombe, G. E. M., 'Thought and Action in Aristotle, What is "Practical Truth"?', in *New Essays in Plato and Aristotle*, ed. R. Bambrough, London, 1965, 143–58. Also in *Articles on Aristotle*, vol. ii, edd. J. Barnes, M. Schofield, R. Sorabji, London, 1977.

Aubenque, P., 'La prudence aristotélicienne porte-t-elle sur la fin ou sur les moyens?', *Revue des études grecques*, 78 (1965), 40–51.

Demos, R., 'Some Remarks on Aristotle's Doctrine of Practical Reason', *Philosophy and Phenomenological Research*, 22 (1961–2), 153–62.

Ebert, T., 'Praxis und Poiesis, Zu einer handlungstheoretischen Unterscheidung bei Aristoteles', *Zeitschrift für philosophische Forschung*, 30 (1976), 12–30.

Even-Granboulan, G., 'Le syllogisme pratique chez Aristote', *Études philosophiques*, Paris, 1976, 57–78.

Fortenbaugh, W. W., '*Ta pros to telos* and Syllogistic Vocabulary in Aristotle's Ethics', *Phr.* 10 (1965), 191–201.

— — 'Aristotle's Conception of Moral Virtue and Its Perceptive Role', *TAPA* 95 (1964), 71–81.

— — 'Aristotle: Emotion and Moral Virtue', *Arethusa*, 2 (1969), 163–85.

—— 'Aristotle: Animals, Emotion, and Moral Virtue', *Arethusa*, 4 (1971), 137–65.

Gigon, O., 'Phronesis und Sophia in der Nicomach. Ethik des Aristoteles', in *Kephalaion, Studies . . . Offered to Professor C. J. de Vogel*, edd. J. Mansfeld and L. M. de Rijk, Assen, 1975, 91–104.

Henderson, G. P., 'Habit and Reflection in Morality', *Dialogue*, 9 (1970), 20–34.

Hintikka, J., 'Remarks on praxis, poiesis and ergon in Plato and in Aristotle', in *Studia philosophica in honorem Sven Krohn*, Annales universitatis turkuensis, series B, tom. 126, 1973, 53–62.

Höffe, O., 'Wissenschaft "in sittlicher Absicht", Zu Aristoteles' Modell einer eminent praktischen Philosophie', *Phil. Jahr.* 79 (1972), 288–319.

Irwin, T. H., 'Aristotle on Reason, Desire, and Virtue', *JP* 72 (1975), 567–78.

—— 'First Principles In Aristotle's Ethics', *Midwest Studies in Philosophy 3: Studies in Ethical Theory*, University of Minnesota, Morris, 1978, 252–72.

Kenny, A. J. P., *Action, Emotion and Will*, London, 1963, ch. VIII.

Kuhn, H., 'Der Begriff der Prohairesis in der Nikomachischen Ethik', in *Die Gegenwart der Griechen im neueren Denken*, Festschrift für Hans-Georg Gadamer zum 60. Geburtstag, Tübingen, 1960, 123–40.

Miller, Jr., F. D., 'Actions and Results', *PQ* 25 (1975), 350–4.

Pickering, F. R., 'Aristotle on Walking', *AGP* 59 (1977), 37–43.

Schmidt, E. A., 'Sind die aristotelischen Ethiken praktizierte *Phronesis*?', *Philosophische Rundschau*, 17 (1970), 249–65.

Siwecki, J., '*Praxis* et *poiesis* dans l'Éthique Nicomachéenne', in *Charisteria Gustavo Przychocki a discipulis oblata*, Warsaw, 1934, 175–89.

Sorabji, R., 'Aristotle on the Role of Intellect in Virtue', *PAS* 74 (1973–4), 107–29.

Taylor, C. C. W., 'States, Activities and Performances', *Aristotelian Society*, suppl. vol. xxxix (1965), 85–102.

Wiggins, D., 'Deliberation and Practical Reason', *PAS* 76 (1975–6), 29–51.

(N) *Akrasia* (*EN* VII.i–iii)

Etheridge, S. G., 'Aristotle's Practical Syllogism and Necessity', *Philologus*, 112 (1968), 20–42.

Kenny, A. J. P., 'The Practical Syllogism and Incontinence', *Phr.* 11 (1966), 163–84. Also in Kenny, *The Anatomy of the Soul*, Oxford, 1973.

Robinson, R., 'L'acrasie selon Aristote', *Revue philosophique*, 80 (1955), 261–80. Also in English in Robinson's *Essays in Greek Philosophy*, Oxford, 1969, and in *Articles on Aristotle*, vol. ii, edd. J. Barnes, M. Schofield, R. Sorabji, London, 1977.

Rorty, A. O., 'Plato and Aristotle on Belief, Habit, and Akrasia', *APQ* 7 (1970), 50–61.

Santas, G., 'Aristotle on Practical Inference, the Explanation of Action, and Akrasia', *Phr.* 14 (1969), 162–89.

(O) *Pleasure* (*EN* VII.xi–xiv, X.i–v)

Gosling, J., 'More Aristotelian Pleasures', *PAS* 74 (1973–4), 15–34.

Lieberg, G., *Die Lehre von der Lust in den Ethiken des Aristoteles*, Zetemata 19, Munich, 1958.

Mansion, S., 'Le plaisir et la peine, matière de l'agir moral selon Aristote', in *Images of Man in Ancient and Medieval Thought*, Studia Gerardo Verbeke ab amicis et collegis dicata, ed. C. Laga, Symbolae 1, Louvain, 1976, 37–51.

Owen, G. E. L., 'Aristotelian Pleasures', *PAS* 72 (1971–2), 135–52.

Ricken, F., *Der Lustbegriff in der Nikomachischen Ethik des Aristoteles*, Hypomnemata 46, Göttingen, 1976.

Rorty, A. O., 'The Place of Pleasure in Aristotle's Ethics', *M* 83 (1974), 481–97.

Urmson, J. O., 'Aristotle on Pleasure', in *Aristotle*, ed. J. M. E. Moravcsik, New York, 1967, 323–33.

(P) *Friendship* (*EN* VIII–IX)

Adkins, A. W. H., '"Friendship" and "Self-sufficiency" in Homer and Aristotle', *CQ* 13 (1963), 30–45.

Annas, J., 'Plato and Aristotle on Friendship and Altruism', *M* 86 (1977), 532–54.

Cooper, J. M., 'Aristotle on the Forms of Friendship', *RM* 30 (1977), 619–48.

—— 'Friendship and the Good in Aristotle', *PR* 86 (1977), 290–315.

Gigon, O., 'Die Selbstliebe in der Nikomachischen Ethik des Aristoteles', in *Dōrēma* Hans Diller zum 70. Geburtstag, *Dauer und Überleben des antiken Geistes*, Griechische humanistische Gesellschaft, Internationales Zentrum für klassisch-humanistische Forschung, Zweite Reihe: Studien und Untersuchungen 27, Athen, 1975, 77–113.

Hoffmann, E., 'Aristoteles' Philosophie der Freundschaft', in *Festgabe für Heinrich Rickert*, ed. A. Faust, Bühl/Baden, 1933, 8–36. Also in *Ethik und Politik des Aristoteles*, ed. F.-P. Hager, Wege der Forschung 208, Darmstadt, 1972.

Voelke, A., 'Le probleme d'autrui dans la pensée aristotélicienne', *Revue de théologie et de philosophie*, 4 (1954), 262–82.

(Q) *Phantasia, sense awareness, and desire*

Cashdollar, S., 'Aristotle's Account of Incidental Perception', *Phr.* 18 (1973), 156–75.

Freudenthal, J., *Ueber den Begriff des Wortes Phantasia bei Aristoteles*, Göttingen, 1863.

Kahn, C. H., 'Sensation and Consciousness in Aristotle's Psychology', *AGP* 48 (1966), 43–81. Also in *Articles on Aristotle*, vol. iv, edd. J. Barnes, M. Schofield, R. Sorabji, London, 1979.

Kosman, L. A., 'Perceiving That We Perceive: *On The Soul* III, 2', *PR* 84 (1975), 499–519.

Lycos, K., 'Aristotle and Plato on "Appearing"', *M* 73 (1964), 496–514.

Nussbaum, M. C., 'Essay 5: The Role of *Phantasia* in Aristotle's Explanation of Action', in her edition of the *De Motu Animalium* (see under (E) above), 221-69.

Schofield, M., 'Aristotle on the Imagination', in *Aristotle on Mind and the Senses*, edd. G. E. R. Lloyd and G. E. L. Owen, Cambridge, 1978, 99-140. Also in *Articles on Aristotle*, vol. iv, edd. J. Barnes, M. Schofield, R. Sorabji, London, 1979.

Addenda to bibliography
The book was written in spring 1980. More recent literature includes:

Ackrill, J. L., *Aristotle the Philosopher*, Oxford, 1981.

Hardie, W. F. R., *Aristotle's Ethical Theory*, Oxford, 1980^2.

Hursthouse, R., 'A False Doctrine of the Mean', *PAS* 81 (1980-1), 57-72.

Kahn, C., 'Aristotle and Altruism', *M* 90 (1981), 20-40.

McDowell, J., 'Virtue and Reason', *Monist*, 62 (1979), 331-50.

Nilstun, T., *Aristotle on Freedom and Punishment*, Lund, 1981.

Price, A. W., 'Aristotle's Ethical Holism', *M* 89 (1980), 338-52.

Rorty, A. O. (ed.), *Essays on Aristotle's Ethics*, Berkeley, 1980.

Sorabji, R. R. K., *Necessity, Cause, and Blame*, London/Ithaca, N.Y., 1980.

Wedin, M. V., 'Aristotle on the Good for Man', *M* 90 (1981), 243-62.

GENERAL INDEX

Ackrill, J. L., 3, 4, 5, 19, 30n, 33n, 64n, 102n, 105-6, 114n
Allan, D. J., ix, 4n, 265, 267n
ambition (*philotimia*), 81-3; a second order attitude, 82; its connection with high-mindedness, 82-3; and acting for the sake of the noble, 83
anger (*orgē*), and good temper, 83-6; defined, 83, 140
Anscombe, G. E. M., x, 21n, 30n, 262n
anthrōpikos (human), a special sense of, 110
Apostle, H. G., 38n, 48, 62n, 89n, 99n
appetite (*epithymia*), as instance of desire as against emotion, 133; analysis of, 139-40; 'practical' character of, 141
Aubenque, P., 267n
Austin, J. L., x, 6n
authekastos, see self-assurance

Bien, G., x
Bonitz, H., 62n, 73n
Brochard, V., 262n
Burnet, J., 25n, 38n, 67n, 88n, 99n, 205n

choice, *see prohairesis*
Clark, S. R. L., 261n
cleverness (*deinotēs*), its relation to *phronēsis*, 228-9
community (*to koinon*), and noble action, 40, 46, 47-8, 73-4; and laws, 54
Cooper, J. M., vii, 3, 4-5, 20, 80n, 94n, 102n, 107n, 108n, 199-200n, 205n
courage (*andreia*), 65-8; and nobility, 48-9, 52, 65-6; cowardice distinguished from injustice, 58; and the good of others, 65-8;

allows for passions but governed by reason, 83-4

deliberation (*bouleusis*), for means, and for components, parts, and constituents of wholes, 4-6; and *phronēsis*, ch. 7; presupposes an end which is kept fixed, achievable by action, determinate, 191-2; implies a problem and is a search, 191; for 'poietic' means in particular situations, 192-4; but may also be 'practical', 192, 198-9; proceeds at universal level, 192-3; rationalizes perceptual knowledge, 202-4; as engaged in by the *phronimos*, 218-19; means and ends in that type of deliberation, 219-21
Denniston, J. D., 137, 204n
desire, Aristotle's analysis of, 130-8; includes evaluative cognitive state of desiring person, 136; as assertion of evaluative predication, 137-8; 'full' and 'bare' type of, 138; and *phronēsis*, ch. 6; how changed, 172-83; and practical principles, 183-7
Dirlmeier, F., 38n, 62n, 88n, 99n

Ebert, T., 27n
ēlithios, see ignorance
empeiria (experience), 145-50, 154-6; affinity with *phantasia* and memory, but specific to humans, 145-6; defined 146-7; implies 'implicit' grasp of universal, 147-9; last step before rational ('explicit') grasp of universal, 155; but in itself non-rational, 155-6; and deliberative search of *phronimos* for means, 200, 202-8, 221n; and grasp of *phronimos* of ends, 211-19

passion (*cont.*)
　　and the courageous man, 83-4;
　　'mean-states in passions', 91-2;
　　Aristotle's list of, 132-3; includes
　　both desire and emotion, 133; a
　　species of desire (*orexis*), 135-6,
　　142; may be rational as well as
　　non-rational, 139; is 'practical',
　　139-42; how it may be changed,
　　178-80; living in accordance with,
　　178
Pears, D. F., 64n
perception (*aisthēsis*), Aristotle's way
　　of accounting for perceptual
　　awareness, 131-2; and universals,
　　156-7; and *phronēsis*, 201, 204-8;
　　and deliberation, 203, 220-1n;
　　its 'richness' when compared with
　　reason, 208-11; *see also empeiria*
phantasia (imagination), and per-
　　ception, 131-2; and desire, 132-3n,
　　134-6; perceptual and calculative,
　　135; of good as due to one's
　　moral state, 251-2
phronēsis (moral insight), utility of,
　　96-7, 98-101, 225, 227-35;
　　relation to *sophia*, 97, 98-101;
　　difficulty in Aristotle's account
　　of its value as being also 'poietic',
　　101; its resolution, 102-4; always
　　considered an independent con-
　　stituent of human happiness,
　　105-11, 118-20; is the cognitive
　　element in 'genuine moral virtue',
　　164, 232-4, 236-7; includes
　　universal grasp of types of act to
　　be done, 163-4, 196, 229-30;
　　how this grasp is acquired, 211-18,
　　230-1; the grasp also includes
　　references to *eudaimonia*, 231-2;
　　presupposes a state of desire, 165;
　　the reason for this, 168-70; the
　　state of desire must be present
　　independently of any rational
　　grasp, 170-2; always true, 189;
　　unerring guide to action, 189-91;
　　involves deliberation, 196, 201;
　　problem raised by this, 198-9;
　　is also insight into particulars,
　　199-208; sense of this, 201-2;
　　this insight acquired 'naturally',
　　216-17; and *empeiria*, 200,
　　202-8, 211-18; a sort of per-

ception, 201, 205-7; and 'noetic'
　　perception of particulars, 215;
　　and justification of grasp of what
　　should be done, 223-4; its pos-
　　session ensures that a man performs
　　praxeis, 231-2; necessarily moti-
　　vational, 238-9
pity (*eleos*), as instance of emotion as
　　against desire, 133; analysis of,
　　139-40; 'practical' character of,
　　141
poiēsis (production), Aristotle's
　　distinction of *praxis* and, 4, 27,
　　29; sense of the 'severance' of act
　　and act-result in Aristotle's de-
　　finition of, 34-5
'poietic', sense of utility of *phronēsis*
　　and *sophia*, 97-8, 100; vocabulary
　　reinterpreted in 'practical' sense,
　　197
'practical', sense of utility of *phronēsis*
　　and *sophia*, 99; character of pas-
　　sions, 139-42; thought and truth
　　necessarily leads to action, 169-70;
　　type of deliberation, 198-9
praxis (action proper), wider than
　　'moral act', 3; Aristotle's distinction
　　of *poiēsis* and, 4, 27, 29; sense of
　　choosing it 'for its own sake', 28;
　　related directly to *eudaimonia*, 29,
　　35-6; and act-descriptions that in-
　　clude a reference to an act-result,
　　32-4; as the direct expression of
　　character even when a *kinēsis*,
　　34-6; sense of the denial of the
　　possibility of 'severance' of act
　　and act-result in Aristotle's defi-
　　nition of, 35
prohairesis ('choice', decision), general
　　sense of, 14, 21-2; sense of *pro-*,
　　14n; lacking in certain 'mean-
　　states in passions', 92; distinctive
　　rational character of, 150-3; as
　　actualization of genuine moral state,
　　163, 166; importance of, 269

Rackham, H., 38n
Ramsauer, G., 8n, 38n, 67n, 73, 99n
reason, and argument for noble action,
　　44-5, 51; right reason (*orthos
　　logos*), 64, 69; and desire, 172-81;
　　living in accordance with, 178;
　　rationality defined, 149-54; its

INDEX LOCORUM